A Black Odyssey

A Black Odyssey

JOHN LEWIS WALLER
AND THE
PROMISE OF AMERICAN LIFE, 1878-1900

Randall Bennett Woods

THE REGENTS PRESS OF KANSAS   *Lawrence*

PUBLICATION OF THIS BOOK HAS BEEN AIDED BY A GRANT
FROM THE NATIONAL ENDOWMENT FOR THE HUMANITIES

Library of Congress Cataloging in Publication Data

Woods, Randall Bennett, 1944-
    A black odyssey.

    Bibliography: p.
    Includes index.
    1. Waller, John Lewis, 1850-1907. 2. Afro-
Americans—Kansas—History. 3. Afro-Americans—
Social conditions—To 1964. 4. United States—Race
relations. 5. Afro-Americans—Biography. 6. Poli-
ticians—Kansas—Biography. 7. Diplomats—United
States—Biography. I. Title.
E185.97.W134W66   978.1'00496073   80-18965
ISBN 0-7006-0207-0

TO

WILLARD B. GATEWOOD, JR.

Teacher, Colleague, Friend

Contents

List of Illustrations

Acknowledgments

Research for this book was conducted primarily at the National Archives and Library of Congress in Washington, D.C., the Kansas State Historical Society at Topeka, Kansas, and Mullins Library at the University of Arkansas. As usual, the archivists in charge of State Department records at the Archives and the staff of the manuscript division of the Library of Congress proved both efficient and resourceful. My debt to the historians, librarians, and archivists who staff the Kansas State Historical Society is immense. Joseph Snell, Robert Richmond, and Forrest Blackburn gave me not only expert advice but continuing support and encouragement. Joan Roberts, reference librarian at the University of Arkansas, guided me through a labyrinth of serial sets and bibliographies with consummate skill and patience.

All the photographs were obtained from the Kansas State Historical Society and are used here with permission.

A National Endowment for the Humanities summer stipend and grants from the American Philosophical Society and the Research Reserve Fund at the University of Arkansas provided monies for travel and microfilming. Jeanie Wyant typed the manuscript and made numerous editorial suggestions.

A Black Odyssey is dedicated to Willard Gatewood not only because of his general contributions to my career but also because of aid rendered on this particular project. It was a footnote in Gatewood's *Black America and the White Man's Burden* that first brought John Lewis Waller and me together. During the five years of preparation that followed, my colleague's enthusiasm for the project and his faith in me proved endless. He read the manuscript numerous times and made helpful suggestions on sources, content, and style.

My wife, Rhoda, and my children, Jeffrey and Nicole, have borne closed doors and long separations with patience and understanding. Without their love and support this project would have remained forever unfinished. Any errors of fact, style, or interpretation are, of course, mine, and mine alone.

Introduction

Black Americans everywhere anticipated that the triumph of "Union and Liberty" would bring in its wake unparalleled opportunities for their race. The egalitarian rhetoric loosed by the Emancipation Proclamation appeared to herald a new age. Afro-Americans of all conditions, classes, and sections eagerly looked forward to the fruits of full citizenship. Rather quickly Negroes realized that the North's commitment to equal rights was transitory and that the South was merely biding time, waiting for the chance to exclude the freedman from participation in the political process and relegate him to servile status in the region's economic system. By 1876 North and South were ready to make their peace. Northern businessmen, a dominant element in the Republican party, were anxious to finance the industrialization of the South and were more than willing to abandon the Negro in return for that privilege. Believing the campaign for black suffrage and equal rights to be a threat to "orderly economic development" and to the survival of the Republican party in the South, Northern business leaders announced that the racial question was now *passé* and urged the nation to move on to the more pressing problems connected with industrialization and commerce. Thus, reconciliation and nationalism became the order of the day, but they were accomplished at the expense of the Afro-American.[1] Following the Compromise of 1877, the black man's condition deteriorated not only in Dixie but throughout the country. "When the mantle of slavery was lifted," cried a prominent black journalist in 1884, "it was believed that the lifetime enemy of the black man was chained to the cold, jagged rocks of death as Prometheus to Mount Caucasus. . . . But not so, for even today we find ourselves confronted, nay, surrounded by an impenetrable fog of race prejudice, which is more gigantic, more widespread and equally as destructive to the welfare and progress of the people as the other—slavery."[2] Increasingly, this prejudice manifested itself in the form of lynchings, discrimination, and systematic segregation.

The Negrophobia that began building with the fall of Radical Reconstruction culminated in the late 1880s and 1890s. Mississippi in 1890, followed by South Carolina in 1895 and Louisiana in 1898, incorporated disfranchisement provisions into its constitution.[3] In the 1880s there was legal separation in southern schools and discrimination in the distribution of school funds. Jim Crow laws for railroads were enacted during the 1880s and 1890s. The convict lease system, a reincarnation of slavery, became widespread throughout the South. Lynchings reached an all-time new high, averaging more than 100 a year during the eighties and nineties, reaching a peak of 162 in 1892. The situation was better for blacks in the North, but even then they increasingly encountered extralegal discrimination and segregation. Their economic situation became ever more precarious as competition from millions of European immigrants forced blacks out of even menial jobs.[4]

Not content with physical separation, disfranchisement, and economic exploitation of the Negro, a group of ultraracists emerged in the 1890s to argue that the very presence of the black man in America was a threat to the wealth and safety of the white majority. In an 1884 symposium on "The Future of the Negro," appearing in *The North American Review*, Senator John T. Morgan of Alabama argued that an increase in black wealth, intelligence, and capacity for industrial, commercial, and political activity was inevitable but potentially disastrous because it could only lead to increasingly bitter competition with whites. Because race prejudice would "forever remain as an incubus on all their individual or aggregate efforts," the only alternative for Negroes was to flee to Africa.[5] Cruder white supremacists such as James K. Vardaman of Mississippi hinted rather unsubtly that the only solution to the Negro problem was a revival of the "peculiar institution."

Black responses to post–Civil War racism were many and varied, but as historian Martin Dann points out, they can all be reduced to two categories: inclusion—the desire for full citizenship, within an egalitarian society, involving a commitment to the American system; and exclusion—the rejection of American society through racial separation, generally expressed in movements for domestic or foreign colonization. A number of blacks, however, were caught between these two approaches for remedying the unacceptable present. In certain areas of the United States limited economic and political opportunity had produced an upwardly mobile black elite which sought power and influence for itself and the race through emulation of the American creed of self-reliance, industry, thrift, and material accumulation. They accepted fully the Social Darwinism and *laissez faire* economics of the time.[6] "It is simply a case of the survival of the fittest," declared the black editor of the *American Citizen* in 1899. "The race would be able to command respect and be acknowledged in a business way by the Anglo-Saxon race if it possessed more real estate, business enterprise, and government bonds."[7] The racism that became increasingly explicit in America following the Compromise of 1877 posed a dilemma for these individuals. Most had enjoyed minor political office, limited economic success, and influence within the black community and, to a degree, among whites. Despite lynchings, discrimination, and segregation they remained committed to capitalism, democratic institutions, and the American creed.[8] But their success had generated not only a positive attitude toward America, it had also led to expectations of something more. Their rising expectations, if not their acceptance of the American way of life, were threatened by the brutal racism of the 1880s and 1890s.

A number of these hopeful but increasingly frustrated Afro-Americans responded to their predicament by seeking a new life in the American West. Blacks were no less influenced by late nineteenth-century popular myths regarding the frontier than whites. Moreover, the siren call of the West affected not just the downtrodden, exploited masses of the South; educated, upwardly mobile Negroes such as Mifflin W. Gibbs of Pennsylvania and Edward P. McCabe of New York also perceived the West as a land of opportunity and individuality where a man was valued for his achievements, not his lineage or the color of his skin. Believing that Afro-Americans would be able to acquire wealth and exercise political power in the sparsely populated and economically underdeveloped areas beyond the Mississippi, a group of lawyers, journalists, teachers, and economic opportunists moved to California, Kansas, Montana, and Nebraska in the 1870s and 1880s. In some regions and in some activities these immigrants did enjoy greater freedom than they had either in the North or South. In Kansas, for example, blacks encountered discrimination in public services, in the administration of justice, and in employment. They were segregated in hotels, restaurants, and theaters; and were excluded from white hospitals, churches, and neighborhoods. And yet during the same period there were integrated schools at one level or another in all sections of the state, public facilities were open to Negroes on both an integrated and segregated basis, and blacks were protected in their effort to vote. With one exception, legally mandated segregation was nonexistent. Influenced themselves by the prevailing popular image of the frontier, by the West's free soil tradition, and by American Protestantism, a majority of whites in Kansas and other western states made a commitment to racial advancement in the form of parallel development. That is, they were willing to leave blacks alone, allowing them the right to vote, to own property, and to enjoy the benefits of a public education. Beyond this, however, the state felt no obligation to the black man. Indeed, "charity"—direct relief and free land grants, for example—would only undermine the Negro's individual initiative and retard the progress of the race. In reality, the doctrine of parallel development merely froze the *status quo*. It left blacks without the land and capital necessary to collective economic advancement. In addition, because white westerners perceived poverty as a badge of moral depravity and wealth as a symbol of divine favor, the concept of parallel development tended to exacerbate racial prejudice. Thus, by the 1890s a number of the upwardly mobile blacks who had come west some ten to fifteen years earlier found themselves disillusioned, frustrated, and confronted with the same dilemma that had compelled them to immigrate initially.

Caught between a desire to work within the existing political and economic framework, thus realizing the promise of American life, and a desire to reject the system, thus escaping the racial prejudice to be found in the American milieu, these members of the black middle class once again sought the best of both worlds by turning to America's New Empire then emerging in the nonwhite, underdeveloped regions of the world.[9] For these men, participation in the nation's burgeoning and far-flung commercial network seemed the perfect solution to the cruel dilemma of the 1890s. By establishing rubber plantations, obtaining mining concessions, and founding trading corporations in nonwhite areas, the black entrepreneur could simultaneously escape the prison of race prejudice while retaining the blessings of American citizenship. This third approach, they believed, would not only enhance their personal power and prestige but, by adding to the collective wealth of the black community, also contribute to the welfare of the race as a whole. And it would prove that blacks as well as whites were proper vehicles for the spread of civilization. These men were not separatists. Although fully aware of the racial injustice that characterized American society, they remained convinced that the Constitution, the free enterprise system, and the principles of the Declaration of Independence offered the best opportunity for the

xvi

black man to achieve political power and equality of economic opportunity. Yet, they were men on the make, impatient to fulfill their destiny. In short, acceptance of the moral and material values of late nineteenth-century America by these disciples of Horatio Alger impelled them toward duplication of white society while racism compelled them to pursue the American dream in isolation, apart from the society to which they were committed.

No black American was more determined to realize the promise of American life nor more frustrated by his inability to do so than John Lewis Waller. Politician, lawyer, journalist, and diplomat, Waller, whose first twelve years were spent in slavery, overcame his humble beginnings and to a remarkable degree realized his potential as an individual. Migrating to frontier Kansas in the late 1870s, he quickly rose to a position of leadership in the black community and became an important figure in the state Republican party. His political career came to an abrupt halt in 1890, however, when the Republicans rejected his bid to be nominated as the party's candidate for state auditor. Frustrated by his inability to break into the inner circle of power and convinced that his defeat was due to the rising tide of racism both in Kansas and throughout the nation, he searched frantically for an option that would allow him further growth and achievement. Waller was a true product of the late nineteenth century. He fully accepted the conservative, Social Darwinist, and *laissez-faire* economic views of his times. A hard-money, high-tariff Republican, he believed in the Gospel of Wealth and the Protestant Ethic as vehicles for both personal fulfillment and racial uplift. Expatriation was, therefore, out of the question. Participation in America's rising commercial empire, on the other hand, would permit him to continue to enjoy the privileges of American citizenship (as he perceived them) and at the same time avoid the discrimination that dogged the footsteps of blacks as they sought to exercise their civil rights and compete for the economic rewards available in a free society.

Specifically, Waller hoped to establish a vast plantation in some nonwhite, underdeveloped region of the globe that would simultaneously serve as a vehicle for his own ambitions and as a haven for other oppressed but upwardly mobile Afro-Americans. An opportunity to realize this dream came in 1891 when President Benjamin Harrison appointed him United States consul to Madagascar. For three years he curried favor with the native monarchy, and then in 1894 Waller retired from the consular service and obtained a huge land grant from the Malagasy government.

The ex-consul's plans, however, were to be thwarted once again by racism, this time in the guise of French imperialism. Africa in the 1890s was the site of an intense colonial rivalry among the major European powers. This was true no less of Madagascar than the Congo or Northwest Africa. By 1895 France had elbowed its way to the front in the competition for control of the huge east African island. Viewing Waller and his plans for the founding of a black utopia as a threat to their hegemony in Madagascar, French authorities in 1895 quashed the concession, arrested Waller, and sentenced him to twenty years in prison.

To France's surprise, expropriation and incarceration of the black entrepreneur provoked a full-scale diplomatic confrontation with the United States. Such diverse interest groups as the black press, white commercial expansionists, black Democrats, and, of course, the Republican party, saw in the case an opportunity to advance their own particular causes. Responding to pressure from these sources, President Cleveland's administration labored mightily throughout 1895 and early 1896 to secure Waller's liberation and to protect his land grant. Unfortunately for Waller, the price Paris demanded for his release was American acquiescence in the French protectorate over Madagascar. When the government in Washington subsequently met France's terms, Waller found himself an empire-builder *sans* empire. Just as his drive in the United States to achieve power and prestige for himself and his brethren through political participation had been blunted by domestic racism, so his program of personal and group advancement through overseas business enterprise was thwarted by international racism in the form of European imperialism.

This book, although touching both subjects, is neither a comprehensive study of the black community in Kansas nor an in-depth inquiry into race relations at the turn of the century. Rather, it focuses on the career of a single individual—an ambitious, resourceful black American —and his efforts to realize personal fulfillment in a racist world. John Waller was both a product and a victim of his times, and thus, I believe, his tale deserves to be told.

A Black Odyssey

CHAPTER ONE

"A Young Man of Good Character"

According to John Waller's own account, he was born in slavery on January 12, 1850, in New Madrid County, Missouri. His owner was "J. S. Sherwood, a wealthy and prominent planter" of southeast Missouri.[1] Apparently, Waller's memory was faulty as to both his age and the name of his owner. A resolution passed by the Missouri House of Representatives and submitted to the State Department in 1895 while Waller was in prison lists his age as forty-three, which would place his birthday in 1851 or 1852. More importantly, the 1860 Missouri Census, Slave Schedule, does not record a male bondsman ten years of age being owned by any of the three Sherwoods listed. Marcus S. Sherwood did list one black male nine years of age, who almost certainly was John. In his later recollections Waller also erred as to the precise name of his owner, referring to him as J. S. rather than M. S.[2]

Marcus Sherwood's father, Eli Sherwood, was a Connecticut Yankee who migrated first from New England to Mississippi in the late 1830s or early 1840s and then to Missouri sometime in the 1850s. A farmer by trade with some capital to invest, he purchased land in Mississippi, acquired several slaves, and became a planter. What prompted the elder Sherwood to move to New Madrid County, located in southeast Missouri, adjacent to the Mississippi River, is a matter of conjecture—soil exhaustion, the lure of new horizons, or perhaps a personal tragedy. Indications are that Eli Sherwood was married twice; his first wife either died or the two were separated during his residency in Mississippi.[3]

The census indicates that as of 1850 Eli Sherwood, at the age of forty-eight, was a well-established planter worth at least $20,000 in land alone. Evidently, he turned over part of his estate to Marcus in the form of a stake. By 1860 Marcus had enlarged his original holdings and acquired most of the family plantation from his father, who had gone into semiretirement.

The Missouri Slave Schedule for 1850 indicates that Marcus Sherwood owned twenty-five slaves, among whom were Anthony, 31, and Maria, 25, and a son, John. All three were listed as black rather than mulatto, which would indicate that Anthony rather than Marcus Sherwood or some other white man was John's biological father.[4]

John's childhood was as secure as it could be within the confines of slavery. The petition from Buchanan County, Missouri, filed with the Cleveland administration during Waller's period of incarceration, states that not only were Anthony and Maria household servants but that their parents before them had served in a similar capacity. Maria was probably the Sherwood family's cook and Anthony its carriage driver and handyman. Anthony must have labored in the fields during some period in his life, however, because the vocation he turned to immediately after emancipation was farming.[5]

Young John was able to enjoy two benefits denied to so many other bondsmen: a degree of protection from the arbitrary exercise of power by his white master, and a stable family life. As house servants, Anthony and Maria occupied a special position within the plantation community. Masters throughout the South were to a greater or lesser degree dependent upon their personal servants for the orderly functioning of the household. According to more than one source, Anthony and Maria fulfilled their duties—cooking, housecleaning, maintenance of horse and buggy, rearing of the Sherwood children—with "obedience, faithfulness, and truth."[6] There were in turn rewards—however slight by contemporary standards—for those who made possible the gracious lifestyle enjoyed by the southern aristocracy. Household slaves and their children usually enjoyed better food and clothing than the field hands. They were necessarily accorded a degree of trust and some freedom of movement within and without the plantation. In addition, house servants generally sat atop the social hierarchy within the slave community. As personal servants of the "massa and missus," Anthony and Maria were in a position to intervene—if ever so subtly—in behalf of bondsmen who had offended the Sherwoods. They served as funnels to the other slaves of news of the larger world outside the plantation. In short, they were probably the most confident and knowledgeable members of the slave community.[7] That they were able to serve the Sherwoods well without compromising themselves in the eyes of their fellow bondsmen is testified to by the fact that following emancipation the Sherwood slave community chose to remain together for a generation.[8] As a result of his parents' privileged status, John was able to escape the backbreaking monotony of field labor, the constant threat of the overseer's whip, and the trauma of family separation.

Indeed, it is reasonable to assume that John's achievements as an adult stemmed in part from the confidence he gained through growing up in the bosom of a closely knit and loving family. He never had to confront bastardy as did so many other bondsmen; John's eleven brothers and sisters were not sold away; the family remained intact throughout slavery, confiscation, emancipation, and reconstruction. Letters between John and his mother, brothers, and sisters written in later years seem to indicate that the passage through slavery had created within the family a special bond. The trauma of emancipation and the struggle to make the transition to freedom served as additional centripetal forces fusing Anthony, Maria, John, and the other family members into an interdependent whole that only death would fragment.[9]

The slavery years no doubt had a profound impact on John's developing personality. The restraints, the racism, the poverty were all there. He was whipped at least twice by whites, once at age six and again at thirteen. The young black could not help but fear and distrust whites. Yet John's experience in bondage did not produce personal disintegration, passivity, hopelessness—to the contrary. His parents' confidence and relatively positive self-image were transferred to their son. He was allowed, as few other young slaves were, to explore the world around him. For example, his father often took John with him when he drove the Sherwoods into New Madrid, where the young Negro witnessed the hustle and bustle of life in a Missouri river town.[10] Yet widened horizons and an increased capacity for growth produced as much pain as pleasure because they led to a rising level of expectations, a thirst for further development and self-realization that simply were not possible within the context of slavery.

Fortunately, the young black was not to be confined within the "peculiar institution" for the rest of his life. Because his mother had access to table talk in the Sherwood household, and his father to conversations between whites held during extended buggy rides, John and his siblings must have been able to follow in at least a rudimentary way the growing rift between North and South in the late 1850s. John first became aware that war had actually broken out in August, 1861. During

5

a trip to New Madrid, the young slave, who was then trusted to drive Mrs. Sherwood and her children about the countryside, was amazed to see the river lined with steamboats packed with Confederate troops and flying the stars and bars. According to a story (almost certainly apocryphal) circulated during a state political campaign in 1890, John, upon seeing a rebel officer haul down a United States flag and replace it with the Confederate ensign, shouted, "Lincoln's men will put it back again," a *faux paus* for which he was allegedly severely punished.[11]

From the very outset of the Civil War, the Union armies operating in the border regions were inundated with thousands of slaves who had either run away from their masters or who had been abandoned by them. The Sherwood family slaves became "contrabands," the name given by General Benjamin Butler to ragged black refugees who flooded Union camps, almost as soon as the Emancipation Proclamation was enunciated. Whether the Sherwoods voluntarily manumitted Anthony, Maria, John, and their other bondsmen or whether they were confiscated by Union troops is unclear. Whatever the method, John, his parents, and more than a hundred slaves from New Madrid County became free men and women in mid-November, 1862, and attached themselves to Company H of the Thirty-Second Iowa Infantry.[12]

Captain John Scott, commander of Company H, arranged for the settlement of his charges in Tama County, Iowa, situated in the south-central portion of the state near Cedar Rapids. Local residents were alerted, and a group of philanthropic whites headed by A. B. Mason, a Sioux City attorney, greeted the shivering, penniless blacks with hot food and a wagonload of clothes. With the aid of Mason, Anthony subsequently obtained a small farm, which he hoped would produce crops sufficient to support himself, his wife, and his numerous offspring. During the move from Missouri to Iowa, literally from slavery to freedom, Anthony and Maria adopted their surname—Waller. Whether the name was chosen to commemorate the illustrious Virginia Wallers or to remember a kindly family encountered during the flight to freedom is unclear; there were no Wallers in New Madrid County. By February, 1863, the Wallers of Tama County, Iowa, had settled down to a life of rural poverty.[13]

Liberty brought many benefits to the four million black Americans released by the Emancipation Proclamation—freedom to move about at will, freedom to choose an occupation, the opportunity to grow materially and intellectually. Emancipation carried with it, however, another freedom that often rendered these benefits meaningless—the right to starve. The years immediately following the move to Iowa were the most difficult the Waller clan had yet experienced. Indeed, Anthony Waller found it impossible to support his large family without another source of income, and in 1863 he hired John out to a local white farmer, William Wilkinson.[14]

Separation from his family was no doubt painful for the twelve-year-old freedman, but his association with the Wilkinsons was to be one of the more fortuitous events in his life. During the summer of 1863 Mrs. Wilkinson taught John Waller to read and write, all the while encouraging him to acquire as much formal education as possible. In the fall of 1863 the Wilkinson's hired hand attended his first public institution of learning, a one-room rural schoolhouse in Tama County. After four years of study, interspersed with long hours of farm labor, John was admitted to the high school at Toledo, Iowa, a small community adjacent to his parents' and the Wilkinsons' farms.[15]

It is impossible to ascertain whether his mother and father, Mrs. Wilkinson, one of his high school teachers (possibly a Mrs. Caldwell, who spent hours with him each week after class), or all of them urged John to enter Cornell College in Mount Vernon, Iowa. Apparently, sometime during his high school years John had apprenticed himself to a barber and learned the trade. For when he moved to Mount Vernon in 1870 or 1871, he immediately went to work in a barber shop in order to support himself while he pursued his studies. No sooner had he settled down in this sleepy college town with its tree-lined avenues and meandering pace, than disaster struck the Waller family. Some type of disease, cholera or smallpox perhaps, ravaged the community around Toledo in the early seventies. Learning that his father and several of his brothers and sisters were desperately ill, John abandoned his plans for college and rushed home to tend the family farm. During his first year back, four brothers and sisters died. The epidemic passed, however, and by 1874 the elder Waller was once again well enough to look after his crops.[16]

The years at home must have been intensely frustrating. The thirst for knowledge evident in John as a teenager was merely augmented by his early schooling. Even if his teachers did not indicate such to him explicitly, young Waller must have realized that he was a gifted student. A college education would enable him to convert the possibilities of freedom into realities. But how to pay for this invaluable key? While the three-year interregnum on the farm may or may not have demoralized John, it most certainly left him penniless.

Finally abandoning plans for college, John Waller in 1874 left the family farm and moved to Cedar Rapids, the largest city in the area.

Apparently, he arrived without any long-range plans, for he immediately began barbering at one of the local shops for blacks, and the "tonsorial arts" remained his sole visible means of support during his four-year stay in Cedar Rapids. Waller's high school education and his native intelligence made him a leader within the black community almost overnight.[17] The twenty-four year old ex-slave began speaking and writing on various topics, particularly civil rights. The Cedar Rapids *Evening Gazette* later recalled that the young black man from Toledo was especially interested in "the relation of his race to the government."[18] Almost certainly he became active in local politics. Late in 1874 Judge N. M. Hubbard, senior partner in the law firm of Hubbard, Clark, and Deacon, wrote the young freedman and asked him to appear on a given date at his office. According to Waller, he had never met Hubbard before. When the young black barber-politician arrived for his interview, the judge questioned him about his education, his values, his hopes for his people. What about a career, Hubbard asked. Would not a thorough knowledge of the law allow Waller to advance his own interests and those of his race simultaneously? When John agreed, Hubbard threw open the doors to his extensive law library and invited Waller to read with him until he was ready to take the bar examination. Securing such an invitation was no mean achievement. Hubbard, Clark, and Deacon was one of the best-known law firms in Iowa, handling virtually all legal business for the Chicago and Northwestern Railroad.[19] Waller proved to be a diligent and capable student. One of the partners recalled in later years that Waller was "a young man of good character, industrious and energetic, and working hard to succeed in life."[20] For the next three years Waller interrupted his legal studies only long enough to administer the shaves and haircuts that paid for his room and board. At Marion, Iowa, on November 15, 1877, the twenty-six year old freedman was admitted to the bar.[21]

Exactly why Hubbard chose to befriend Waller is a mystery. More than likely a combination of philanthropy and politics was responsible. By taking in Waller, Hubbard could simultaneously aid a worthy Negro struggling to better himself and make a potentially powerful political ally within the black community. Waller may have been astounded by Hubbard's proposal, as he later claimed, but he had no reservations about accepting. The former slave from Missouri had over the years acquired a knack for getting along with and winning the respect of whites. "Honest, upright, and faithful" were some of the adjectives used by those who had known him as a youth. G. R. Struble, a Toledo lawyer acquainted with Waller during his high school days, recommended him

John Lewis Waller

as "an exemplary and reliable young man."[22] Waller's facility for getting along with whites was probably due more than anything else to experience. As house slave, hired hand, student, barber, and then legal scholar, he came into daily contact with those on the other side of the color line. While he could be circumspect, there apparently was no obsequiousness in Waller. Rather, it was his earnestness, honesty, hopefulness, and desire to get ahead that impressed his contemporaries. No doubt these traits were real and not merely feigned; nonetheless, Waller could hardly have escaped the fact that whites valued them, especially in blacks.

When John Lewis Waller entered the legal profession, he was twenty-seven years old. Six feet tall, 180 pounds, and barrelchested, Waller physically was an imposing man. He remained clean shaven until middle age, when he began to sport a thin moustache. Closely cropped hair, a prominent forehead, dark skin, and piercing eyes were his most prominent features. After his admission to the bar Waller's public attire remained essentially the same throughout the rest of his life. He wore a tight-fitting, single-breasted black suit that always appeared one size too small for him, and a black tie. His only departure from this costume was the military uniform he donned during the Spanish-American War. In conversation Waller was articulate and forceful, although his language tended always to be a bit formal. Sensitive and intelligent, he possessed a facility for empathizing with others and a propensity for lost causes. If John Waller possessed a sense of humor, there is no record of it.[23]

Waller was eager to explore the world and realize the possibilities opened up by his new profession. To a young man anxious to make his mark in the world, the Cedar Rapids area appeared singularly unpromising. It was, among other things, oversupplied with bright young lawyers. Moreover, there was always the chance that his father's health would fail and he would be called back to the farm. Reports within the black community of a mass migration of Negroes to Kansas, reputedly a land of economic opportunity and civic equality, stirred Waller's imagination. He subsequently fell under the influence of Benjamin "Pap" Singleton (or at least Singleton's propaganda), who in 1874 had established the Tennessee Real Estate and Homestead Association with a view to promoting black migration to Kansas. During the mid-1870s Waller became one of Singleton's most ardent advocates.[24] Deciding that the torrent of humanity he was certain was about to descend upon the Sunflower State would require the services of a lawyer and, more importantly, would have the means to pay for them, Waller took his own advice and in the spring of 1878 set out for Kansas.

CHAPTER TWO

Law, Politics, and Leavenworth: A Beginning

The black community in Kansas actually began taking shape between 1860 and 1870 when several thousand Negroes moved to the state. Newly emancipated slaves who had come to view the home of John Brown as something of a promised land, a haven from oppression and exploitation, made up the bulk of the immigration. Even before the end of the Civil War, rumors began circulating among Negro contrabands that blacks and whites lived side by side in Kansas, free of animosity, and that the climate and soil were as beneficent as the racial atmosphere. These ex-slaves were joined by a smaller number of free blacks from the North who perceived Kansas to be a land of political and especially economic opportunity. Mining, railroading, the meat-packing industry, land development, and other areas of endeavor beckoned to Negroes who for generations had been relegated to menial jobs in the North. The census of 1870 showed a total black population of 17,108, a gain of 16,481 and an increase of over twenty-seven times the 1860 number. These immigrants, in spite of their large numbers and the fact that most were initially destitute, were able to find work and become self-sustaining. A significant number, taking advantage of the Homestead Law, moved to rural areas and began farming, but most settled in the larger towns of eastern Kansas such as Leavenworth, Atchison, Topeka, and Lawrence.[1]

The train that brought John Waller west from Cedar Rapids that day in May, 1878, made its first scheduled stop in Kansas in Leavenworth; Waller chose to go no farther. Situated on the Kansas-Missouri border,

11

just west of the Missouri River, Leavenworth was one of the largest, oldest, and wildest towns in Kansas. Established by a group of Missouri slaveholders in June, 1854, the community subsequently became one of the principal proslavery centers in the state prior to the Civil War, and it remained a stronghold of the Democratic party in Kansas throughout the last quarter of the nineteenth century. The federal military reservation, the state prison at nearby Lansing, several coal mines, the levees, and a number of small manufacturing establishments served as the foundation of Leavenworth's economy and supplied the town with an abundance of skilled and semiskilled jobs. The site of several breweries and distilleries, Leavenworth was the antiprohibition capital of the state; and even after passage of the prohibitory amendment in 1880, two hundred saloons continued to operate.[2] Intimidated by the voting power of Leavenworth inhabitants and the economic clout of the liquor interests, Kansas governors, both Republican and Democratic, proved unwilling to enforce the ban on alcohol—much to the chagrin of the drys. "I realize that 'tis almost like subduing the South," complained a W.C.T.U. official to Governor E. N. Morrill in 1896, "but that law [prohibition] was meant for Leavenworth too."[3]

Despite the city's politics and its relative lawlessness (a situation that invariably spelled trouble for blacks), Negroes were drawn by the abundance of jobs and flocked to Leavenworth in the 1860s. By the end of the decade the black community was the largest in the state, numbering nearly 5,000. The black population, most of whom were employed in the mines, at the prison, on construction jobs, or on the levees unloading steamboats, lived almost exclusively in two enclaves, one in the south, known as Cincinnati, and one in the northern part of the city. Despite the fact that most blacks had lived in Leavenworth only a few years, social organization among the Negro populace was fairly complex, and by 1870 a cluster of separate institutions had emerged. There were five black churches: the African Methodist Episcopal (the largest), the First Baptist, the Mount Olive Baptist, the Independence Baptist, and a small Catholic congregation, Holy Epiphany. Serving the cultural and economic needs of the population were at least three literary societies and a number of fraternal and benevolent lodges.[4]

As soon as he got his bearings Waller took a room at a boarding house on the south side of Metropolitan Avenue between Thirteenth and Fourteenth streets. Fully convinced that he could support himself practicing law, Waller made arrangements for an office, hung out his shingle, and began advertising in the Topeka *Colored Citizen* (Leavenworth had no black newspaper during this period). Presenting letters of recommendation from Hubbard, Clark, and Deacon to Judge Robert Crozier, Waller was duly admitted to practice in the First Judicial District.[5]

Professionally and hence economically, Waller's first year in Leavenworth was one of struggle and disappointment. In late nineteenth-century America virtually all black professionals faced a daily struggle for financial survival, and lawyers perhaps fared worst of all. Negro attorneys suffered from the fact that many communities were oversupplied with lawyers, that Negroes could rarely afford to resort to litigation, and that the prejudice shown blacks in general by whites led Negroes to believe that they would fare much better in court with a white lawyer than a black. Moreover, blacks were often as suspicious as whites of the qualifications of Negro lawyers. Typically, Waller's practice suffered because of prejudice exhibited by both whites and blacks. In August the young attorney became embroiled in a controversy with Charles H. Langston, a prominent black resident of Lawrence, over the qualifications of Negro professionals. During an industrial and business convention held in Kansas City in the summer of 1878, Langston had exhorted his fellow blacks to avoid Negro lawyers and doctors who did not have a degree from a professional school. Leavenworth blacks must have taken Langston's advice in seeking legal aid because Waller's practice languished. Indeed, so precarious became his position that Waller wrote a lengthy letter to the *Colored Citizen* in rebuttal. "Some of our most worthy young men are not able to remain at a professional school the five or six years that are necessary to graduation; . . . one half the white lawyers admitted to the bar . . . came . . . holding the same kind of certificates he [Langston] so ardently denounces."[6] Waller's protest did nothing to improve his business. When he did persuade a Negro client to hire him and when the case came to court in Leavenworth, Waller, no less than his colleagues in other regions, suffered from the prejudice, often blatant, displayed by white lawyers and jurists.[7]

There were, however, some successes. In August Waller began catering to the several hundred black veterans of the Grand Army of the Republic living in Kansas. Many of these men, he discovered, had just claims against the government for back pay not received or against lawyers who had compelled the War Department to disburse back wages and then cheated their clients out of a portion. On August 9 a "Notice to Colored Soldiers" appeared in the *Colored Citizen*. "If you have any claim against the government for bounty or back pay," it read, "John L. Waller, the colored lawyer of Leavenworth proposes to collect for you at greatly reduced rates."[8] The appeal brought Waller a number of cases, one of which led him into a courtroom confrontation with one of

Leavenworth's most prominent white citizens. In October, 1878, William Clark, a veteran of the Seventh United States Colored Infantry, called on the "colored lawyer of Leavenworth" and, presenting his discharge papers, asked Waller if he had received all that was due. Waller compared Clark's discharge with those of one Joseph Carris who had served in the same regiment and who was enlisted and mustered out on the same dates as Clark. His client, Waller discovered, was $100.00 short. An inquiry directed to the auditor of the Treasury in Washington brought news that Clark had been allowed $351.64, the same as Carris. If Clark had not received said amount he should recover from the lawyer who had represented him at the time.[9]

Clark had a good case, but Waller must have been hesitant to press the matter, for the veteran had been represented originally by Colonel Thomas Moonlight, one of Leavenworth's leading white attorneys, a man who would twice receive the Democratic nomination for governor. Ironically, he was the commander of one of Kansas' two colored regiments during the Civil War. Moonlight's prestige notwithstanding, Waller decided that if he were going to maintain his credibility with the black community, he would have to proceed. The black attorney brought suit for exactly $100.00 in district court—and won.[10]

Perhaps out of disappointment with the volume and character of his cases, but most certainly because he was an educated black with a rapidly developing race consciousness and a strong sense of personal destiny, Waller inevitably turned to the activity perhaps most typical of upwardly mobile blacks during the post-Reconstruction era—politics. Because the black community, even in the West, existed at the caprice of the white, politics assumed special significance for Negroes. As William Chafe has pointed out, the attitude of white politicians toward their black counterparts served as a barometer of the white citizenry's feelings toward the race and as a signal to the populace in general of the Negroes' status within the larger society. Thus, blacks came to view recognition of individuals through patronage and political office as tantamount to recognition of and protection for the entire race. Waller fully shared this point of view. Like so many of his contemporaries, he was firmly convinced that, once Negroes were excluded from voting and holding office, they would be vulnerable both economically and legally to white supremacists.[11] "I would not care a fig for my citizenship," he remarked in 1888, "if I did not have the right to vote."[12] In short, Waller viewed political activism as a means for enhancing his personal status among both blacks and whites, and as a technique of racial uplift.

Not surprisingly, Waller pledged his allegiance to the Republican party as the group most likely to allow the Negro a voice in its affairs and to reward loyalty through elective and appointive public office. Protection and recognition were the primary reasons Waller joined the party and the yardsticks by which he continued to measure the organization and its leaders. During his twenty years as a Republican, he labored unceasingly to see that only those who were proven friends of the Negro reached the top.[13] He denounced Chester A. Arthur in 1882 and 1883 for his treatment of black officeholders and his lily-white policies in the South. "We challenge his right as the executive of this country to experiment upon the colored citizens of these United States, for the purpose of advancing his own chances for the future," he wrote in 1883. Just because Arthur was a Republican president and he, Waller, was a loyal member of the same party, he would not condone the "infamous acts" and "wholesale insults" visited upon the black community by the chief executive.[14] Whenever Republicans strayed from their traditional commitment to democracy and human rights, the black Kansan never failed to remind the party leadership of its duty. When, for example, James G. Blaine advised southern blacks in the 1880s to abjure all topics except the tariff, Waller wrote to President Harrison that he admired Blaine and respected his opinion, but "[I am] not willing to close my mouth and eyes to the frauds committed against the suffrage of nearly a million colored voters in this country."[15] An editorial in the *Western Recorder*, the first of Waller's newspapers, perhaps best summed up his views on political loyalty and his adopted party. "We have acted with the Republican party all the time, not because of the name . . . but from a principle. . . . While we do not favor everything championed by the Republican party, yet we are satisfied beyond all doubt that the party is in advance of all others in the development of one of the grandest civilizations known in the annals of history." He would remain loyal to the party of Lincoln, he continued, "but we expect to claim . . . our right to the class or kind of men we want for office."[16]

Although Waller embraced the Republican party primarily because it promised a degree of participation and protection to Negroes, there were other dimensions to the relationship. He, like many of his educated contemporaries, identified with the conservative leadership within the party. The American creed of free enterprise, self-reliance, and unlimited material acquisitiveness expressed by Republican leaders seemed to Waller to be the key not only to his own progress but to that of the race as a whole.[17]

If Waller saw opportunity in the party of Lincoln, Kansas Republicans in turn perceived political profit in the Negro vote in general and

Waller in particular. Although blacks never comprised more than 4.75 percent of Kansas' total population in the nineteenth century, they formed anywhere from 15 percent to 30 percent, varying over time, of the inhabitants of the state's five largest counties. In 1880, for example, Douglas County (Lawrence) was 17.4 percent black, Shawnee (Topeka) 22.6 percent, and Wyandotte (Kansas City) 31.5 percent.[18] The black vote was of obvious importance in city and county elections in these areas, and it could be vital in statewide contests in case a party stalemate devoloped.

More than likely the attribute that first brought John Waller to the notice of Kansas Republicans was his speaking ability. His powerful voice, his education, and his seemingly imperturbable self-confidence made him an effective, at times awesome, orator. W. F. Jaques, a white man who lived some six years in Kansas City while Waller was active in state politics, recalled the Negro lawyer's impact on him: "He is one of the most eloquent men your correspondent ever heard address an audience. . . . In fact, his ability as an orator and public speaker is such that to our mind no one could listen to him speak any length of time without being convinced that no mediocre mind is housed beneath his black skin."[19] His addresses at black social functions and public ceremonies were often historical, tended to engender race pride, and were heavily laced with flowery phrases. During the course of a speech given at Blue Rapids in 1883 in which he paid tribute to the black soldiers who had fallen in the Civil War, Waller gave full reign to his voice and imagination. "Their [Union veterans'] Graves are all covered with autumn leaves, they are at peace now, sleeping sublimely sweet, they are still on guard, watching in their stillness, the destiny of our country, they clinch as in battle the musket and the sabre. . . . Oh grandest and most sacred patriotic dead! let the Nation rest in peace upon their sacred and hallowed ashes; come here all Nations and assist this great people in doing honor and adoration to these sacrifices, these blood offerings to Union, Liberty, and fraternal universal freedom."[20] His political addresses, particularly when delivered to racially mixed audiences, tended to be shorter and more hard-hitting, with an emphasis on logical argument.

By the time Waller arrived in Kansas black Republicans were already numerous and well organized. Every city of any size had a Negro "flambeau" club which mobilized local blacks for torchlight parades and rallies, and every black precinct had a Republican "captain" ready to turn out the vote on election day. In the late 1870s there was no clearly recognized leader or boss among the state's black Republicans; instead the black and tan's quota of nominations and appointive offices was controlled by a quadrumvirate of ambitious and colorful politicians. Heading the list was the intensely race-conscious and militant William Bolden Townsend of Leavenworth, who was born a slave near Huntsville, Alabama, in 1855. He and his mother, after being manumitted by their master, who was also William's father, moved to Kansas in 1857. Townsend completed a common school education, taught for a period, and became increasingly active in Republican politics. When Waller met him, Townsend held an appointive post in the Leavenworth Post Office and controlled black Republican patronage throughout the county. He would later edit two race journals and earn a law degree from the University of Kansas. The second member of the quartet was John M. Brown of Topeka. A graduate of Oberlin College in Ohio, Brown first entered public life in Mississippi where he taught school, served as sheriff of Coahoma County, and became colonel of the First Mississippi Colored Militia. Migrating to Kansas sometime in the mid-1870s, he settled in the state capital and began a lifelong quest to be recognized by the Republican party as the political spokesman for Kansas blacks. A 100-acre farm, acquired somewhat mysteriously while he was serving as general superintendent of the Kansas Freedmen's Relief Association from 1879 to 1881, provided "the Colonel" with a handsome income throughout his life.[21]

Next in importance to Townsend and Brown in black Republican circles were William L. Eagleson and T. W. Henderson, co-editors of the Topeka *Colored Citizen*. Eagleson, considered one of the pioneer black journalists of the West, was born in St. Louis in 1835. Completing his apprenticeship to a printer, he quit St. Louis, headed west, and in 1872 established the *Colored Citizen* in Fort Scott, Kansas. (He moved the paper to Topeka some six years later.) Political opportunist extraordinaire, Eagleson was always on the lookout for the main chance. In the late 1880s he would defect to the Democrats and become an ardent advocate among blacks of "political independence." T. W. Henderson, an ordained minister, was born in Greensboro, North Carolina, and migrated to Kansas from Oberlin, Ohio, in 1868. He was pastor of the A.M.E. churches in Lawrence and Topeka respectively and served as chaplain of the House of Representatives in the early 1880s. A leader of the black community in Topeka, Henderson would found along with Eagleson the Kansas Colored Emigration Bureau and would become one of the black directors of the Kansas Freedmen's Relief Association.[22]

Townsend and Waller became close friends and political allies almost as soon as the Iowan arrived in Leavenworth. They remained so for thirteen years until a political disagreement ended their relationship. Waller was evidently never close to Brown—few men were—but he managed to remain in Brown's good graces until 1890. One of the most experienced and ruthless politicians in the state, a man particularly adept at interracial politics, Brown would stop at nothing to control the black vote and whatever patronage Republicans were willing to distribute among Kansas Negroes. Waller evidently got along well with Eagleson and Henderson initially, but their penchant for political independence would soon lead to mutual alienation.[23]

Largely at the urging of Townsend, Brown, Eagleson, and Henderson, Cyrus Leland, chairman of the Republican state central committee, invited Waller to tour eastern Kansas in October, 1878, and speak in support of the Republican ticket then headed by gubernatorial candidate John P. St. John. The Republican slate swept Kansas, and Waller received the plaudits of both blacks and whites for his efforts on the stump.[24] Waller may or may not have realized it, but the campaign of 1878 marked the beginning of a twenty-two year political career during which he would become one of the most prominent black politicians in Kansas.

CHAPTER THREE

The First Frontier: Kansas and the Great Exodus

John Waller arrived in Kansas on the eve of what was surely one of the most significant population movements of the nineteenth century: the three-year migration of tens of thousands of oppressed blacks from the South into Kansas known as the Great Exodus of 1879–1881. Although he preceded the main body of exodusters and though his economic and educational level ranged far above that of the great majority of immigrants, Waller was part of the movement; he was influenced both by the forces that were responsible for the exodus and, more importantly, by the movement itself—the propaganda it produced and the utopian dream that underlay it. The exodus focused his attention on the plight of southern blacks, which in turn heightened his sensitivity to racial conditions and to problems of the larger black community. In coming to Kansas, moreover, many exodusters were responding to a desire for racial uplift by following a scenario in which blacks would remove to a sparsely populated, economically underdeveloped frontier area. Once there, Negroes could act out their lives relatively free of racist restraints, accumulating wealth and exercising their civil and political rights. These successful colonies would improve the lot of both those who came and those who stayed behind. Such a dream had probably played a significant role in luring Waller to Kansas in the first place, but his fantasy had been personal, not communal. As the movement progressed, Waller came to view it not as something accidental but rather a divinely ordained social experiment that promised individual and collective salvation for

Afro-Americans everywhere.

Further, the exodus implanted in Waller's mind a plan for Negro advancement suitable, he believed, for implementation within a biracial frontier such as Kansas. This scheme originated in part in the white community's response to the black in-migration. At first apprehensive over the influx of poverty-stricken and sometimes disease-ridden Negroes in 1879 and 1880, whites began to accept the presence of the exodusters once it became apparent that the movement was limited both in size and duration. In caring for the hungry and homeless, state authorities, religious groups, and secular philanthropists developed a plan for peaceful co-existence. Influenced by the prevailing popular image of the frontier, ity of white Kansans made a commitment to racial advancement in the by the West's free soil tradition, and by American Protestantism, a major-form of parallel development. That is, they were willing to allow blacks their civil and political rights, but they rejected amalgamation and long-term economic aid. Ignoring the fact that they controlled at least 95 per-cent of the state's wealth, whites chose to believe that blacks had the op-portunity to compete with them on an equal basis and that if they failed, Negroes had no one to blame but themselves. Ironically, at the same time they were imprisoned by the myth of parallel development, Waller and many of his middle-class brethren came to accept and advocate it as a viable method of racial uplift particularly appropriate to the Kansas frontier.

The exodus actually began in the mid-1870s when, at the urging of two ex-slaves, Benjamin "Pap" Singleton of Tennessee and Henry Adams of Georgia, several hundred downtrodden Negroes left the South and established colonies in Kansas. In their search for protection, civil equality, and economic opportunity Singleton and Adams looked to a new frontier. Kansas, they believed, was a land in which blacks could leave the past behind and develop their individual potentials to the fullest. Dunlap Colony, established in May, 1878, on the eastern edge of Morris County in eastern Kansas, was Singleton's largest effort. Consist-ing of about 200 Negro families, the settlement was situated on 7,500 acres of government land acquired at $1.25 an acre. Each colonist was required to purchase his own land, and the farms varied in size from 40 to 160 acres. A group of Kentucky Negroes, probably indirectly influ-enced by "Pap" Singleton, established two colonies in Kansas in 1877. The first of these was situated in Hodgeman County in the west-central part of the state. The colonists originally intended to found a town, and to this end they filed articles of incorporation for the Morton City Town-ship Company and began to lay out streets. At its largest, however,

John Sumner residence built in 1880s, northeast of Dunlap, Morris County

Morton City consisted of three houses, nine dugouts, and a frame build-ing intended to be used as a general store.[1] It was also a group of Kentuckians who established Nicodemus, the best known of the black colonies. Founded by a group of Lexington, Kentucky, blacks led by W. R. Hill, a white man, Nicodemus was located in Graham County in western Kansas near the Solomon River. Established in September, 1877, the colony claimed 600 settlers by 1879. As of that year there were twenty-five houses in Nicodemus and two churches, Methodist and Bap-tist. In the early 1880s the colony, anticipating the construction by Missouri Pacific of a rail line through its midst, experienced a boom period. Following a flurry of construction, the village boasted "two drugstores, three grocery stores, a bank, a hotel, two newspapers, and other business enterprises."[2]

Although the black colonies established by Singleton, Hill, and others in central and southern Kansas have received a great deal of attention from scholars who have seen them as the backbone of the exodus, the bulk of those who participated in the migration to Kansas did not settle permanently in these independent colonies. Rather, they wound up as farm laborers or farm owners scattered throughout the state, or more frequently as laborers, craftsmen, or owners of small businesses in one of the state's larger towns.[3]

The 1870–1882 migration of blacks to Kansas, particularly the much-

21

publicized post-1878 phase of the movement, was the product primarily of the deteriorating racial climate in the South following the collapse of Reconstruction. By 1879 all of the Radical Republican governments had fallen and the last remaining federal troops had departed. The freedmen were left to the mercy of those white southerners who were determined to deny them their civil rights and to reduce them to virtual peonage. Using a variety of techniques, including the crop-lien system, lynching, and *de facto* disfranchisement, white supremacists achieved both goals. Among the numerous corollaries and consequences of the caste system in the South were the lack of opportunities for education and self-improvement, and a court system that would not protect the Negro in the few rights left to him. Exclusion and discrimination convinced many Negroes that the South could never be anything but a land of "violence, oppression, and want," and impelled them to consider emigration as an alternative.[4] It was a series of specific events in the late 1870s, however, that crystallized black dissatisfaction and served as catalysts for the Great Exodus.

Among the most important was an 1878 crop failure, which caused widespread suffering and intense economic frustration among black sharecroppers. The depression produced inquiries from southern Negroes about economic opportunities in Kansas, and responses to these letters were generally encouraging. Writing to R. H. Lanier of East Carroll Parish, Louisiana, in June, 1879, Governor John P. St. John advised that land for farms was plentiful in central and western Kansas. Refugees wishing to take advantage of the homestead laws of the United States could lay claim to 160 acres for fees totaling about $18.00. Land prices ranged from $1.25 an acre in the west to $40.00 an acre in the east. Credit was available, he assured Lanier, and any man willing to practice "honesty, industry, and sobriety" could succeed in Kansas.[5]

In addition to the economic factor, blacks in the South, particularly in Louisiana, believed that constitutional proscription was imminent and that they had best leave while they still had the freedom to do so. Once their rights were no longer guaranteed by law, the door would be open for the resurrection of slavery.[6]

Still another spur to migration was the resentment among southern whites created by the movement itself. Fearing loss of their labor force, whites went to great lengths to discourage Negroes from migrating. A black exoduster from Texas wrote to Governor St. John in November, 1879, that many of his fellow migrants had left their families behind "to keep them from being murdered."[7] Another Texas Negro desirous of coming to Kansas wrote that whites in his area were threatening local blacks suspected of encouraging the exodus. Several had been beaten. "White pepel say if aney of the collerd pepel do get out they will make it as hot as hell for the rest."[8] Nonetheless, he reported, he and 500 of his neighbors were planning to leave immediately. Thus, paradoxically, white hostility to the movement only served to further stimulate it.

Also contributing to the exodus was the pressure exerted by special interests that would profit from rapid population of the West, and by unscrupulous individuals who sought to take advantage of the blacks' discontent. Land companies, railroads, and colonization societies distributed thousands of circulars and colorful chromos depicting the bountiful opportunities available in Kansas.[9]

No less significant was Kansas' historical appeal. Proponents of immigration never tired of portraying Kansas as the "promised land." Kansas, the home of John Brown, had never permitted slavery and had consistently voted for the party of Lincoln. Thus, those Negroes who came to the state in the 1870s, no less than those who migrated in the sixties, expected to find an open society, one characterized by racial tolerance, social justice, and equality of economic opportunity.[10]

It is quite possible, however, that the exodus, particularly the post-1878 phase, would never have materialized had it not been for a phenomenon Nell Painter calls the Kansas Fever idea. According to Painter, southern blacks responded to the racial violence, proscription, and economic exploitation that was their lot in the 1870s by developing and proclaiming the Kansas Fever idea, which promised all black people who wanted to go to Kansas free transportation, free land in Kansas, and free supplies and subsistence for the first year from the federal government. The idea that they would be provided for stemmed from a predilection that freedmen shared with most other disadvantaged Americans of the Gilded Age—that of soliciting Congress for aid. The Kansas Fever myth seemed to offer the impoverished a way out of the South to a utopia where blacks would know true freedom. The federal government would usher in the millenium—a time and place where their lives would be transformed and they would be in a position to enjoy full citizenship. The concept served as a catalyst or enabling factor which provoked downtrodden southern Negroes into pulling up stakes and risking the unknown.[11]

In early February, 1879, boatloads of indigent blacks began to arrive in St. Louis. By the end of the month groups of exodusters ranging in size from 50 to 600 were arriving daily, and by March 19 there were more than 1,500 such refugees in the city, waiting for transportation to the "New Canaan." Anxious to rid themselves of these "riff-raff," St. Louis municipal officials decided to finance the trip to Kansas. As a result, in early April steamboats and barges loaded with expectant Negroes, together with their bedding, livestock, plows, and household utensils, began landing regularly at Kansas' Missouri River ports. Not all were destitute. Some exodusters not only had farm equipment and livestock but also money to invest. These fortunate few started businesses—grocery stores, barber shops, delivery services—in the towns of eastern Kansas or purchased improved land in the eastern part of the state.[12]

Most, however, were poverty stricken and suffering from malnutrition and exposure. Because there they could be sheltered and cared for, these migrants also tended to remain in cities in the east, particularly during 1879. The exodusters' primary port of entry into Kansas was Wyandotte. As the population swelled, creating a strain on the resources of city and state, newcomers were sent on to Lawrence, Topeka, Atchison, and Leavenworth. Those who remained in the east established or expanded existing black ghettos within each of the towns. In Kansas City, Quindaro had been a black community since the Civil War when runaway slaves fleeing Missouri had settled on the bluffs overlooking the Missouri River. Several thousand exodusters, deciding upon their arrival at the Wyandotte levees to go no farther, joined Quindaro's original residents and created a thriving, all-black city. In Kansas City proper, exodusters established Mississippi Town and Juniper Bottoms in the east, Rattlebone Hollow near Jersey Creek, and Hogg's Town at the extreme western border of the city. In Topeka there were several major Negro settlements. The oldest one, founded in the 1850s, was a four-block area on the south bank of the Kansas River known as The Bottoms. On the east side exodusters settled in Ritchies Addition; in North Topeka, Redmonsville; in the southeast portion of the city, Mudtown; and in the extreme west, Tennesseetown.[13]

In October and November of 1879 a large number of exodusters, primarily from Texas, settled in Labette County in southeast Kansas, most of them in the towns of Chetopa, Oswego, and Parsons. An estimated 1,500 to 2,500 migrants came to Parsons alone and settled in districts which came to be known as Mudtown and Scuffletown. Others moved on to settle in and around Baxter Springs.[14]

The vast majority of those refugees who fled the South in 1879 and 1880 hoped to become landowners. To this end, a number of the more ambitious blacks moved to the already established rural colony of Nicodemus and to Morton City. Others founded new settlements such as the one established by 125 Texas blacks at Burlington, Coffey County, in the spring of 1879. After an epidemic broke out among cattle in the

A 1900 scene in Tennesseetown, a black section in west Topeka

Burlington community, many of the inhabitants abandoned their home-steads and migrated to Independence and Coffeyville. In May, 1887, the Reverend Alfred Fairfax, an ex-slave, Union veteran, and an ordained A.M.E. minister, led some 200 families out of Louisiana and into south-ern Kansas where they established Little Caney Colony in Chautauqua County.[15]

The number of blacks who arrived in Kansas during this period is difficult to calculate with any precision. Although some estimates are as large as 80,000, most sources state that between 40,000 and 60,000 mi-grants made the trek. The total population for the decade increased by about 26,000 while the black population increase for 1880–1890 was only 6,603, much of which took place in 1880–1881. The estimate of 40,000 seems accurate when one considers the many deaths and the great number of migrants who returned South.[16]

The black community's initial reaction to the exodus was quite positive. Leaders such as Eagleson and Henderson believed that an immigration of blacks from the South would increase the political and economic power of the Negro population. "We want 50,000 colored voters in Kansas in less than two years," Eagleson wrote in the *Colored Citizen* in September, 1878.[17] As the towns of eastern Kansas became glutted with ragged refugees in the spring of 1879, however, many began to have second thoughts. Some feared that the newcomers would take jobs away from black residents of the state or, worse, that white laborers, fearing job competition from the burgeoning black community, might seek total exclusion of blacks from the packing houses, mines, retail stores, and service establishments. "We think it an outrage on the workingmen of this city, both black and white, to allow these refugees to compete with them in the matter of cheap labor," editorialized the *Kansas Blackman* early in 1880. "Of late we have heard a great deal of complaint among the working classes in regard to the refugees being the direct cause of the great reduction of wages that have been made in this city [Topeka] . . . ."[18] Actually, most black Kansans were ambivalent toward the movement. Negro leaders could not help but sympathize with the sufferings of their southern brethren. Most believed that, relatively speaking, Kansas was a land of freedom and opportunity. Migration was a viable alternative to proscription, lynching, and the crop-lien system, and it was an option which, if taken, would benefit both those who came and those who remained behind. Yet many upwardly mobile, "respectable" members of black society feared that the ragged, destitute, ignorant, and sometimes diseased exodusters would actually increase prejudice among whites and in the long run lead to greater discrimination than already existed. Too, the black middle class consciously or unconsciously feared that the pressure of the exodusters would tend to decrease their own social standing, particularly among whites. At a convention of black men held in the House of Representatives in Topeka in April, 1880, a series of lengthy debates on the exodus mirrored the deep split that existed among black Kansans. The convention nearly deadlocked over the question of whether it should issue a proclamation inviting all oppressed blacks of the South to migrate regardless of their economic state, or promulgate a decree that encouraged only those with money enough for a stake. The assemblage finally passed a resolution deploring the violence and oppression that characterized race relations in the South and also advising prospective émigrés not to come without some money.[19]

Waller's attitude reflected little ambiguity toward the exodus; he was an outspoken and active supporter of the movement. He must have shared the misgivings of other members of the black bourgeoisie about the possible adverse impact that the influx would have on the economic and social status of blacks already residing in Kansas, but such fears were overshadowed by other factors. His early speeches and writings were fairly idealistic, filled with paeans to duty, honor, courage, and selflessness. It was the destiny of his generation, Waller believed, to elevate the race as it struggled to slough off the cultural blight imposed by slavery. He and his contemporaries should acquire skills—expertise in the law, for example—that would prove of concrete benefit to the race and should adopt life-styles that would serve as guideposts to the ignorant and profligate.[20] "Allow me to plead with the young men of my race," he wrote in the *Colored Citizen* in 1878, "to lead virtuous lives, to leave off gambling and other dissipations, and be real gentlemen in deed as well as appearance. . . . Be true to your manhood and yield to nothing that in any way compromises your dignity."[21] Kansas, as a northern state with a heritage of freedom, and black Kansans in particular, had an obligation to help the "bleeding race of the South."[22] The young lawyer was acutely aware of the lynchings, burnings, and whippings endured by southern Negroes, and he could not avoid identifying with them in their tribulation. "Our manhood is not even respected [in the South]; our people are murdered without mercy; our schoolhouses are burned; our families are outraged; we are in debt at the end of every year because white men take advantage of our ignorance and prey upon our generosity . . . . What people on God's green earth have suffered so much," he wrote to John P. St. John in 1879.[23] The blacks of the South had two alternatives available to them: armed revolution or colonization in the West. While he believed bloodshed was fully justified by the treatment meted out to Negroes in the South, Waller's religious scruples and his hope for ultimate reconciliation between the races led him to reject "bloody carnage" as a viable option. Migration and colonization were the answers. The exodus, he wrote in the *Topeka Commonwealth*, was not temporary and spasmodic but revolutionary and long-term. The migratory movement constituted a conscious decision by blacks to endure discrimination in the South no longer but to seek a new world in which their deep desire for liberty, so long frustrated, could be satisfied.[24]

As a major Kansas riverport, Leavenworth became one of the principal assembly points for the exodusters. City officials made arrangements to house the neediest in an old abandoned warehouse at the corner of Third and Choctaw streets. Municipal relief funds were quickly exhausted, and by late April the mayor was beseeching the state for aid. Throughout the spring and summer of 1879 Waller busied himself soliciting funds for the newcomers and organizing meetings to encourage even more black southerners to flee to the promised land. On the evening of March 13, 1879, a number of prominent blacks gathered at Old Market House to discuss immigration. Waller was chosen chairman of the meeting and spent the evening convincing his fellows of "the necessity of encouraging emigration." Earlier, in the *Colored Citizen*, Waller had called for a state convention of colored men to meet in Topeka to discuss the best means for attracting and locating Negro refugees pouring into the state. At that gathering held in April, he was appointed to the statewide executive committee. A week later Waller wrote to St. John asking that his administration encourage the movement and provide food, shelter, and clothing to the suffering hundreds who had aleady arrived.[25]

While the federal government refused to respond to Waller's appeals, Governor St. John, other prominent Republicans, and various religious groups ranging from Quakers to Presbyterians plunged into the business of relief and launched a nation-wide campaign for funds. From the beginning their goals were first to care for the basic needs of the exodusters and then to convert them into useful members of society.[26] In the course of their relief activities these political and religious philanthropists developed a philosophy of race relations and Negro uplift that would gain wide acceptance, not only among whites but blacks as well. By mid-1879 the plight of the newly arrived freedmen was truly deplorable. "Our city is now crowded with colored refugees far beyond its capacity for accommodation," reported the *Emporia Ledger*. "To make things worse, they brought with them . . . a very malignant type of measles, which has not only proved a very sad affliction among themselves, but has spread disease widely over the city . . . . The condition of these negroes is truly alarming. All the old tumble down buildings in the city—unfit for white men to live in—are crowded with these poor people. Half clad, half-starved . . . negro children swarm the streets and beg from door to door for cold victuals and old clothes."[27] On April 15 a group of prominent whites gathered at the Opera House in Topeka to decide what to do about the exodusters. Governor St. John, who chaired the meeting, declared that the causes of the movement should be of no concern. Reminding his listeners of Kansas' historic devotion to liberty, he proclaimed that the state should and would live up to its reputation as a land of mercy and opportunity. The conclave subsequently decided to create the Central Relief Committee under St. John to receive and distribute among the exodusters the contributions that were then pouring in from various quarters. The meeting, Republican almost to a man, passed resolutions denying charges by Democrats that the exodus was a plot designed to add a huge bloc of easily controlled votes to the Republican column and promising black leaders that under no circumstances would the state militia be used to bar further immigration.[28]

Not to be outdone, a group of prominent colored Topekans met on the evening of April 21 at the Baptist Church and established a committee of five to aid the Central Relief Committee in raising funds, in finding houses for the newcomers, and in securing the means for exodusters to make an "honest living." Included on the committee were John M.

John P. St. John

Brown, John Jones, a black lawyer, and J. M. Eagleson, brother of William. Then, on May 3, T. W. Henderson and William Eagleson founded the Kansas Colored State Emigration Bureau to aid immigrants already in Kansas and to correspond with southern blacks desirous of migrating, advising them what to expect.[29] In establishing their own organization Topeka blacks were responding to a number of motives—fear that a white-dominated relief movement might not operate even-handedly, a simple wish to aid their impoverished brethren, and the desire among some, particularly Brown, to increase their visibility and thus promote their individual political careers.

29

In early May, St. John decided to expand the original committee to include a larger number of representative whites as well as prominent blacks. He had come to realize only too well that the effort to aid the exodusters was fraught with political danger. The Democrats were already charging him with conspiring to Africanize the state, and blacks were hinting that the administration was holding back in its relief effort. In addition there would inevitably be charges of corruption against those engaged in distributing moneys and supplies. In an effort to deflect present and future criticism, St. John authorized the reorganization of the Central Relief Committee into the Kansas Freedmen's Relief Association. According to its charter, the association was to purchase land upon which the exodusters could settle and to supervise their activities until they became economically independent. The association promised to advance funds to enable the indigent to make a first payment on their land; but after that, according to an association circular, each man was to "hoe his own row." Among the directors were A. B. Jetmore and L. A. Beck, prominent attorney and wealthy Topeka banker, respectively; the Reverend W. O. Lynch, a leading black Methodist minister of Topeka and head of the Kansas Methodist Freedman's Work; and John M. Brown. The first secretary of the Kansas Freedmen's Relief Association was Laura S. Haviland, one of a number of transplanted New Englanders living in Kansas whose philanthropy and stewardship were fully aroused by the exodus. The guiding light and driving force behind the association, however, was Governor St. John.[30]

In making plans for the care and settlement of the exodusters, St. John and officials of the K.F.R.A. were apparently greatly influenced by one Stephen A. Hackworth, a white southerner and Radical Republican then living in Brenham, Texas. Considering himself an expert on the character and habits of the southern Negro and on colonization in general, Hackworth wrote St. John a series of lengthy letters from May through August, 1879, advising the governor on how best to care for his new charges. The freedmen of the South, he wrote, fell into three categories. The first, comprising one-tenth of the population, had been well treated by their masters, trained in a specific vocation, and were now industrious, thrifty property owners. The second, embracing four-tenths of the freedmen, had been well cared for but untrained. This segment had become the tenant population of the South, hard-working but gullible and poor. The third class, about one-half the aggregate, had been ill treated and ill trained, and consequently as freedmen they were "thriftless, often dishonest," and "entertained small respect for morality and moral obligations." Obviously, the first two groups should be encouraged to immigrate and the last discouraged. Hackworth went on to lay down certain rules to govern the state in its dealings with the exodusters. The supervising authorities, after converting each head of household into an independent yeoman farmer, should closely supervise the Negro population's social and economic activities, refraining from outright charity whenever possible. Blacks, Hackworth advised, were easily organized and disciplined, and worked diligently if dealt with honestly.[31]

In conformity with Hackworth's advice St. John and the K.F.R.A. first attempted to settle the exodusters on farms in rural Kansas, either as independent farmers or as agricultural laborers. By late June, 1879, the association had started a colony in Wabaunsee County. The state agreed to sell university land to blacks coming to Wabaunsee in forty-acre plots at $2.65 an acre. Under the agreements signed, the black settlers were to pay one-tenth down and the balance in nineteen years at 7 percent interest. By June 28, thirty black families had taken advantage of the offer. For these first colonists the K.F.R.A. furnished teams, agricultural implements, a barracks, and rations. The association also agreed to make the first installment payment on each forty-acre farm.[32] Colonization was imperative, the K.F.R.A. believed, if the exodusters were not to become liabilities of the state. "Our pecuniary interest demands that we aid these people to become self-supporting as soon as possible," Laura Haviland wrote an unknown correspondent in 1879.[33] Moreover, if the exodusters remained in the towns and cities of the east where they would compete with white labor, probably unsuccessfully, both whites and blacks would blame the K.F.R.A., the St. John administration, and the Republican party.

Kansas officials also followed Hackworth's advice in encouraging freedmen of the "first and second class" to immigrate and in discouraging those of the "third." All who came to Kansas, St. John advised a prospective immigrant in 1879, could expect to enjoy "rich soil, healthy climate, full protection to life and property of every law-abiding human being, free schools, and a free ballot." There was a condition, however: "All those who come here . . . should understand that they will be expected to be self-supporting and not a charge upon the charities of our people."[34]

Unfortunately, the St. John administration and the K.F.R.A.'s goal of seeing all the exodusters become independent, self-reliant yeomen farmers was difficult to realize. In the first place, colonization on the Hackworth-Wabaunsee plan was expensive, and by July the K.F.R.A. had received only $5,819.70 in contributions. In the second, the number of immigrants entering Kansas had become so great by mid-1879 and their physical condition was so appalling that merely feeding, clothing, and providing medical care for the new arrivals occupied all of the K.F.R.A.'s resources. By fall, 1879, the exodusters arriving in Wyandotte and Leavenworth who did not have plans and means of their own were simply sent on to Topeka where they were housed in a large, two-story barracks maintained by the K.F.R.A. on the fairgrounds in the northern part of the city.[35]

According to a study published in late May, 1880, anywhere from 15,000 to 20,000 blacks had settled in the state during the previous twelve months. "About one-third are supplied with teams and farming tools and may be expected to become self-sufficient within another year; one-third are in the towns employed as house-servants and day laborers and can take care of themselves so long as the market for their labor is not overcrowded; the other one-third are at work in a desultory fashion for white farmers and herders, and doing the best they can but powerless to 'get ahead' and achieve homes and assured support without considerable assistance." This article, which appeared in the *Topeka Commonwealth*, went on to estimate that the surplus proceeds of the exodusters' own efforts during their first year in Kansas amounted to approximately $2.25 per capita. Despite "their disposition to work, and to be honest and sober and frugal," blacks would have to face the fact that it took a minimum of a hundred dollars to take up, maintain, and improve a farm in Kansas, and thus "an annual increase of $2.25 a head will not soon make Kansas Negroes economically independent."[36]

If the exodus could not be limited to the proper classes of freedmen and if those who had arrived could not be converted into independent farmers or self-sustaining tenants, the only alternative was to end or, better yet from a political standpoint, deflect the exodus to other areas. Accordingly, in mid-March the K.F.R.A. dispatched W. O. Lynch to Cairo, Illinois, "to use such means as [Lynch] may deem prudent and expedient to turn the tide of immigration from the South into other States than Kansas." Lynch composed and then distributed throughout the South circulars warning prospective emigrants of overcrowding and depressed economic conditions in the Sunflower State. Throughout the remainder of the year Lynch and other agents of the K.F.R.A. met hundreds of exodusters at Cairo and funneled them into Illinois and Iowa.[37]

By May, 1881, the flood of black immigrants into Kansas had started to dwindle; by the end of the year the exodus was, for all intents and purposes, over. But what of the thousands who remained, particularly those in central and southeast Kansas, who were particularly destitute and generally ignored by the K.F.R.A. They, for the most part, were cared for by and, indeed, became wards of the Kansas Quakers. The

Quakers, committed since the seventeenth century to bettering the condition of Afro-Americans, at first strongly supported the exodus, believing migration to be the only answer for the oppressed and exploited black masses of the South. Staunch Republicans and ardent supporters of St. John (they were particularly attracted to the governor's outspoken support of prohibition), the Quakers were very much aware of the political harvest to be reaped from the exodus.[38] Although the massive suffering endured by many of the migrants eventually caused reservations among some Quakers, they persevered in their relief efforts and, in the process, dramatically influenced the white community's view of the Negro.

Almost as soon as the Kansas Freedmen's Relief Association was founded, a number of prominent Kansas Quakers offered their services. Among those whom the organization employed directly were Wilmer Walton, who headed up relief efforts in Labette County; John M. Watson, who supervised the association's efforts in Columbus, Kansas; and Daniel Votaw, a prosperous farmer who represented the K.F.R.A. in and around Independence. All of the Quakers were imbued with a sense of mission and had definite ideas about how relief should be distributed and the exodusters treated. Walton was typical. Upon arriving in Parsons (Labette County) he asked all freedmen to assemble in Hughes Hall. The Negroes, he later wrote to St. John appreciatively, were neat in appearance, quiet and orderly in their deportment, and respectfully attentive. For over an hour he harangued the blacks on their responsibilities and obligations as free citizens in "this noble—long sought for—State of Kansas." It was incumbent upon them to pursue "a straight forward, honest, truthful, strictly moral, virtuous course of life—ever accompanied with habits of industry, economy, and uncompromising temperance."[39] Charity should be shunned and self-reliance cultivated. The meeting ended, Walton consulted with local whites and "the more intelligent colored people," and then instructed the members of the black churches in Parsons and all those not belonging to a church to vote for one man and one woman to sit on a committee of certification to examine applications for aid. In ranking the applicants, the committee should give first priority to the sick, the aged, orphans, widows, and victims of natural disaster. Those who were willing to work, but through no fault of their own were unemployed, would next be allowed to draw from available food, clothing, and equipment. Those "who have no more self respect and ambition than [to] idly and lazily hang around the street corners, or visit liquor or gambling saloons" were to be entitled to draw from the "leavings." Thus, Walton, as did other Quakers, clearly discriminated in the distribution of aid in such a way as to discourage certain behavior by the blacks and encourage the development of other clearly defined traits.[40]

Early in 1881 the Friends began to break away from the K.F.R.A. and operate independently. Elizabeth Comstock, a midwestern Quaker who had immigrated to Kansas after the Civil War, had collected funds for the K.F.R.A. throughout 1879 and 1880. In January, 1881, the Yearly Meeting of Friends decided to take control of and administer funds collected by Comstock and others. Pursuant to this goal Quaker leaders established the Kansas Friends Yearly Meeting Committee to Advise and Assist E. L. Comstock. Its officers were instructed to use the funds at their disposal to provide food, clothing, medical care, and, when practical, education for the freedmen. Comstock and her co-workers proved far more successful fund raisers than St. John and his lieutenants, for by 1882 more than $18,000 had been collected.

As the Friends' committee became increasingly active in efforts to care for and educate (in the broadest sense) the exodusters, the K.F.R.A. began to wind down its operations. St. John was more than happy to have the Quakers identified with what was becoming an increasingly divisive issue. Then, in April, the K.F.R.A. decided to self-destruct as of May 1. Before disbanding, the directors named a caretaker committee to take charge of the association's business, specifically to receive and distribute all goods and money contributed after May 1.[41]

No sooner had the K.F.R.A. dissolved than a deep split developed among the Quakers as to how money collected in behalf of the freedmen should best be spent. In April, 1881, Comstock and Laura Haviland persuaded the Friends' committee to commit all incoming funds to an institute to give agricultural and industrial aid to black people. The committee subsequently purchased 400 acres of land four miles from Columbus in Cherokee County and began constructing barracks, barns, and other necessary buildings.[42] The Agricultural and Industrial Institute provided instruction for men in farming, carpentry, and stock raising and for women in cooking and general domestic service. Students were paid for their labor, and thus the institute provided temporary employment for the freedmen as well as industrial and agricultural education. Comstock and Haviland, perhaps because they had both worked for the K.F.R.A., won the support of the caretaker committee and St. John. Much of the food, clothing, and implements collected by the K.F.R.A. committee after May, 1881, were funneled to the A. and I. Institute.[43]

Opposing establishment of the Agricultural and Industrial Institute were Daniel Votaw and a group of blacks in southeastern Kansas who believed that the leftover moneys and supplies as well as the funds being

Daniel Votaw

donated by eastern Quakers should be used to satisfy the immediate needs of the exodusters. The Agricultural and Industrial Institute, Votaw believed, was premature. Blacks in southern Kansas, whom he described as "honest, industrious, moral, religious, and temperate," needed shoes and coal before industrial education and moral uplift. Many Kansas Negroes agreed. The first week in June, 1881, blacks from Bourbon, Cherokee, Labette, Montgomery, Chautauqua, Shawnee, Wyandotte, and other counties met in Independence and fashioned a circular denouncing the concept of the A. and I. Institute and calling on the K.F.R.A. to commit its resources to direct relief. To the black community's way of thinking, the Quakers at Columbus were appropriating supplies and funds donated to the exodusters and forcing them to work for what was already theirs.[44]

Officials of the institute were slow to respond. According to S. W. Winn, Votaw and his supporters were actuated by jealousy and prejudice. Votaw's weakness for "absolute charity" would undermine the individual initiative of the exodusters and put off indefinitely their ability to become self-reliant, Comstock wrote to St. John from New York. The institute's traveling agents subsequently urged eastern Quakers to withhold funds for Votaw, and in late June Comstock and Haviland managed to enlist the aid of the *Christian Worker* and *Friends' Review* in the struggle with their detractors.[45]

Finally, in April, 1882, Votaw and his supporters founded a second Kansas Freedmen's Relief Association, which employed Votaw as secretary and hired John M. Brown as traveling agent. Eventually, Votaw raised enough money to start a colony, which bore his name. He and his black emissaries continued to compete with agents of the institute for the support of eastern philanthropists until the two experiments collapsed in the mid-1880s. The A. and I. Institute ceased operations in 1885; and the Votaw Colony, situated as it was on extremely poor land, simply lost its population as black homesteader after black homesteader failed to make a go of it.[46] As the history of race relations in Kansas was to reveal, however, the philosophy of education and self-help, with its opposition to "charity" and its emphasis on self-reliance and material accumulation, had clearly carried the day. White attitudes toward the Negro and white views on the best approach to "racial uplift" would parallel Comstock and Haviland's beliefs rather than Votaw's.

The exodus of 1879–1881 compelled white Kansans, many for the first time, to think about Afro-Americans and to define their role in society. Initially, the influx of blacks generated a great deal of anxiety among whites and exacerbated existing prejudices. A large number feared the exodusters would infect Kansas with disease and poverty, an attitude particularly prevalent among eastern city-dwellers. "Suffice it to say," wrote a white resident of Wyandotte to Governor St. John, "that most of them [refugees] are penniless, many are sick, and their dead are scattered along the way. . . . If they remain in crowds, in filth, poverty, actual want, in a very short time malignant and contagious diseases will break out."[47] In addition, most working-class whites and poor farmers opposed the movement. Railroad laborers, miners, packing house employees, all feared job competition from the exodusters and the possibility that the influx of blacks might depress wages. Destitute homesteaders who had been pleading with the state for relief perceived that the Negro immigrants might absorb public funds that would otherwise be channeled to them. "I think you will [i.e., should] take more interest in the white people and let the colored people go for god sake," wrote one irate sodbuster to St. John. "Let the nigger go and help the white people."[48] By the end of 1881, however, it was becoming clear that the influx was temporary, that Kansas would not be Africanized, and that blacks, even after the exodus, would constitute only a small percentage of the overall population. In the wake of this realization a fairly distinct philosophy of race relations began to emerge within the white community.

Waller and other blacks living in Kansas after 1881 had to deal with a white population whose attitudes toward them ranged across a broad continuum. There was, of course, a group of extreme Negrophobes made up of ex-Confederates, Irish immigrants, manual laborers, and destitute farmers who had opposed the exodus and who subsequently sought to block Kansas Negroes in their bid for economic and political advancement. To one degree or another, the social status of the Negrophobes, as perceived by them, depended upon the maintenance of an ironclad caste system. Writing to Governor George Glick in 1883 a former Confederate expressed the view that Negroes were no better than "stock" and should be treated as such. Most Kansans identified by their contemporaries as antiblack were, however, more sophisticated. Drawing from the Darwinian concepts so often invoked by the white supremacists of other regions, the *Kansas Democrat* expressed the view that Negroes should be allowed to challenge the Anglo-Saxon for supremacy in economic, military, and cultural endeavors, but dismissed as absurd the idea that he could ever succeed in any field.[49] "The Anglo-Saxon blood is in possession of the government and its wealth. No race has ever yet been able to stem the progress of the Anglo-Saxon, and no race ever will. . . . The Negro race in America will never become assimilated or absorbed by it."[50] Blacks were regarded by their detractors in Kansas as submissive, imitative, stupid, lazy, and generally incompetent in all fields of endeavor save "industrial pursuits," that is, unskilled and semiskilled labor.[51]

The extreme Negrophobes were in a minority, however. Most white Kansans simply did not feel particularly threatened by the black community. For this reason comparisons between racial attitudes in the South and in Kansas are not particularly useful. There was (except perhaps briefly during the height of the exodus) never any fear of black political or economic domination. Kansas had not experienced Reconstruction; there was no debt to settle with Negroes, carpetbaggers, and scalawags. Moreover, Kansans were self-consciously Western, convinced that they had a reputation to maintain for frontier hospitality, openness, and freedom. And as Kenneth Wiggins Porter has suggested, the fluidity and individuality of the frontier may have contributed to the relative freedom Negroes enjoyed in Kansas.[52] "If a man, white or black, is decent, respectful and respectable," insisted a prominent white newspaper editor and Union veteran, "he should be treated in a decent and respectful manner."[53] The extreme prejudice against the Indians that prevailed in Kansas during the last quarter of the century[54] may also have worked in the blacks' favor. At least blacks were capable of farming and laboring; at least they had sense enough to try to learn the white man's ways, to try to become assimilated.

As evidenced by the activities and rhetoric of those associated with the Kansas Freedmen's Relief Association, the Kansas Friends Yearly Meeting Committee, and other philanthropic groups, the attitude of the most articulate and influential white Kansans toward Negroes was ambiguous. On the one hand they were animated by a sense of duty and obligation. Kansas was to the freedmen of the South what America was to the European peasant and laborer: a refuge from tyranny and oppression; a land where equality before the law and equality of economic opportunity were inalienable rights of all citizens.[55] Despite the fact that "white men had heretofore subdued the frontier,"[56] Kansas could not use the Negro's poverty nor his color to deny him an equal chance; "the soundness of our laws, the sincerity of our religion are at stake."[57] And yet there was a fine line between justice and charity which if crossed would destroy the individual initiative of the Negro and negate any real chance he had for independence and self-reliance. The Negro was not, most believed, genetically inferior. He had the capacity for intellectual development, moral growth, and material advancement common to all human beings. Whites had an obligation to provide their black brethren with an education and moral training, but whites also had a duty to then leave them alone to pull themselves up by their own bootstraps.[58] "The black man has now in his hands in this country all the resources of progress and future power," editorialized the *Kansas City Star*. "If he chooses to remain ignorant, he will be cheated and despoiled; . . . but if he chooses to walk up the ascending way . . . , then he sees into the high atmosphere of freedom and enlightenment and a greater prospect spreads all around him. . . ."[59] But this commitment to civil and political equality did not stem fom egalitarian assumptions. As George M. Frederickson has pointed out, equality before the law was in theory compatible with a very conservative type of society; in England it had been formally guaranteed for centuries without conflicting with flagrant forms of social and economic inequality. This concept of equality was in fact doubly flawed in its application to the Negro. The idea that equal rights led to equal opportunities was based on the assumption that all competitors started at approximately the same place. Whites, however, had not had to deal with slavery, sharecropping, the crop-lien system, and the color prejudice that pervaded both North and South. Moreover, the white population's confusing of civil rights with the opportunity to achieve wealth and power enabled it to exploit the Negro politically and economically without having to call into question the "bourgeois ideology" of self-help and equal opportunity.[60]

Further hindering Kansas blacks in their struggle for survival and growth was a paradoxical prejudice against the poor found among those Quakers and secular philanthropists who took an interest in the Negro. Like the English and Dutch settlers who colonized America in the seventeenth century and who came to control its mores and institutions, these white Kansans believed that poverty, particularly long-term poverty, was a sign of inner depravity and moral worthlessness. Charity would only reinforce the individual's negative characteristics. God helped (and blessed) those who helped themselves, and his disciples could only do likewise. Negrophiles proved during the years following the exodus ever ready to abandon those who did not succeed in helping themselves.[61] Thus, in their dealings with the white man, Kansas Negroes, particularly the poor and uneducated, were caught in a vicious circle. Material success promised to elicit a degree of respect and acceptance; but the white community's commitment to the doctrine of parallel development, together with its prejudice against both charity and the poor, meant that a majority of blacks could never attain the status expected of them by whites.

Waller followed—and for the most part, approved—the activities of the K.F.R.A. and Quakers in behalf of the exodusters. He had but two reservations about the various relief and rehabilitation programs: there should be more black control in general, and he himself should play a larger part. More importantly, the exodus and the way in which white Kansans reacted to it profoundly affected Waller's world-view and his philosophy of racial and personal advancement. The movement occurred during a time in Waller's life when he was becoming sensitized to the Afro-Americans' place in the nation's past and when he was searching for a means to prevent the Negro from reliving that past. Fond of drawing analogies from the life cycle in his musings on the black experience, he asserted that by the 1880s the race had left the cultural and psychological infancy of slavery behind and was entering early manhood. It was incumbent upon him and his generation to perceive and accept the responsibilities that manhood implied: self-sacrifice, self-improvement, exemplary living, faithfulness to principles such as truth, honesty, and courage, and above all a commitment to racial uplift.[62] Not surprisingly, the blueprint for racial uplift that began to take shape in Waller's mind grew out of the events and rhetoric that swirled about him. Many of the blacks who came to Kansas during the 1878–1881 period were reacting to a utopian image. They were searching for an economically underdeveloped region, a frontier area where respect for the individual, equality of opportunity, and the democratic creed overshadowed color prejudice. In this ideal social setting blacks would be allowed to grow and achieve, to realize, at last, their potential as human beings. This image of the ideal society, already partially formed in Waller's mind when he came to Kansas in 1878, was massively reinforced by the exodus and the rhetoric associated with it. And in fact he was to spend large portions of his adult life in search of an idealized frontier. Moreover, during this period Waller internalized white society's criteria for success and acceptance. He sensed both that blacks could not succeed economically and politically in America without white aid, or at least tolerance, and that a majority of his white fellow-citizens in Kansas equated poverty with inner depravity and moral worthlessness. By 1881, as a result, he had come to view material accumulation as a means not only to raise the group's living standard and increase its economic leverage, but to win approval from white society as well. Indeed, it may be argued that he had come to accept white society's social yardstick as his own.

By the spring of 1879 Waller was disillusioned with Leavenworth. His law practice was not going well, he needed to widen his circle of acquaintances within the Republican party, the city administration in Leavenworth was Democratic and would probably remain that way, and there he had little opportunity to participate actively in the great freedmen's aid project that was then preoccupying so many Kansans, both white and black. In considering alternative places to settle, Waller quickly ruled out Nicodemus, Morton City, the Votaw Colony, and other rural black communities. He had come to recognize during his exile to the family farm in the early 1870s that agriculture was not his calling. No, if he moved it would have to be to another urban community. Waller eventually settled on Lawrence, the next town of any size as one moved westward into the state.

CHAPTER FOUR

All Things Possible

Saunders Redding traces the beginning of mass black awareness and self-assertion to the publication of W. E. B. Du Bois' *The Souls of Black Folk* in 1903. Du Bois' famous volume, he writes, "may be seen as fixing that moment in history when the American Negro began to reject the idea of the world's belonging to white people only, and to think of himself, in concert, as a potential force in the organization of society."[1] For John Lewis Waller that moment came during his five-year stay in Lawrence. A number of recent psychological and sociological studies have shown that the ability of a black child to adapt and achieve depends to a large extent on his parents' attitude toward being black.[2] Inculcation of a positive racial identity builds self-esteem, which is associated with a characteristic called assertiveness. According to sociologists, assertiveness may be defined as functional aggressiveness (i.e., competitiveness that enables the individual to manipulate his environment successfully). Despite slavery, discrimination, and poverty, all of which could be traced to racial prejudice, Waller's parents obviously accepted their blackness. Anthony and Maria rejected the slaveholder's myth of black worthlessness, and they transferred their sense of race pride to their children. But self-esteem is also associated with dysfunctional aggressiveness (i.e., fighting and crime). The critical factor in determining which type of assertiveness is followed is the individual's sense of internal control. In turn, internal control depends in large part on the individual's perception of his environment and his ability to control it. During Waller's residence in Lawrence he was accepted as a member of the city's black middle class, he played a prominent role in the biracial effort to "uplift" and educate the exodusters, he participated in the political campaign that elected Kansas' first black state official, and he founded the city's first black newspaper. The barriers to personal and racial fulfillment were great—that prejudice and discrimination existed in Kansas is undeniable—but by the time Waller left Lawrence in 1884 he was convinced that blacks could grow and achieve within the Kansas milieu.

Situated in Douglas County halfway between Topeka to the west and Kansas City to the east, Lawrence in 1880 was a milling and grain storage center with a population of some 15,000. Wheat and potato farmers throughout the surrounding countryside sold their produce there and bought farm implements, seed, clothing, and other manufactured items they could not produce. As a result, retail trade was the community's main business. Those not occupied in farming, milling, or commerce worked at the University of Kansas.[3]

Douglas County's black community as of 1880 was second in size only to Leavenworth's. The area around Lawrence was inhabited by dozens of independent, prosperous Negro farmers. Most of the black population of Lawrence, concentrated in enclaves in the northern and southern parts of the city, worked for the city, the university, one of the flour mills, or for white families as domestics. Moreover, the town possessed a relatively large number of black businesses, including two grocery stores. One was run by Charles Anderson, the first free black to come to that community, and the other by Charles H. Langston, brother of the distinguished Virginia politician and civil rights leader John Mercer Langston. In addition, there were a boot and shoe shop, two printing shops, a hotel, several restaurants, and an employment agency. Meeting the spiritual needs of black Lawrence in 1880 were four churches: two African Methodist, a Baptist, and a Congregationalist. Superimposed on the educated and relatively affluent Negro element were several hundred impoverished exodusters, most of whom had either been ejected from Wyandotte and Leavenworth or had been unable to make a go of it as homesteaders in the southeastern part of the state. Nearly all were illiterate and impoverished, living in makeshift shanties thrown up in the black sections of town.[4]

By the time Waller arrived in Lawrence he had acquired a family. After he left Leavenworth, the young lawyer had returned to Cedar Rapids and married Susan Boyd Bray, the widow of T. D. Bray of Urbana, Ohio. Waller had evidently met and courted Mrs. Bray before coming to Kansas; it seems unlikely that he would have had time to do so during his brief return to Iowa in 1879. Susan Bray was an articulate, forceful, and educated woman. She helped support the family by giving music lessons, taking in boarders, and sewing. Although well-informed and astute, she chose, as did most active women of her era, to live for and through her husband. Despite being an outspoken woman-suffragist, for example, she several times rebuffed acquaintances who urged her to run for the school board and other local offices. Aware of the power centers and shifting interests within both the black and white communities, Susan Waller not only helped broaden her husband's political contacts but also planned his various campaigns.[5] In September, 1890, the *Topeka Capital* observed of her: "There is not a colored woman and very few white ones in Kansas better posted in political and race matters than Mrs. John L. Waller."[6] Perennially active in church and social affairs, she sponsored innumerable benefits, lawn parties, teas, banquets, and other activities to raise money for the organizations to which she belonged and for her husband's political campaigns.[7] She had two children, Paul and Minnie, from her previous marriage.

As was the case when he moved to Leavenworth, Waller's first task in Lawrence, particularly pressing now that he had a family, was to secure a steady means of income. Once again he attempted to earn a living practicing law. He first rented offices over Charles Anderson's grocery store and then purchased space in several local papers announcing his competency to buy and sell real estate, collect bills, and "Practice in all the State Courts."[8] Clients, however, continued to be few and far between. In 1881 the parents of one George Green, a convict in the military prison at Leavenworth, hired Waller to secure a pardon for their son. In addition, he once again represented several black veterans with claims against the federal government for back pay. For the most part, though, the income derived from his practice did not even cover the rent. As a result, he returned to a trade learned during his youth in Iowa—barbering. Pursuit of the tonsorial arts proved to be much more profitable than practicing law. By the time he left Lawrence, Waller had acquired a chain of barber shops. Like George Knox, editor of the *Indianapolis Freeman*, and other politically active blacks who were also barbershop proprietors, Waller found his business a useful means of cultivating influential whites and lobbying in the interest of the race.[9]

The Wallers naturally gravitated toward the "respectable element" within the black community and in the process became involved with two institutions, which more than any others served both as avenues to power and badges of middle-class status within Negro society. The church in late nineteenth-century Kansas no less than in other areas was for blacks more than just a haven from the cares of the world. It was a meeting house where temporal as well as spiritual affairs could be discussed and acted upon. It served as a training ground in organization, cooperation, management, finance, and self-government for black leaders. Moreover, because religion was one of the few areas where Negroes controlled their own destiny, the church and church-related activities provided an outlet for the suppressed creative and organizational impulses of black members. Finally, not only did church membership satisfy the black Kansan's need for a sense of belonging and drive for self-realization, but it also constituted a badge of respectability within both the black community and the white. The best-organized and wealthiest denomination in Kansas was the African Methodist Episcopal with sixty-eight churches and an adult membership in 1890 of 3,641. The A.M.E. churches were the home of the black elite, the educated, the economically independent. Services were fairly reserved, and there was a great reverence within this denomination for conventional behavior and the accumulation of wealth. From the ranks of the A.M.E. congregation came a corps of ambitious and articulate clergymen and laymen—Henderson, Lynch, Brown, Langston, and Townsend were all affiliated with the A.M.E., for example—who were to play a key role in black political and civic affairs. Larger if not as politically oriented or influential were the black Baptists. True to the denomination's tradition, each black congregation in Kansas was independent, but each offered services characterized by literalism, emotionalism, and baptism by total immersion. The poor and illiterate, those who were particularly oppressed, found in the Baptist church a sense of release and total involvement that they could not in other denominations. Not surprisingly, the Wallers joined the A.M.E. church in Lawrence. In 1880 the 200-member congregation elected John secretary of the Board of Trustees. During his tenure in office, Waller, among other things, successfully liquidated a five hundred dollar indebtedness.[10]

Waller's religious commitment was deep and enduring. As disillusionment with Christianity and outright agnosticism increased among blacks during the remainder of the century, he refused to fall away. Waller believed in a personal God, a beneficent hereafter, and the Christian ethic. His Deity was not a wire-pulling manipulator, however. God endowed man with a free will and responsibility for his own material and spiritual well-being. Christ's life was the ultimate blueprint for human development, but it was up to the individual as to whether or not to follow it. Apparently, Waller was reared a Christian; while in Cedar Rapids he became active in a racially mixed church, probably

Presbyterian or Methodist, and for two years taught Sunday school. His students were about evenly divided between whites and blacks.[11] He found the Baptists in Kansas too "radical" in their theology and liturgy, and opted for the A.M.E. At one point the Wallers decided that even the A.M.E. was not conservative enough and temporarily affiliated with the Congregational Church.[12] Jennie Maria Waller, born in 1880, and John Lewis Waller, Jr., born in 1882, were both baptized into this body.[13]

Church membership was only one symbol of social class in black Kansas, and not a completely satisfactory one at that. A segment within the black community—the Townsends and Bruces of Leavenworth, the Browns and Hendersons of Topeka, the Andersons, Langstons, and Wallers of Lawrence—were determined to establish social distance between themselves and those of their brethren who were less educated and less tied to conventional patterns of behavior. "In all our church gatherings, our socials, entertainments, picnics, we are huddled together both the moral and immoral of our race," lamented the *Colored Citizen*. "It should not be so . . . . There is some of us that have children, and do not want them to associate with the loafers, thieves, bummers, harlots . . . . Let us make a line, and keep within it and those that steps over, ostracize them from our society."[14] Dozens of editorials appearing in black newspapers during the last quarter of the nineteenth century proclaimed that all Negroes were not alike, that there existed an educated and cultured elite which deserved to be treated with respect by both black and white. The fluidity of society in frontier Kansas, the upheaval caused by the exodus, and the notorious collection of pimps, prostitutes, gamblers, and thieves that inhabited the river front in Leavenworth, the stockyards in Kansas City, and the railroad yards in Topeka made respectable blacks especially desirous of establishing a clearly recognizable class structure. Among the most important symbols of the black elite in other, older communities were wealth, place of residence, family heritage, and skin color; in Kansas the badges of the middle class were education and conventional behavior. Particularly important in setting the "better class" apart was membership in one or more literary societies. Kansas City had the Negro Author's Literary Club and the Columbian Literary Society; Topeka, the Interstate Literary, Pleasant Hour Literary, and Palace Reading Clubs; Baxter Springs, the John R. Lynch Lyceum; and Lawrence, the Lawrence Progressive Club, the Whittier Literary Society, and the Union Literary Lecture Association. Women participated in auxiliary organizations or separate societies like The Coterie in Topeka. These societies held weekly meetings at which the works of Alexander Pope, Victor Hugo, and Walter Scott were read and discussed. Often members re-

A ladies' club, Tennesseetown

searched and debated philosophical topics—"Do Circumstances Make the Man," for example—or traded rhetoric on contemporary subjects. In the larger cities some of the societies performed plays such as *Julius Caesar* and *East Lynne*. Membership in these organizations was fairly exclusive, with education, manners, dress, and conventional moral behavior being the most pervasive criteria. Waller was an active member of the Union Literary Lecture Association in Lawrence and, subsequently, the Pleasant Hour and Interstate Literary Associations in Topeka. His specialty was debate.[15]

The black middle class in Kansas to which the Wallers belonged was ambiguous in its attitudes toward the ignorant and destitute of their race. Some were totally insensitive; contact meant social contamination, and they avoided the "lower class" whenever possible. Others, Waller included, felt a sense of *noblesse oblige* toward the less fortunate. Like the Quakers and white philanthropists who had managed the K.F.R.A., these Negroes were convinced that worthless, profligate Negroes could be drawn up into the respectable stratum through education, discipline, and moral training. Thus, Waller and those of like mind wanted to remain socially aloof from the unregenerate but were willing to participate actively in the process of regeneration.[16] An opportunity to do just that presented itself not long after Waller moved to Lawrence. In January, 1880, Mrs. Mary E. Griffith, a white philanthropist and temperance worker from Ohio, was asked by Scottish clergyman George Gladstone, then head of the International Order of Good Templars, to go to Kansas and establish Good Templar Lodges among the blacks. There were already a number of Good Templar Lodges in Kansas, but evidently, despite their claims to the contrary, they banned Negroes from membership. By April Griffith had established chapters in Lawrence, Manhattan, Topeka, Wichita, Kansas City, and a number of other locations. In September black Kansans under the tutelage of the Ohio philanthropist organized a state-wide Grand Lodge. Waller endorsed Griffith's views on temperance and became one of her most outspoken supporters. Partly as a result, in February he was chosen Grand Master of the Lawrence Templars and in September Grand Treasurer of the state organization. Waller, W. O. Lynch, Charles Langston, E. H. White, editor of the *Topeka Tribune*, all agreed with Griffith and other temperance workers that liquor was one of the principal causes of poverty, crime, and disease among the black population. The self-discipline necessary to abstain from liquor would also lead to a life of virtue that would command the respect of white and black alike. Moreover, temperance would check the violent prejudices of the Irish and other Negrophobes within the white community. Drinking led to crime, and Negroes inevitably suffered when there was widespread disregard among whites for the law. Waller's conversion to the temperance cause was due more to a belief that abstinence would promote racial uplift than to a conviction that drinking was morally evil.[17]

Griffith was concerned with more than the drinking habits of black Kansans. On February 7, 1880, she and a group of local do-gooders organized and obtained a charter from the state for the Freedmen's Educational Society. The society's goals were to establish a system of free night schools for colored adults, to found industrial schools in which "girls and women shall be trained for household work and fitted for the duties of cooks, chambermaids, seamstresses, and housekeepers," and to finance free libraries and reading rooms.[18] Waller proved instrumental in selling the concept of a night school to the black community. After Griffith persuaded the Lawrence School Board to allow her to use one of the public school buildings, classes opened with an initial enrollment of 130. Like the K.F.R.A. and the various racial uplift operations established by Kansas religious groups, the Society was based on the belief that self-help was the Negroes' only hope for salvation. Unless blacks acquired "intellectual and moral training" they would be barred from useful citizenship and remain wards of the state.[19]

A number of Kansas Democrats charged that the Good Templar

Lodges and the Educational Society established by Griffith were front organizations for the Republican party. In a sense this was true, although temperance rather than the success of the party was the primary consideration for Griffith. Nonetheless, the two were inextricably bound together. By 1880 the prohibition wing of the Republican party, headed by Governor St. John, was in firm control of the Kansas G.O.P. The legislature had passed and would submit during the fall election a constitutional amendment prohibiting the manufacture and sale of alcoholic beverages. Officers of the Good Templar Lodges and the Educational Society did not fail to point out the connection between the party of Lincoln and temperance. Waller was certainly aware of the relationship. Indeed, one of the reasons Waller advocated temperance is that he anticipated that such support would endear the black community to the prevailing powers within the Republican party. Similarly, he became active in both the Templars and the Educational Society not only out of a desire to elevate the race but because he perceived both as vehicles that would advance his personal political interests.

As the state elections of 1880 approached, Negro politicians were, as usual, hungry for recognition. Eagleson, Brown, Townsend, and Langston had been embittered by the Republicans' refusal in 1878 to nominate T. W. Henderson for lieutenant-governor. Following Henderson's rejection (he received just seventy-two ballots on the final vote[20]), J. C. Embry, an A.M.E. minister and political activist from Fort Scott, summed up the black community's sense of frustration: "Democracy ascendent means political and social death to the Negro—and in politics, and in civil administration, a close monopoly. Republican ascendency means a general drift along in trust to providence. . . . The old party that we loved so much has lost its energy and youth. . . . It is a confirmed coward. . . . Concerning our relation to the party as an element, it can be said with truth, that we have been treated more shabbily in Kansas than in any other Republican state."[21] Blacks were only slightly placated when Eagleson was named assistant doorkeeper in the House and Townsend was chosen assistant sergeant at arms in the Senate.[22]

A number of factors combined to convince black politicians that 1880 might be the year a Negro was nominated and elected to state office. In 1879 several Republican county conventions nominated and then succeeded in electing blacks to local office. The Republican convention which met April 2, 1880, to elect delegates to the national meeting chose Townsend and Columbus M. Johnson, a black who was a former associate of Singleton's and now a prominent Topekan, as alternates. Moreover, the exodus had swelled the black electorate considerably. The state census of 1880 showed 43,789 blacks in Kansas. Approximately 21,895 of these were adult males. White voters in the state had averaged about two-fifths of the population, but probably a much larger percentage of blacks than whites voted. In South Carolina during Reconstruction, for example, three-fourths of the blacks who were eligible did in fact cast their ballots. Given the higher literacy rate for blacks and the lack of any concerted effort to keep them from the polls, the percentage, even taking into account voter apathy, might have been even higher in Kansas than in South Carolina. Too, St. John had gone to great pains to indicate his friendship for the Negro populace. Finally, indications were that many temperance workers considered the black vote essential to adoption of the prohibitory amendment.[23]

Early in 1880 black political leaders decided to meet separately and select one man to present to the Republican convention for nomination on the state ticket. Accordingly, they notified eligible voters to meet and elect representatives to a state convention of blacks, which in turn would select a suitable candidate for state office and plot strategy for the Republican state convention scheduled for September. The Douglas County convention, which met in Lawrence, was typically uproarious; the delegates argued, shouted, pleaded, and pouted for more than twelve straight hours before finally settling on nine candidates. The meeting fractured along two lines: church affiliation and selection of a candidate for state office. Each of the congregations demanded maximum representation at the state convention, and their representatives haggled over every delegate. A small number of those present were pledged to support Colonel John M. Brown. The majority, headed by Waller, were determined to see a local man, Charles Langston, chosen at the state convention. After a bitter, name-calling free-for-all, the anti-Brown forces prevailed, with Waller being chosen chairman of the meeting by a vote of forty-two to twelve. James R. Johnson, one of Brown's minions, was elected vice-chairman. Needless to say, the nine individuals (which included Waller) chosen as delegates were all Langston men.[24]

Although Waller had been a resident of Kansas for only two years, the State Convention of Colored Men which met in Topeka on August 4, 1880, named him chairman of its central committee. The delegates spent most of their time and energy reemphasizing the need for blacks to mobilize and descend *en masse* on the Republican state gathering scheduled for September 1. "The colored race must secure this recognition under all circumstances," resolved the delegates; the "safety and advancement of the entire community depend upon it."[25] Although the convention met on John Brown's home turf, and despite the fact that the powerful Shawnee delegation was pledged to support the black boss of Topeka, Kansas Negroes selected Langston as the convention's choice for a place on the Republican state ticket, a significant victory for Langston, Waller, and Douglas County.[26]

The last week in August Waller made a personal appeal in the *Topeka Tribune* to every member of the black central committee to attend the Republican convention and "present the claims of 35,000 colored voters."[27] On September 1 Waller arrived in Topeka to attend his first state convention. Despite Waller's resounding speech nominating Langston for lieutenant-governor, Kansas Republicans would have none of him. The Lawrence grocer received fifty-one votes on the first ballot, and his total declined steadily thereafter. Republican bosses privately apologized to Waller and other black delegates; nomination of a black man, they feared, would arouse the latent prejudice of white voters and lead to the defeat of the entire Republican ticket and the prohibitory amendment. As a sop to Negro Republicans, the convention elected John Waller to the Republican state central committee, the first black in Kansas history to be so honored.[28]

Negro voters were not placated. Langston; William D. Matthews, a former steamboat captain and Union Army officer who settled in Leavenworth after the war; William D. Kelley, an aspiring young politician also of Leavenworth; and William Eagleson had all warned prior to the convention that Langston's rejection would mean a bolt of the party by blacks. On September 3, the black central committee called a convention of black men to meet in Lawrence and nominate Langston as an independent candidate.[29] Waller refused to sign the call and on September 4 published an open letter addressed to W. L. Eagleson and other members of the central committee. While "feeling keenly" Langston's defeat in Topeka, Waller advised his colleagues to refrain from running his fellow townsmen as an independent. To do so might mean the defeat of St. John and the entire ticket. "That," he wrote, "we cannot afford to do."[30] The decision to dissent had been a most difficult one for Waller. As a member of the Republican central committee and a party loyalist, he felt he must support the regular nominees. Yet he sensed and to a degree shared his black brethren's feelings of alienation. Caught up between two antagonistic constituencies, one white and one black, the young lawyer from Lawrence was faced with the black politician's classic dilemma. The same day he published his open letter, Waller wrote to St. John: "I must in justice to yourself support the ticket as nominated at Topeka but in doing so I will incur the condemnation of some of the leading men of my race. . . I expect this thing will kill me politically. . . It will alienate the colored men of weight from me and the white Republicans will have no sympathy in my behalf when I am done."[31]

Despite Waller's efforts, the black protest convention was held in Lawrence on September 20. Matthews, Eagleson, Kelley, and Langston were very much in evidence. Matthews delivered a "stirring speech" condemning the Republican party, and the delegates passed resolutions urging black men in every county to organize and run Negro candidates for state and local office. Representing Waller's viewpoint was E. H. White. A native of Tennessee, a graduate of Oberlin College, and a one-time member of the Howard University law faculty, White agreed with Waller that a black independent movement would be an exercise in futility and would end all chance of meaningful recognition of the black man within the Republican party. After a heated debate the delegates narrowly defeated a resolution nominating Langston for lieutenant-governor.[32]

Disgruntled though they were with the party of Lincoln in 1880, blacks really had nowhere else to turn. Republicans would not let them forget that in July at a Democratic meeting in Leavenworth a prominent white Democrat expressed the view that the federal government should never have extended the franchise to blacks. Nor did they fail to note that Democratic "whiskey interests" (German antiprohibitionists) worked to defeat W. D. Matthews, who had had second thoughts about rebelling against the Republican party and decided to run for the state legislature. Democratic county officials tried to close the polls early during the Republican primaries in October and then, when that failed to stop Matthews' nomination, defeated him in the general election by appealing to the racial prejudices of whites and distributing silver among unprincipled blacks.[33] Consequently, just as Republican leaders had anticipated, St. John, the Republican ticket, and the temperance forces enjoyed almost solid black support in their victories in November.

No sooner had the dust settled from the 1880 campaign than Waller and his contemporaries began to lay plans for 1882. A number of black political leaders, the same ones who had been responsible for the September, 1880, protest convention, believed that Kansas Negroes had too long submitted passively as Kansas Republican bosses shoved them to the back of the political bus. On June 1, 1882, 150 black men met in the old Senate chamber in Topeka. Chaired by William D. Kelley of Leavenworth, the conclave passed a series of resolutions complaining of past neglect and demanding recognition at the forthcoming state convention. The debt of gratitude owed the Republicans for their efforts in behalf of the Negro during the Civil War had been fully repaid; blacks had proved their loyalty "by the faithful performance of all menial and subordinate party service imposed upon us by party leaders"; the "independence, numbers, character, intelligence, interests, education, and general welfare of the colored population" deserved recognition through nomination of a black for state office. The convention did not, as in 1880, select a man to run for a state position but did name the Reverend Alfred Fairfax of Chautauqua County as its choice for congressman-at-large on the Republican ticket. Waller was conspicuous by his absence.[34]

Republicans in 1882 were not as confident as they had been in 1880. St. John was planning to violate Kansas' two-term tradition and seek a third two-year stint in the statehouse. Some Republicans feared that this would provide the antiprohibition element within the party with an excuse to bolt, temporarily fuse with the Democrats, and support an antiprohibition, anti-third-term ticket. A number of St. John supporters and temperance workers had come to the conclusion by 1882 that a solid black vote was imperative. It was true that, despite their dissatisfaction with Langston's rejection, blacks had voted overwhelmingly Republican in 1880, but whites feared that in 1882 blacks would either support an antiprohibition ticket or stay away from the polls altogether. White political observers in central, south, and northwest Kansas reported that hundreds of exodusters felt that the St. John administration had prematurely abandoned them. Black disaffection in rural areas was fed by the Democrats, who spread stories to the effect that St. John was still collecting funds in the East in the name of the black refugees of Kansas, and that these moneys were going not into medical supplies, food, and clothing but St. John's campaign chest. To reverse this trend, to save prohibition, and to earn St. John a third term, Republican drys believed that the party should nominate a black either for state auditor or secretary of state.[35]

In the summer of 1882 black Republicans and their white supporters settled upon Edward P. McCabe, the county clerk of Graham County, as the man to nominate, and decided upon auditor as the proper post for him to fill. A New Yorker by birth, educated, intelligent, and ambitious, McCabe migrated first to Chicago where he was active in Cook County politics for a short time, and then to Kansas in the late 1870s. In Chicago McCabe had met A. T. Hall, and the two men, hearing of the exodus, decided to go west and make a fortune as land developers. In 1878 they settled in Nicodemus and immediately purchased a sizable tract of land, which they subdivided and sold to new arrivals. McCabe first came to the attention of the St. John administration in 1880 when he and Hall made a deal with the whites of Graham County to support Hill City, a white community, rather than Nicodemus for county seat. In return white Republicans voted for him for county clerk and named Hall as census taker.[36]

Throughout 1882 Waller toured the state urging blacks to mobilize in support of McCabe's candidacy and whites to accord their Negro fellow-citizens the recognition they so richly deserved. Despite his efforts, white Republicans who gathered in Leavenworth on August 10 were split on the question of McCabe's nomination. Because they believed black support to be absolutely essential to the party's success in November, temperance delegates overwhelmingly endorsed him. In addition, a number of anti-third-termers hoped that a black on the ticket would lead to St. John's defeat and so were willing to vote for the Negro from Graham County. A sizable group of party loyalists, equally convinced that a Negro nominee would torpedo the entire ticket, opposed him. By the second ballot McCabe had accumulated 169 votes, 13 short of the number needed for nomination. St. John's closest supporters, including the statehouse staff, then secured an adjournment and lobbied all through the dinner hour against his nomination. Despite the treachery of St. John's lieutenants, when the delegates reassembled McCabe received 7 votes on the third ballot and was subsequently nominated on the fourth amid "deafening applause."[37] Though St. John was defeated in the fall elections by Democrat George Glick, McCabe won. The 1882 campaign marked the beginning of a close if brief political friendship between McCabe and Waller, who delivered a total of fifty-four speeches in behalf of the Republican nominee for auditor. Given the fact that McCabe's election (and reelection in 1884) brought him to prominence within the larger black American community and attracted the attention of the national Republican leadership, the relationship proved of considerable importance to Waller's later career.[38]

In late nineteenth-century Kansas, just as in other areas of the country during this period, it was virtually impossible for men of affairs within the black community, particularly those with political ambition, to avoid involvement in the issue of discrimination and segregation in public education. Waller was certainly no exception.

Of all the restraints imposed on American bondsmen by slavery, perhaps the most onerous was the ban on education. In the minds of many freedmen education became the bridge that would transport them from slavery to true emancipation; knowledge would protect their children from oppression; learning would earn the respect of whites and persuade them to admit blacks to full citizenship. For many Negroes the willingness of the white power structure to make available a free and equal public education to all regardless of color was even more significant as a symbol of white attitudes and the black man's status in white America than the willingness of the political parties to accord recognition through nomination to office. Indeed, one of the principal factors impelling southern blacks to migrate to Kansas was the lack of educational opportunity in their native land. For many exodusters the state's readiness to make available public schooling without discrimination was an important selling point for the "New Canaan."

In Kansas, unlike the southern states, there was no deep-seated prejudice against Negro education. Some whites were indifferent, but most favored public instruction for blacks. It became quite obvious during the exodus that the white community believed primary school education together with industrial training were essential if blacks were to become independent, self-reliant citizens and lift themselves out of poverty. An educated black populace would, in addition, reduce the crime rate and lower state expenditures for charitable purposes. On the question of integration, however, the desire of the white community to see the Negro learn his three R's conflicted with its fear of "social equality." Consequently, whites were divided not on the question of the necessity of education but on the relative value of mixed versus segregated schools.

The framers of the 1859 Wyandotte constitution clearly intended that institutions of learning should be segregated by race; it established a dual system and stipulated that tax moneys collected for school purposes were to be kept separate and each race was to enjoy facilities and instruction that they could pay for directly. The Kansas legislature that ratified the Fourteenth Amendment did not believe that it applied to public education, and it made no attempt in 1868 to alter the state's legally mandated system of segregation. Subsequently, however, the tide of public opinion began to turn in favor of integration, and in 1874 Kansas solons passed a civil rights act that made it a crime for "the regents or trustees of any state university, college, or other school or public institution [to] make any distinction on account of race, color, or previous condition of servitude."[39] The triumph for the advocates of mixed schools seemed complete when in 1878 the state legislature eliminated the word "white" from the school provision of the 1859 constitution. The very next year, however, a Republican legislature enacted a measure giving cities of the first class (10,000 population or more) the authority to establish separate primary schools for white and black.[40]

This, then, was the *de jure* situation as of 1879, but Kansas school districts did not always follow the letter of the law during the remainder of the century. Cities of the first class generally provided separate pri-

Sheldon Kindergarten, Tennesseetown

mary schools for blacks. In Leavenworth, for example, black children of elementary school age were educated in the North and South Leavenworth Colored Schools. The building in the northern part of the city was evidently quite inferior, being described as a "hut" situated in a "low, dirty looking hollow close to a stinking old muddy creek, with a railroad running almost directly over the building."[41] After Kansas City absorbed Armourdale and Wyandotte, it maintained a separate school, the Lincoln School, which was one of the better all-black facilities in Kansas. In Topeka in 1865 city authorities hired a small frame building to be used as a primary school; blacks were taught in the attic while whites learned their ABC's in the lower rooms. By the 1881–1882 school year there were fourteen elementary schools in the capital, two of which, Lane and Lincoln, were all black. In 1885 Tennesseetown had its own school, Sumner, a dilapidated structure that served the Negro children of that ghetto. Wichita and Lawrence in the 1880s and 1890s and Atchison in the 1890s were the only cities of the first class in Kansas that afforded mixed schools at the primary level.[42]

Cities of the second class, such as Fort Scott, were divided into wards, and each ward had its own elementary school. Because blacks were concentrated in one of two wards, *de facto* segregation was the result. In most instances cities maintaining ward schools forced blacks living outside predominantly Negro wards to attend black facilities, no matter how far they might have to travel. Grade schools in some towns, such as Hiawatha and Emporia, were fully integrated, but in nearly all cases the faculty was white. As was the case in cities of the first class, separate facilities in the smaller towns of Kansas were grossly inferior.[43]

Rural counties were divided into school districts. Usually each had a single schoolhouse with all elementary grades taught in one room. These schools were usually mixed, although by the late 1880s the number of blacks living in central and western Kansas outside the black colonies was relatively small.[44]

High schools in the larger cities and some Kansas colleges were integrated. Indeed, in cities of the first class the black community graduated proportionately only slightly fewer children from high school than did whites. Ironically, it was more difficult for blacks to gain admittance to secondary schools in towns of the second and third class. Wathena admitted colored students to its high school for the first time in 1895, and even then a number of whites strenuously objected and pressured the school board to expel them. In Jefferson County the superintendent made certain that the high school remained all white by requiring black applicants to take a special examination. Although Washburn College and the Emporia State Normal School both admitted and graduated blacks on a regular basis, the medical school refused to admit Negroes throughout this period.[45]

Those Negro children who attended mixed schools did not always consider themselves fortunate. One white schoolteacher in Lawrence discriminated in the manner and degree of punishment he administered; he whipped white transgressors with a switch and black with a cowhide. Others made derogatory statements about Negroes in class and discriminated in grades. A white instructor in the rural school at Gladden near Wathena installed separate water buckets for whites and blacks. When several Negro students partook of the water for whites, he expelled them. Some black leaders claimed that white instructors in all-black primary schools were ordered by their school board to neglect their students, thus retarding their progress and keeping them out of the mixed high schools.[46]

A minority of Negroes, led by Blanche K. Bruce, nephew and namesake of the ex-senator from Mississippi, and principal of the South Leavenworth School for blacks, and C. H. J. Taylor, politician and editor in the early 1890s of the *American Citizen*, advocated separate schools in order, they said, to protect black children from racist instructors and provide Negro teachers with jobs. Most black Kansans, though, viewed segregated schools as a racial slur and an obstacle in the path of their children as they sought to acquire a functional education. This was as true of the ignorant exoduster as the educated elite. When white school officials in Independence attempted to confine black students to a single room in the schoolhouse, the "collored citizens" of that town withdrew their children and petitioned Governor St. John for relief. Kansas Negroes also objected to segregation because it often required black students to walk several miles in the mud, rain, and cold, past white schools situated much closer to their homes. As they passed through white neighborhoods, moreover, black children were often subjected to harassment and abuse. In 1880 members of the black community initiated the first in a long series of civil suits designed to secure integration throughout the public school system. In October of that year one James Phillips filed suit in district court against the Topeka School Board claiming that his children had been barred from the Clay Street Elementary School because of their color and that according to the 1874 Civil Rights Act, this was unlawful. Phillips was represented by a black attorney, John H. Stuart.[47] The Clay Street case proved nothing, however, for the court subsequently threw out Phillips' case on a technicality.[48] When they did decide to act in a case, the district courts and Supreme Court consistently blocked efforts by cities of the second and third classes to establish separate systems. In *Board of Education* v. *Tinnon* the Supreme Court ruled against the school board of Ottawa, a city of the second class. The board in justifying the establishment of separate schools for the two races cited section 170 of the *Compiled Laws of 1885*, which gave to school boards sole control over schools and school property. The Court ruled that the Ottawa board could not force blacks to accept separate facilities, even if equal in every respect, because that power had not been specifically delegated by the legislature.[49] Blacks had no luck, however, in their attempts to have school segregation *per se* declared unconstitutional. The right of the legislature to provide for segregated schools was consistently upheld by the courts. In 1903 in *Reynolds* v. *Board of Education of Topeka*, the Supreme Court asserted that the law allowing segregation in cities of the first class did not conflict with the constitutional requirement for maintenance of a common school system.[50]

In the course of editing two race journals (1883–1885 and 1888) and in giving hundreds of speeches around the state, Waller became familiar with the status of blacks in various Kansas school systems and aware of the significance of the "mixed school question" in the minds of his brethren. He shared their concern. Literacy meant protection from exploitation; knowledge would help bring wealth and respect. In a speech delivered to a group of black Baptists in August, 1880, he urged his audience to teach their sons and daughters "how to read, write, and cipher. . . . Do this and the time is not far distant when there will be positions for your children that will call them to the highest stations of life."[51] Convinced that racial mixing was the only real guarantor of equality, he crusaded throughout his residence in Kansas for integrated schools. In the absence of mixed institutions, however, he felt the least the white community could do would be to provide equal facilities, and he repeatedly insisted that it do so. Almost as soon as he moved to Lawrence in 1879 Waller began incorporating appeals for integrated education in his speeches. Partially as a result, he was elected to the school board in 1882, defeating Joseph Riggs, a prominent white Democrat. Waller subsequently used his position on the board to ensure that Lawrence remained one of the two Kansas cities of the first class in the 1880's with integrated primary and secondary schools.[52]

In the mid-eighties Waller helped plan legal strategy for the various court battles initiated by Negroes in behalf of integration and/or equal facilities, and then in 1888–1889 he joined with two other prominent race leaders in a campaign to compel the legislature to modify the 1879 law pertaining to cities of the first class. His colleagues in the struggle for integration were Alfred Fairfax and William Abram Price. Both men were born into slavery and both were active in Radical Republican politics following the close of the Civil War, Fairfax in Louisiana and Price in Texas. Fairfax was self-educated, while Price was formally trained as a lawyer. In 1888 Fairfax, who had established a colony in Chautauqua County during the exodus, became the first black in Kansas history elected to the state legislature. Fairfax and Price met in Peru, Kansas, in the late 1870s and shortly thereafter became acquainted with Waller at the black men's convention of 1880. For a period in the late 1880s Waller and Price were law partners in Topeka.[53]

In 1888 a white legislative acquaintance of Waller and his associates introduced into the House of Representatives a bill drawn up by black leaders providing that separate and equal facilities could exist in Kansas only when two-thirds of the black and white citizenry, voting separately, approved. This was not to apply to the high schools, where integration would continue to be mandatory. In no case would a parent have to send his child past a school where his grade was being taught. On February 9, 1889, Fairfax delivered on the floor of the House an impassioned address—written by Waller and Price—in which he argued in the name of Christianity, history, and American citizenship that whites had a duty to provide blacks with every educational opportunity and that separate

58

facilities were degrading and unequal. In 1891 segregationists launched a counterattack by introducing a bill that would give cities of the second class the same right to discriminate as cities of the first. The segregationist measure did not pass, but neither did the Fairfax bill. As a result, in mid-February, 1891, Price warned blacks that the black community should focus its efforts on preventing a further extension of segregation.[54] Waller and his co-workers in the cause of integrated education had not been totally unsuccessful. True, the forces of segregation and even exclusion remained strong in Kansas, but even through the turbulent nineties there were integrated schools at every level in every region of the state.

During his first two years in Lawrence, Waller was frequently distracted from his political and educational battles by personal problems. In June, 1880, he wrote to St. John asking if there was a reform school or home of correction for young people in Kansas. Minnie, then fourteen, was headed for "wrongdoing," it seemed, and was "very determined."[55] To add to the family's problems "Johnny" suffered more than fifty convulsions during his first year of life.[56] Minnie's deportment and the health of John, Jr., evidently improved with age, however. During the late 1880s Minnie graduated from the Emporia Normal Institute, while John survived his infant maladies to grow into a bright and precocious schoolboy.

In March, 1883, Waller established the *Western Recorder*, which served as a forum for his views for the next two and one-half years. The *Recorder* was evidently the fifth black newspaper established in Kansas. The first was Eagleson's *Colored Citizen*; it was followed by the *Kansas Herald*, which became the *Herald of Kansas*, and then E. H. White's

Topeka Tribune. The *Recorder* was a four-page, four-column, "patent back" sheet; that is, two of the four pages consisted of syndicated state and national news purchased from a news service. A single copy sold for five cents, while a year's subscription was $1.50. Waller hired agents to peddle his papers in most of the larger towns in Kansas, and in several cities in Colorado, Iowa, and Missouri.[57] Physical facilities were no problem; he simply converted his law office over Anderson's grocery store into a press room. According to an introductory article in the initial issue, the *Recorder* was established in response to the overriding need to advance "a nobler, wiser, a more virtuous, a more self-assertive manhood and womanhood."[58] No doubt Waller was committed to racial advancement, but his real motives for going into journalism were probably more selfish. Money, in terms of revenue earned through advertisements and subscriptions, was not the answer. "There is not a Negro paper in Kansas making any money," one Negro editor remarked. "Whoever says there is tells an untruth."[59] It is possible that the Republican county and state committees subsidized the *Recorder*, although there is no evidence of this. Waller's constant appeals for new subscriptions and for payment by old subscribers indicate that any monetary aid rendered by the party was nominal. More than likely, Waller started the *Recorder* in order to advance his own personal political interests. Nothing would put his name and views before the black community or attract the attention of white political leaders more effectively than a successful race journal.

The *Recorder* was filled with church news, obituaries, and detailed accounts of various social functions. Black editors had to be just as careful not to offend their readers by failing to cover an excursion or describe a wedding as by expressing controversial views on racial matters. The bulk of the *Recorder*'s editorial page was devoted to excoriating the local Democratic regime of Mayor J. D. Bowersock. Bowersock had sinned in Waller's eyes, not so much because he was a Democrat—Waller was not averse to giving credit to local and state Democratic leaders who were in his estimation able and fair—but because Bowersock discriminated against blacks. In 1883 the city administration ordered one Edward Washington and his entire family to move to a small island close to the south bank of the Kansas River, just east of Lawrence. The city was then threatened by a smallpox epidemic and the Washingtons had been exposed. They were denied access to the regular "pest house," where patients were attended by medical personnel, simply because they were black. When Washington, who was a childhood friend of Waller's in Iowa, subsequently died, Waller launched a crusade to defeat Bowersock for reelection. As a result, the editor ran afoul of the city administration and the *Lawrence Standard,* the local Democratic sheet. Several black political rallies called by Waller prior to the 1883 city elections in behalf of Republican J. S. Crew were broken up by a gang of Democratic "toughs." Bowersock won the election, but at Waller's prodding the city eventually paid Sarah Washington, Edward's widow, $175 in damages.[60] His crusade earned Waller the respect of the black community in Lawrence and throughout the state.

John Waller spent his first two years in Lawrence sinking roots in the local community, broadening his circle of acquaintances throughout the state, and generally increasing his political visibility. Desirous of taking their places among the black "upper crust" in Lawrence, John and Susan cultivated the well-to-do merchants, farmers, and mechanics, and became active in those two most middle class of Negro institutions—the church and the literary society. Responding to a deep-seated need to serve the race, Waller joined wholeheartedly in supporting Mary Griffith's crusade for temperance and adult education among blacks. Bolstered by a supportive wife and a steady income earned through his barber shops, Waller began to play an increasingly active role in state Republican affairs, joined the campaign for equal education, and established Lawrence's first black newspaper. These were years not of frustration and disillusionment, as was so often the case for young, upwardly mobile Negroes in the late nineteenth century, but a time of growth and rising expectations. Waller was once described by a white acquaintance as above all "hopeful."[61] His quest for power and influence for himself and his people had only begun. Despite the discrimination that existed in the Sunflower State, Waller believed that in Kansas all things were possible.

CHAPTER FIVE

Materialism and Militancy

By 1883 politics had come to play an increasingly important role in John Waller's long-range plans. The young lawyer-journalist hoped ultimately to succeed McCabe as the chief black officeholder in Kansas, a position that automatically made its occupant the recognized leader of the Negro community. He realized, however, that a direct challenge to his friend would be counterproductive in every way. Consequently, with an eye to the future, Waller contented himself with extending his contacts among black and white Republicans in Kansas and establishing lines of communication with the national Negro leadership. During these years he developed and articulated a comprehensive philosophy of race relations that was, if irrelevant, typical of the black middle class in Kansas during the last quarter of the nineteenth century. Influenced by the Protestant ethic and the self-help philosophy espoused by the Quakers, the Kansas Freedmen's Relief Association, Mary Griffith, and other white philanthropists, by the rags-to-riches myth so prevalent in America during the Gilded Age, and by his conviction that Kansas was a frontier area where the Negro could control his own destiny, Waller fashioned a stratagem calling for civil rights militancy, political activism, and black capitalism.

In July, 1883, Waller attended the Colored Men's Press Convention in St. Louis where for the first time he met such black dignitaries as John Mercer Langston of Virginia, ex-Senator B. K. Bruce of Mississippi, and Frederick Douglass.[1] Apparently, the young Kansan was not overawed. According to the *St. Louis Advance,* Waller, "though not as well known as others, proved himself to be among the most brilliant debators in the convention. . . . Clear, incisive, active, he cut a clean swath through all the questions he handled."[2] Despite the *savoir faire* he exhibited in St. Louis, Waller returned to Lawrence deeply impressed by the new acquaintances he had made and determined to play a larger role in national affairs. Another opportunity was not long in coming.

The State Convention of Colored Men that met in Lawrence on August 30, 1883, directed most of its efforts toward electing and instructing delegates to a national Negro convention to be held in Louisville on September 24. Waller, as secretary of the meeting and chairman of the committee on resolutions, was in a strategic position to influence both the composition of the Kansas delegation and the priorities that were to guide it. Waller, Captain William D. Matthews of Leavenworth, Charles Langston, J. H. Stuart of Topeka, and a majority of those in attendance supported resolutions urging the national body to dedicate itself to agitation and protest. "So long as colored men are discriminated against all over this country in their accommodations, at public schools, hotels, theaters, and other public places common to other citizens because of race," Waller and his committee declared in their report, "it is the sacred duty of intelligent men of the race to meet together in convention and devise whatever laws they deem best to awaken a public and national sentiment that will make it impossible to continue such unjust discrimination."[3] A number of dissenters attacked the proposals as being implicitly critical of the Republican party. After a vigorous defense by Waller of the tradition of agitation and protest among both black Americans and Republicans, the resolution recommending vigorous civil rights agitation passed by a wide margin. As he had hoped, Waller was chosen one of the four delegates to Louisville.[4]

The meeting in Kentucky constituted, according to Waller, an assemblage of the most "representative men of the race in the United States . . . fine looking . . . men of intelligence, learning, industry, and familiarity with parliamentary laws."[5] Distinguished though the delegates were, the meeting proved to be a rowdy affair. Many were disgruntled with the Republican party because President Arthur, in an attempt to build a durable following in the South, had appealed to anti-Negro, white independents. Not only did the meeting refuse to adopt a resolution endorsing the party, but a faction led by the Tennessee delegation even launched an attack on the venerable Douglass. The charges leveled at the "leader of the race" were contradictory. Some accused him of having promised to support Democrat Benjamin Butler for the presidency in 1884; others maintained that he was indifferent to the implications of the Compromise of 1877 and had become too faithful a Republican for the good of the race. Waller supported Douglass and the Republicans throughout the deliberations. The Kansan was named to the committee on resolutions and played a central role in hammering out a set of recommendations that urged the federal government to enforce the various civil rights laws then on the books, demanded abolition of the "plantation credit mortgage system," and endorsed the religious and moral training of black youth.[6]

Most of the race leaders whom Waller met during his travels in 1883 and 1884 were past or present residents of Washington, D.C., the cultural and political mecca of late nineteenth-century Afro-America. Like many ambitious young Negroes of the Gilded Age, Waller was ambivalent toward the national elite and the black colony in Washington. On the one hand he was immensely proud of the Douglasses and Bruces. Their political positions, their social pretensions, and their conspicuous consumption were all vicariously satisfying. He continually applauded the intelligence and refinement of the national Negro elite, and he viewed any slippage in their perquisites as a threat to the status of the entire race. On the other hand Waller was jealous of the aristocracy, impatient for it to step aside and make way for a younger generation, or at least to take cognizance of the achievements and opinions of black leaders in the West and Midwest.[7] Despite occasional grumblings, Waller, politician that he was, managed to stay on good terms with the graybeards of the race.

In July, 1884, for reasons that are unknown, Waller moved his family to Atchison, a rough-and-tumble railroad center and riverfront town on the Missouri. Immediately after his arrival, he began campaigning for a place on the Kansas delegation to the Republican national convention. In spite of his strenuous efforts in his own behalf and the active support of a number of influential white newspapers, including the *Lawrence Journal*, the party chose an all-white contingent. Waller's pain of defeat was somewhat assuaged, however, when Blanche K. Bruce, then recorder of deeds, named him Kansas' black representative to the New Orleans World's Fair. Waller's selection by Bruce, who as recorder was *ex officio* chief dispenser of black patronage for the Arthur administration, underscored Waller's position as a recognized, if second echelon, member of the Negro national leadership. On November 7, 1884, Waller sold the *Western Recorder* to H. H. Johnson of Kansas City and set about preparing the state's exhibit for the forthcoming exposition, which was scheduled to open in December.[8]

Participation in racial affairs at the national level was heady stuff, particularly for a man like Waller who had risen from the humblest of origins. But Waller was a realist; he quickly recognized that the benefits accruing from Negro conventions and expositions, especially at the national level, were more apparent than real. After the meeting halls had emptied and the exhibits were dismantled, the black man's political and economic position—and perhaps, more importantly, his image in the white man's mind—had changed not a whit. What Waller wanted was the substance of power, not the illusion. And although he liked to think of himself as a rugged individualist, Waller was forced to realize that because Kansas was a white-dominated society his fate was irretrievably bound up with that of his black brethren.[9] Responding to this perception, the black lawyer-politician articulated in his speeches and editorials a philosophy of racial advancement that he believed was suited to the Kansas milieu, one that would preserve the black man's self-respect and at the same time meet the white man's expectations. That philosophy —civil rights militancy and black capitalism—was surely a product of Waller's background and his unique personality, but it was at the same time both a repsonse to and a reflection of the racial climate and pattern of race relations that prevailed in Kansas from 1880 to 1900.

In April, 1889, the *New West Monthly* promised that blacks intent upon immigrating to the Sunflower State could expect to find "a school for every child; a field to labor;/Respect that sees in every man a neighbor; the richest soil a farmer ever saw/and equal rights to all before the law."[10] The *New West*'s portrait was overdrawn. Black Kansans encountered discrimination in public services, the administration of justice, and hiring; segregation in hotels, restaurants, and theaters; and exclusion from white hospitals, churches, and neighborhoods. And yet during the same period there were integrated schools at one level or another in all regions of Kansas, public facilities were open to Negroes on both an integrated and segregated basis, and blacks were protected in their effort to vote. With one exception, legally mandated segregation was nonexistent after 1887.

Blacks who sought access to public facilities in Kansas might encounter exclusion, segregation, or integration. Hotels applied the color line perhaps more frequently than any other type of facility. When the Shawnee County delegation to the Republican congressional convention in 1886 applied for lodging at the Coolidge Hotel in Emporia, they were turned away because three of their number were black. In 1888 a white innkeeper in Leavenworth denied lodgings to none other than Frederick Douglass. A majority of Kansas restaurants also either excluded or segregated blacks. One of the famous 1833 civil rights cases involved a

Negro, Bird Gee, who was physically ejected from the City Hotel restaurant in Hiawatha.[11] Restaurants in Coffeyville, Lawrence, Topeka, and Leavenworth also refused to admit Negroes. Segregation was apparently less frequent in eating houses than exclusion, but there were Jim Crow sections in some establishments. A letter to the editor of the *Leavenworth Advocate* in 1890 complained of a restaurant "between 4th and 5th streets" that forced a Negro patron to retire to a dark room in the rear of the establishment "with a curtain drawn over him as though he was going to have his picture taken."[12]

And yet segregation and exclusion were by no means universal. Refused accommodations in Leavenworth, Douglass moved on to Topeka where he was received and feted at the largest hotel in the city. Rebuffed by the Coolidge Hotel in Emporia, the Shawnee County delegation sought lodgings at the Merchants Hotel and was welcomed. In 1878 Eagleson in the *Colored Citizen* praised the Tefft House Hotel in Topeka and its restaurant as establishments that "never discriminate as to color."[13] Even in Leavenworth there were hotels and lunch counters open to blacks on an integrated basis. In transportation, the first separate coach for blacks did not appear in Kansas until 1892, and segregation did not become the rule on railroads and streetcars until after the turn of the century.[14]

Black urban dwellers in Kansas, no less than their brethren in Chicago and Detroit, experienced residential segregation and discrimination in public services. Blacks who came to Kansas in the 1860s and 1870s purchased homes in Topeka, Wyandotte, Leavenworth, Atchison, Lawrence, or some other town and tended to cluster together, but they were not excluded from every white neighborhood. The thousands of blacks who poured into the state during the exodus heightened the white community's desire to see blacks restricted to a certain section of a particular city, however, and led to the creation of what could be accurately called ghettos. Just what the tipping point—that is, the percentage of blacks in a given community necessary to trigger segregation—was for each Kansas town is unclear. What is clear is that in each town whose black population totaled 7 percent or more, residential segregation existed.[15] Apparently, in Kansas as in other areas, residential segregation was the product primarily of white hostility rather than black clannishness.[16] Not only did blacks in Leavenworth, Lawrence, Topeka, and Kansas City have to live in designated areas, but they had to endure discrimination in public services as well. Streets in Tennesseetown and Mudville were constantly filled with potholes or went unpaved completely, sidewalks were often nonexistent, and fire departments staffed by whites frequently took two to three times as long to answer a call in black sections as they did to respond to an alarm in white areas.[17]

Black Kansans seeking jobs in the public sector—firemen, policemen, janitors, sanitary workers—and those seeking admittance to state institutions encountered some discrimination, but in these areas it was the exception rather than the rule. In 1879 the black men of Lawrence held a meeting to protest the city administration's neglect of Negroes in hiring. Yet, the police force in every Kansas town of the first class, and some of the second, was integrated. The city marshal of Lawrence in 1895 was a Negro. Some of the urban fire departments were integrated, and Kansas City boasted an all-black fire company. Apparently, all of the "charitable institutions" of Kansas, such as the State Insane Asylum, the School for the Blind, and the Asylum for Idiotic and Imbecilic Youth, were open to blacks. These institutions were extremely crowded, however—waiting lists for each ranged from 50 to 200 in 1890—and not only blacks but whites without political influence found it difficult to gain admission. Once admitted, however, Negroes were usually segregated.[18]

Equality under the law and due process were realities only for black Kansans of property and influence. The poor and the ignorant encountered discrimination at virtually every stage of the legal process. Negroes were more likely to be lynched than whites, although the lynching of whites was by no means uncommon in frontier Kansas. In 1879 the residents of Fort Scott hanged and burned the body of one Bill Howard, a black man and an alleged outlaw. In 1887 Richard Woods, a black youth accused of assaulting and raping a fifteen-year-old white girl in Leavenworth, was taken from the county jail by a mob of white men. His tormentors subsequently attached one end of a rope to his neck and the other to the pommel of a saddle, and dragged him for more than a mile. Blacks accused of raping white women were lynched near Hiawatha in 1889 and Larned in 1892. And yet lynchings in Kansas were rare in comparison to the southern states, and the number each year declined steadily from 1870 to 1900.[19]

Another kind of violence—police brutality—plagued black Kansans throughout the late nineteenth century. In 1889, for example, a white policeman in Leavenworth shot and killed a black youth simply because he would not tell the officer where he obtained a cigarette he was smoking. Five years later in the same city several police, seeing a white man chasing a Negro, joined in pursuit. Without a single inquiry, one of the officers shot the black man, Charles Reed. As it turned out, Reed had been waylaid by a gang of white toughs and was simply running for his life. Similar incidents were reported in Topeka and Lawrence. Because the black community comprised up to one-quarter of the voting population in the state's eastern cities, and because there were nearly always a few black policemen on municipal forces, oppression and brutality by the police were intermittent and, apparently, never systematic.[20]

Lynchings and police brutality were not the only problems confronting Kansas Negroes accused of committing crimes. The state prison at Lansing operated a modified convict-lease system. As of 1890 there were 882 convicts in the state facility; of these all but 125 worked at the prison or in nearby state-owned and -operated coal shafts. The warden leased those who were not employed in the mines to a furniture factory, shoe shop, wagon factory, or brick works in Leavenworth. The $3,000 a month realized from convict leases and the proceeds from the sale of state-produced coal were incentives for state officials to keep the prison full. A disproportionate number of inmates at the state prison—approximately 25 percent of the total throughout the last quarter of the nineteenth century—were black. This imbalance was due to the fact that the crime rate among urban-dwelling blacks, if not rural residents, was higher than among whites. The higher rate, however, was the result not only of a greater tendency toward crime among blacks but also of discrimination in the administration of justice. Blacks were more likely to be arrested as suspects than whites, they were more likely to be convicted, and they were sure to receive longer sentences. In May, 1890, for example, two men, one white and one black, were convicted of the identical crime of selling liquor. The white was pardoned, but the black received a fine and jail term. In 1896 the *Leavenworth Herald* insisted that a Negro man had been sentenced to twenty-six years in prison for breaking into a man's home and stealing a bottle of wine. Others were incarcerated for taking food; often the value of the stolen item was increased in order that the black offender might be convicted of grand larceny rather than a misdemeanor. Whites accused of crimes against Negroes were less likely to be convicted and, if found guilty, more likely to receive a lighter sentence than if the offense had been committed against a white. There was some discrimination in jury selection, but blacks served on state district court juries throughout the late nineteenth century, even in cases involving two whites. In jury selection the determining factor seems to have been economic and social standing rather than color.[21]

Although segregation and exclusion were not universal in any phase of life in late nineteenth-century Kansas, blacks faced the possibility of discrimination in virtually every situation that involved contact with whites. Nearly all the white churches in the state drew the color line, and several Y.M.C.A. chapters discriminated against blacks. The Mutual

Life Insurance Association of Hiawatha refused to sell policies to Negroes. Theater and opera house owners generally insisted on segregating their audiences, except when their facility was being used for a political gathering or a public lecture. Although it was unusual, black individuals and organizations were sometimes excluded from public functions and celebrations. In 1890 a detachment of black veterans was prevented from attending the unveiling of a monument to Ulysses S. Grant in Leavenworth. By contrast most professional organizations, such as the State Teachers Association and the State Bar Association, were integrated. Blacks participated conspicuously in the innumerable political functions that took place during the last quarter of the century.[22]

The word "white" appeared three places in the state constitution adopted at Wyandotte in 1859. As has been noted, the school provision authorized the establishment of an educational system for the state's white children. In addition, Article V limited the franchise to "every white male person of twenty-one years and upward."[23] In 1867 Kansans defeated a constitutional amendment striking the word "white" from section V by nearly a two-to-one vote, and it was not actually removed from the constitution by an amendment until 1918. Nonetheless, blacks were effectively enfranchised in 1870 when Kansans ratified the Fifteenth Amendment to the United States Constitution. Although there were innumerable attempts made by both Democrats and Republicans to buy black votes, no political organization made a concerted effort during the late nineteenth century to disfranchise Negroes. Finally, the constitutional convention at Wyandotte not only barred blacks from voting but also excluded them from serving in the state militia. Although there were "independent" black military units in all the larger cities of the state, the word "white" was not actually stricken from section VIII—the constitutional provision establishing a state militia—until 1887.[24]

The pattern of race relations that emerged in late nineteenth-century Kansas was a product largely of white attitudes toward "social equality," that is, racial mixing in neighborhoods, churches, places of amusement, and other areas not considered essential to the individual's health and safety. Whites did not want it, blacks did not want it, and it was contrary to the laws of God and nature. Equal rights before the law, even equal access to essential public facilities, were the Negro's birthright, but he should for all time occupy a separate niche in society. He should and would develop, but independently.[25] Typically, then, the white Kansan was willing to tolerate the Negro, to recognize his right to equality before the law and to equal access to public facilities such as schools and railroads, but he was adamantly opposed to amalgamation and residential integration.

Blacks responded to discrimination, segregation, and exclusion in two ways. Just as their brethren did in Chicago, New York, Charleston, and New Orleans, Negroes in Topeka, Leavenworth, and Wichita established a system of institutions that would make available to blacks those social services and cultural activities that were open to whites. The black churches and literary societies have already been dealt with. There were in Kansas numerous fraternal and benevolent societies: the Knights of Labor, the Prince Hall Colored Masons, the Knights of Pythias, and the United Order of Immaculates, to name a few. These associations provided members and their families with fellowship and a certain amount of social security. Membership usually carried with it a life insurance policy, which paid, upon the death of the insured, burial expenses and a monthly stipend to survivors. Some of the societies attempted to force their members to live by a well-defined moral code. Adultery was a consensus sin, and offenders were summarily expelled. The fraternal and benevolent societies were more or less exclusive. At one extreme was the Grand Order of Wise Men, open to all classes and to both men and women. The Colored Masons, in contrast, restricted membership on the basis of wealth, education, and/or participation in public life. In addition to the various fraternal and benevolent orders, the black community in Kansas founded a Colored Widows and Orphans' Home in Leavenworth and, in 1898, the Douglass Hospital and Training School in Kansas City. In 1896 W. I. Jamison, James H. Guy, and several other black Topekans established the Industrial and Educational Institute, but because of financial difficulties they were forced to close the school within a matter of months. Much more substantial was Western University, which was established at Quindaro by the A.M.E. Church in 1881. The school struggled along until William T. Vernon, a graduate of Lincoln Institute and Wilberforce University, became president in 1896. Vernon converted Western into an industrial institute and secured state support. By 1902 Quindaro school could boast 9 instructors and 102 pupils. Finally, Kansas Negroes, excluded for the most part from white unions, formed their own trade organizations. Black stonemasons in Topeka, Negro bakers in Kansas City, and black miners in Weir City banded together to discuss common grievances and in some instances to join with white unions in strikes and boycotts.[26]

At the same time the black community was erecting this complex of separate institutions, several prominent Negroes, most notably Waller and W. B. Townsend, stepped forward to insist that the black community must react to segregation and exclusion, not with withdrawal but with increasing agitation and protest in behalf of equal access on an integrated basis to all public facilities. After 1884 Waller's speeches and writings reflected a growing conviction that "separate" could never be "equal." Segregated facilities and institutions were the products of racial prejudice and thus were bound to be inferior. Waller was particularly concerned about the blighting effect the color bar would have on the self-image and self-confidence of Negro youths in Kansas. Pride and achievement were inextricably intertwined; acquiescence in proscription and segregation would inevitably stunt the race's growth. Moreover, Waller recognized that the white community wanted rather desperately to maintain Kansas' reputation as a land of freedom and equality. Widespread violence and proscription directed against blacks might reinforce an image of the state as a lawless frontier wilderness, thus retarding the influx of immigrants and capital from the East.[27] A militant campaign in the newspapers, courts, and state legislature, Waller reasoned, would simultaneously build the black community's confidence and compel whites, sensitive to the state's image in other regions of the country, to eradicate discrimination and segregation throughout the state.

Waller's first public challenge to institutionalized racism in Kansas came in 1883 during a controversy with the Lawrence Police Department over an alleged case of police brutality. On July 21, Green Johnson, a young black man, was arrested on a misdemeanor charge and then released on bail. A white police officer subsequently followed Green to the livery stable where the Negro was employed and beat him unconscious. In a series of editorials Waller denounced the city administration and called for the immediate resignation of the officer. If Johnson failed to take the matter to court, he would be neglecting his duty "as a parent and a citizen."[28] Actually, he did go to court twice, each time losing because of a hung jury. Throughout 1883 and 1884 Waller denounced the Kansas constitutional prohibition against the induction of blacks into regular militia units and demanded, "in the name of equality, equity, and fair play," that the distinction be eliminated.[29] In 1887 he headed the successful drive to persuade the legislature to eliminate the word "white" from section VIII of the constitution.[30]

Increasingly, though, the arena in which Waller and other black activists chose to fight their battles and publicize their cause was the state courts. Litigation received widespread attention in the press, white as well as black; even the lowliest of Negroes could seek redress of his grievances through the courts; and most of the leaders of the civil rights movement were lawyers. Unfortunately, the decisions that resulted from the cases initiated and/or argued by Waller eroded rather than promoted the civil rights of Negroes. Unwilling to admit even that individual citizens operating their own businesses had the right to refuse service on the basis of color, Waller in 1888 represented a Topeka black, who, having been denied service at a local lunch counter, was seeking redress through the Kansas Civil Rights Act. The case was dismissed when one Will Pickett, chief witness for the plaintiff, was bought off and left town just as the trial was about to open. In 1889 a mulatto named Simpson Younger bought two tickets to a performance at the Ninth Street Theater in Kansas City. When he arrived with a woman much darker than he, the management gave him the option of moving to the section reserved for blacks or accepting a refund. Younger rejected both alternatives and subsequently brought suit in circuit court in Kansas City. The plaintiff's brief, which was prepared by a group of Negro lawyers including Waller, Price, and Townsend, failed to sway the presiding judge. In his decision the judge insisted that theaters, like race tracks, were not necessary to the health and safety of the citizenry. Because the denial of access to such facilities resulted only in inconvenience, the proprietors or lessees could exclude any manner of clientele they considered detrimental to their business. Black Kansans' right of access was further restricted when, in a case involving the St. Nicholas Hotel of Topeka, the state district court held the Kansas Civil Rights Act of 1874 unconstitutional. It seems that on August 4, 1892, one J. L. Leonard, colored, showed up at the St. Nicholas dining room and demanded his breakfast. Told that he would be served at the lunch counter but not in the dining room, he left and subsequently brought suit (Waller once again helped prepare the plaintiff's case) under the 1874 law, officially entitled "An act to provide for the protection of citizens in their civil and public rights." This statute stipulated among other things that if the owners or agents in charge of any inn, hotel, or boarding house, or any place of entertainment or amusement should make any distinction on account of race, color, or previous condition, he would be guilty of a misdemeanor. In *State* v. *De Moss and Armstrong* the state court ruled that the 1874 act was unconstitutional on the grounds that the title of the measure (referring to all citizens) and the body of the law (pertaining to a special class of citizens) were incompatible.[31]

Waller's advocacy of protest, agitation, and litigation was based in part on the assumption that the black community could significantly alter its status within the larger, white-dominated milieu. In reality the black man's ability to affect his treatment at the hands of whites was quite limited. True, in several instances blacks successfully resorted to

73

direct action to forestall racial violence. In March, 1892, for example, Will Lowe, a black resident of Coffeyville, was arrested for assaulting a white woman. Despite the fact that Lowe was one of the most respected members of the black community, a mob of whites gathered and decided to "lynch the nigger." When several dozen blacks armed with Winchesters and shotguns subsequently intervened, the crowd quickly dispersed and Lowe was accorded due process. In May, 1897, whites were dissuaded from stringing up William Jeltz, accused of stabbing a white man, when local blacks swore to lynch the lynchers.[32] Moreover, through agitation and protest, black leaders did manage to compel the legislature to strike the word "white" from the state constitution. But the black citizens' right to enter a given restaurant, to attend a certain school, to live in a particular neighborhood, or to attend the church of his choice was governed by the extent of the white community's commitment to the doctrine of parallel development and its determination to avoid social equality. As the court decisions in the Ninth Street Theater and St. Nicholas Hotel cases and the inactivity of the Kansas legislature throughout this period indicate, white lawmakers and jurists were determined that white individuals and businesses did not have to associate with blacks so long as public health and safety were not involved.

In reality the protest editorials, court briefs, and militant speeches that emanated from John Waller's pen affected his status within the black community far more than it did black society's position within the larger milieu. In Kansas, blacks experienced a relatively high amount of physical and psychological freedom, which in turn spawned a sharply rising level of expectations. For people like Waller and Townsend, militancy was a political necessity. Even those Negroes who supported the establishment of a separate institutional life demanded that their leaders challenge segregation and exclusion. In articulating the feelings and venting the frustrations of his less literate brethren, Waller may not have tangibly improved the black subculture's lot within the larger society, but he certainly extended his following beyond the black parlors, churches, and meeting halls of Leavenworth and Lawrence and into the fields, construction sites, and stockyards of central and eastern Kansas.

Waller would never admit in the 1880s that his campaign for protest and agitation was largely irrelevant to the black community's drive to improve its position within the white-controlled milieu, but he was aware that a program consisting purely of civil rights militancy had its limitations. Civil equality was necessary if blacks were to enjoy "life, liberty, and property," but even if Negroes were accorded due process, equal protection, and full access to public facilities, they could still remain underprivileged and disadvantaged. A successful civil rights campaign would not produce the capital and purchasing power necessary for blacks to achieve socioeconomic parity with the white majority. What was needed, Waller recognized, was a comprehensive approach that would go beyond protest and agitation and secure for the Negro not only civil equality but collective wealth and the power that inevitably accompanies it. Predictably, the solution that he came up with called first for economic self-sufficiency and then capital accumulation. "We are free men," he declared in a speech at Tonganoxie in August, 1880. "Let us turn our attention to the great agricultural and mechanical pursuits of life and make for ourselves free homes and free firesides on every hilltop."[33] In an 1888 editorial he urged "our monied men to centralize their capital and use it to the advantage of the race. . . . such men by assimilating their means, could place themselves in possession of valuable real estate, and sell it to the deserving poor. . . . in ten years there will be ten million dollars more property owned by the colored people of the state than they now possess."[34] Anticipating Booker T. Washington and other future proponents of racial uplift through economic self-help, Waller held up the merchant class as a model for the rest of the community. Those who did not have the capital to start a business of their own should invest what spare money they had in corporate enterprises, black or white. Infiltration of the economic power structure would inevitably enhance the power and prestige of the entire race.[35]

In line with his belief that economic development would drive the status of the black man ever upward, Waller assumed, like so many Republicans, past and present, that what was good for business was good for the country, including Kansas Negroes. Accordingly, he supported the high tariff and internal improvement policies espoused by Blaine, Garfield, and McKinley.[36] Waller realized that the bulk of the black population was engaged in farming and manual labor, but he subscribed to the theory that protection would raise wages and create a prosperous home market for agriculturists. "I shall hold out for the protective policy," he editorialized in 1888. "High prices and plenty of work is a million times better for us . . . than no work and low prices."[37] While stumping Kansas for Benjamin Harrison in 1888, he proclaimed: "Free trade means to throw open the markets of the country to European manufacturers, to cheapen the price of labor, to place the laborer of this country on the same level with the pauper labor of Germany, England, France, and Italy."[38]

Waller was a staunch opponent of strikes, boycotts, and other direct-action techniques employed by American workers. Between 1885 and 1886 the Knights of Labor, utilizing the momentum gained from its successful 1884 strike against Jay Gould's Missouri Pacific Railroad, increased its membership from about 100,000 to over 700,000.[39] Ignoring distinctions of color as well as trade, K. of L. organizers made a strong pitch to Negroes, especially in Kansas and Missouri. By 1886 Waller was being inundated with requests for advice from black workers who had been approached by the Knights. Waller was repelled by the violence and destruction of property that so often accompanied late nineteenth-century strikes, yet he was sympathetic to the desire of Negro laborers for job security. During a second, unsuccessful round of strikes against the Gould line in 1886, Waller sought advice from his friend and political mentor Governor John A. Martin. "It is urged," he wrote, "that should colored men take hold of the order [K. of L.] there will be a chance for the young men of the race to become skilled laborers and that the avenues of business and trade now closed against them will be instantly thrown open." Yet, he declared, "the present strike had caused me to form a very unfavorable opinion about the said organization. . . . I shall hesitate to countenance the Knights of Labor or any other organization that cannot control its members and prevent them from destroying property and destroying the commerce and traffic of the country."[40] Martin responded that, although the K. of L. had some admirable objectives and Terrence Powderly (National Grand Workman) was a worthy, respectable man, the organization in Kansas was led by a group of "vicious" and "irresponsible" demagogues. (Martin was caught in a political squeeze between capital and labor during the 1886 strike, which in Kansas was fairly violent.) Given the race's desperate need for "intelligent leadership," the governor concluded that Negroes should shy away from the organization. In the end, like all good politicians, Waller straddled the issue. He lauded the Knights as the best of all labor unions because of its egalitarian policies, while he denounced organized labor in general for its tendency toward illegal and antisocial activities.[41] In calling for a state convention of black men in 1888, Waller proposed that one of the meeting's first actions be to denounce "the annual strikes which appear to strike at the interests of the people of the whole country, rich as well as poor, black as well as white."[42] No doubt his opposition to strikes stemmed from the knowledge that use of blacks as strikebreakers by unscrupulous managers had the ultimate result of provoking cries from white laborers for total exclusion of blacks from the industrial force as well as from a belief that they disrupted the economy and promoted unemployment.

At times Waller's orthodox economic views placed him to the right of the white rank and file of Kansas Republicans. Although he had at one point endorsed state railroad regulation in principle, he came out in open opposition to a bill pending before the state legislature in the 1890s that would establish maximum freight rates. No state owed its prosperity to the railroads more than Kansas, he insisted. Few Kansans had funds invested in the roads, but many earned their living because of them. The rate-control measure would surely frighten capital away and rob the Sunflower State of much-needed jobs.[43]

In part, Waller's economic views were a natural by-product of his membership in Kansas' black middle class. All of the larger towns of eastern and central Kansas contained a handful of black professionals and successful businessmen. Each of the six largest cities in the state could boast at least one Negro doctor and several black lawyers. Each community had its black barbershops, grocery stores, hotels, and restaurants. Occasionally, an ambitious Negro entrepreneur would open a blacksmith shop or a shoe store. In addition, the state could boast two or three black concerns that could legitimately be called corporations. Serving as a model for the rest of the Negro business community was the largest black-owned business in Kansas during the last quarter of the nineteenth century—the A.C.L. Coal Company of Kansas City. This enterprise, incorporated in 1891, sold coal, feed, and flour, both wholesale and retail, and eventually employed an all-black labor force of several dozen men. Second and third to the A.C.L. in size were the Twin City Brick and Building Association of Kansas City, which employed fifteen colored masons, and the Eureka Building, Loan, and Investment Association, an all-black Leavenworth real-estate business, which sold $10,000 in stock during its first year of operation. By the spring of 1890 this enterprise was actively making loans, selling real estate, and building houses. Probably the most successful of all black entrepreneurs in late nineteenth-century Kansas, however, were the saloon owners of Kansas City, Leavenworth, Topeka, and Lawrence. Nick Chiles, a Topeka hotel and tavern keeper, was well-to-do even by white standards. Joining these businessmen in the economic elite were a number of successful farmers who had managed to purchase acreage in the eastern part of the state where the soil was more fertile and the rainfall more frequent than in the west. A number owned 160-acre potato farms in the fertile Kaw River valley. One, H. P. Ewing, known as the "Potato King of Kansas," farmed over 500 acres and produced a crop in 1893 of 75,000 bushels. North and east of Topeka, independent Negro farmers such as Alexander Steele, William Hines, and Clark McPheters raised wheat, corn, hogs, and cattle on spreads that ranged from 80 to 160 acres.[44] Responding to their own success, to the materialistic concepts that pervaded American life in the late nineteenth century, and, no doubt, to the expectations of the white community in Kansas, members of this black middle class advocated, as early as 1880, capitalism and property ownership as techniques of racial uplift. Reflecting the views of the black bourgeoisie, Bill Eagleson in 1878 declared: "The colored people must generally own well-cultivated farms.... We must own railroad and steamboat and bank stock.... We must be able to give checks for labor as well as receive checks for labor.... In short we must acquire wealth and rise above respectable indigence and bread and butter slavery."[45]

In addition, Waller's nostrums reflected the attitudes of the white leadership within the Kansas Republican party. Through his barber shops and his various political activities, Waller came to know such luminaries as Harrison Kelley, state senator and well-to-do landowner; E. N. Morrill, banker, real-estate dealer, congressman, and, later, governor; T. Dwight Thacher, brother of Solon and editor of the *Lawrence Journal*; and John Martin, editor of the *Atchison Champion* and governor from 1884 to 1888.[46] These bankers, merchants, and agri-businessmen were no less committed to the tenets of American capitalism than their fellow Republicans in other parts of the country.

Finally, and perhaps most importantly, Waller's paeans to free enterprise and black capitalism were the result of his association and identification with those white philanthropists who viewed material success as an indication of moral worth. White Kansans continued to recognize and approve—in the press, in the courts, and in the job market —those blacks who were well dressed, well fed, and well mannered. Waller was hardly immune to such reinforcement.

The problem with Waller's plan to augment the black community's prestige and power within the larger white-dominated milieu was that the vast majority of blacks living in Kansas were members of the proletariat or subproletariat, not the middle class. Most Negroes who lived in the cities and towns of eastern Kansas earned their bread as unskilled or semiskilled laborers. The depots at Topeka, Kansas City, Leavenworth, Lawrence, and Atchison all employed blacks as porters and, in a few cases, as clerical personnel. A much larger number of Negroes who lived in the east found temporary work on the railroad construction crews that crisscrossed the state with thousands of miles of railroad track during the 1880s and 1890s.[47] Still others were employed in the repair shops and train yards in Kansas City, Topeka, and Atchison. Another important source of income for urban blacks was the meat packing industry in Kansas City and Topeka. The huge Armour plant in Kansas City at one time employed several hundred Negroes. Blacks could also find work as hod carriers, carpenters' helpers, and waiters. With a few exceptions the only work open to women in the larger towns was as a seamstress, washerwoman, or maid.[48]

Outside the major population centers of Kansas the two most important occupations available to blacks were coal mining and farming. Coal mining was a major industry in Kansas during the Gilded Age, with the largest deposits situated near Leavenworth, Pittsburg, and Oswego. There sprang up around these cities small mining towns such as Weir City, Litchfield, and Cherokee. Nearly all of the mining companies—the Kansas and Texas Coal Company, the Keith and Perry Coal Company, and the Riverside Coal Company—employed black miners. One Riverside shaft near Leavenworth was worked by 126 black and 4 white miners. The whites, of course, all occupied supervisory positions. Most Kansas miners, both black and white, lived very near the subsistence level. Each worker had to buy his own set of tools, which cost up to thirty dollars; top pay for digging was around five cents a bushel; and compensation was usually in the form of scrip redeemable only at the company store. By the late 1880s only a small percentage of Kansas blacks were engaged in tilling the soil. Many of the exodusters who had taken advantage of the Homestead Act and filed claim on 40, 80, or 160 acres in western or southern Kansas were driven back to the cities of the east or completely out of the state by the severe droughts of the late eighties and early nineties. A few, principally in Chautauqua, Labette, Morris, Graham, Pratt, and Wabaunsee counties, did manage to survive until the rains came, but even then their economic situation continued to be precarious.[49]

There was that segment of the community, of course, that could only be classified as unemployed. In 1887 in Topeka 566 people were receiving county welfare.[50] Of these, three-fifths were black. In each black enclave in Topeka, Wichita, Leavenworth, Atchison, Lawrence, and Kansas City dozens of Negro orphans roamed the streets begging and stealing enough food to stay alive. During a walk on the south side of Kansas City in 1897, Dennis Thompson, a reporter for the *American Citizen*, came across what he claimed was not an atypical scene. In a dilapidated shack were "two little girls, orphans so they informed us, aged 18 and 8 years. . . . There was not a sign of anything to eat in the house, no coal, no bed, save a small piece of carpet in a corner behind the stove and no other visible means of subsistence."[51]

Thus, for black Kansans, the outlook for economic opportunity just as for civil equality was mixed. Skilled and unskilled jobs, except during the depression years of 1888–1894, were relatively plentiful. On the other hand blacks were excluded from most white-collar jobs and certainly from the state's counting houses and corporate boards. Waller's plan for racial advancement through free enterprise and capital accumulation was in part predicated on the assumption that blacks in general had the wherewithal to accumulate investment capital. For the most part, in Kansas, as in other areas, they did not. Whites were not willing to provide the massive economic aid necessary to raise the Negroes' living standard to a point where he would be able to participate in life on anywhere near equal footing with whites. Objections to "charity" by white philanthropists and relief officials during the exodus had prevented formulation and implementation of a land reform program that would have put property in the hands of a significant number of Negroes. Subsequently, racism among white employers and white workers kept blacks from filling positions that would enable them to accumulate wealth.[52] True, management did occasionally hire black workers to fill lower level white-collar jobs, but usually at a lesser wage, and with the intention of curbing the wage demands of white workers of similar rank.[53] In short, following a period of intense philanthropic activity (designed to make the Negro "earn" his way to independence), which lasted from 1878 through 1884, white Kansans virtually abandoned the black man to his fate. The few who succeeded in white middle-class terms were singled out for recognition and approbation, but the poor, the semi- or uneducated were shunned as a hopeless cause.

If Waller's plan for racial advancement through black capitalism did not materially advance the political and economic interests of the black community in Kansas, it, like his militant stand in behalf of civil equality, enhanced his political standing with the black subculture. This was true primarily because the doctrine of racial uplift through material accumulation and property ownership was espoused not only by the middle class but by much of the black proletariat as well. A mood of expectation, if not optimism, pervaded the black community in Kansas prior to the turn of the century. Negroes who came to the state from the South, no less than the millions of immigrants who came to America from Europe during the last quarter of the nineteenth century, perceived their new home to be a land of rugged individualism where a man was judged by his accomplishments and not by his family's heritage or the color of his skin. This perception, which endured in spite of the crop failures, wage cuts, and racism that constantly threatened the existence of black Kansans, together with the *relative* economic opportunity to be found in Kansas, the expectations of the white community, and the presence of a handful of conspicuously successful Negroes, led many Negroes to believe, indeed to expect, that they too could become property owners and men of means, when in reality there was virtually no chance for them to do so. Thus, while Waller's advocacy of black capitalism was largely irrelevant to the social and economic needs of his brethren, it was highly pertinent insofar as their expectations and self-image were concerned.

When he arrived in Kansas in 1878, John Waller was a young, inexperienced black lawyer; half of his life had been spent in slavery, and his horizons were understandably narrow. He was largely ignorant of the issues agitating the black community and unfamiliar with the political and economic condition of Negroes both in the West and the nation as a whole. Although ambitious, both for himself and his people, Waller was unsure as to the best method for achieving his goals. During the decade that followed, Waller developed a distinct, if typical, philosophy of racial uplift. Convinced that blacks could achieve power and prestige in America only by working within the existing societal and economic framework, he accepted the individualistic, materialistic concepts of the Gilded Age and combined them with civil rights militancy. He urged his brethren to stand up for their rights, to accumulate wealth, and to render faithful support to the guardian of liberty and property— the Republican party—while at the same time he conducted a personal campaign against discrimination, exclusion, and segregation in all walks of life. Waller was committed to this blend of materialism and militancy, not only because it would lead to power and protection for the race, but because it would enable him to appeal to and reconcile his two principal constituencies, white Republicans and black Kansans.

CHAPTER SIX

The Best Laid Plans . . .

The period from 1886 through 1891 was one of great expectations and disappointed hopes for black politicians in general and for John Lewis Waller in particular. A challenge to Republican supremacy mounted by the Democrats and Populists led many Negro leaders to believe that the party of Lincoln would offer special inducements to blacks in order to retain their allegiance. They reasoned that if blacks could play one political faction against another their leverage would be increased and a new era of equality and opportunity would result. The reality was quite different. While white Republicans were willing to accord minimal recognition to a few blacks in order to keep the Negro vote, they generally refused to respond to threats of ticket splitting. The Democrats and Populists, both separately and in coalition, displayed an inclination to appeal to the black electorate, but by 1894 exclusionist elements had temporarily gained the upper hand in both parties.[1] It was against this backdrop that Waller made an unsuccessful bid for nomination and election to the position of state auditor. Failure and the disillusionment that inevitably ensued caused the frustrated black politician to look beyond Kansas for the ways and means to advance his interests and those of his race.

Waller's year in Atchison was not one of the more propitious periods in his life. The *Western Recorder* proved to be a financial albatross; by the time he sold it, the paper had accumulated more than $500 in debts.[2] Plans for the New Orleans World's Fair were cancelled shortly after

Waller was named director of the Kansas Negro Exhibition. There was a silver lining, however. Soon after his arrival in Atchison the lawyer-turned-journalist made the acquaintance of John A. Martin, wealthy editor of the *Atchison Champion* and one of the leading Republican politicians in the state. Waller's relationship with Martin, in turn, led directly to his recognition by white Republicans as black Kansas' chief political spokesman.

In 1884 the Republicans wanted desperately to regain control of the governorship, lost to the Democrats in 1882. A group of younger men, headed by Martin and Cyrus Leland of Troy, was determined not only to defeat the Democrats but also wrest control of the party from the clique that had directed it since the Civil War. With Leland, who was Kansas' national committeeman from 1878 to 1917, working tirelessly in his behalf, Martin managed to garner the gubernatorial nomination. The Democrats chose Glick again and, just as they did in 1882, came out in favor of resubmission of the prohibition amendment to the electorate. A group of antiprohibition Republicans, headed by David Overmeyer, fused with the Democrats after being given the right to name the Democratic nominee for lieutenant-governor. In the election Martin defeated Glick by a vote of 146,777 to 108,284. Waller delivered a number of speeches during the campaign in behalf of Martin, McCabe (who was renominated), and the entire Republican ticket. According to one observer, Martin received a larger percentage of the black vote than any previous gubernatorial candidate. Whether or not Waller's attacks on the Democrats were related to Republican successes in 1884 is unclear; he managed, however, to convince Martin that they were. Indeed, by the time of his inaugural in 1885, the new governor viewed Waller as his personal representative within the black community, the man who above everyone else could hold Negroes in line in 1886.[3]

As a reward for his efforts in behalf of the ticket in 1884, Martin secured for Waller a position at the Kansas State Prison at Lansing. Waller moved his family to Leavenworth in May, 1885, and eagerly began his duties as assistant steward. His salary was a respectable $60 per month plus room and board. The competition for positions at the prison among the rank and file of the Republican party was fierce. Waller's appointment was significant, especially given the fact that he was neither white nor a member of the Grand Army of the Republic.[4]

The state penitentiary was an imposing structure even in 1885. The inmates, who numbered nearly a thousand, one-quarter of whom were black, were housed in four cellblocks situated around a central courtyard. Nearly all of the convicts worked. As previously noted, some were hired

John A. Martin

out; others labored in various prison facilities; and still others toiled in the state-owned coal mines just outside the gates. All types of criminals, from mass murderers to embezzlers, were housed under the same roof.[5]

Waller's duties at the prison consisted of securing, storing, and distributing supplies to the various prison departments. In addition, every morning at 3:30, he unlocked the gate of the south block to allow those prisoners assigned to extramural labor to leave for their duties. Waller evidently got along well with the warden, Captain John H. Smith, and with his white co-workers. At one point he even intervened with Governor Martin in behalf of Martin J. Cuff, an Irish Republican ward heeler from Atchison. When Cuff, who was fairly elderly, found his duties as nightwatchman arduous and a threat to his health, Waller succeeded in having him assigned to a position in one of the shops. With the people of Lansing and with the deputy warden, John Higgins, however, the assistant steward did not fare so well. Because no white in Lansing would rent to him, Waller was forced to settle Susan and the children in Leavenworth while he lived on the prison grounds. In addition, from

Kansas State Penitentiary, Lansing

May, 1885, until his departure in the fall of 1886, Waller wrote a steady stream of letters complaining of his treatment at Higgins' hands. On one occasion the deputy warden had Waller called before Captain Smith on charges that he had been selling copies of the *Leavenworth Times* to an inmate (convicts were allowed reading materials only as a reward for good behavior). As it turned out, the inmate, a young half-breed, had been placed in solitary confinement on Waller's order and was simply seeking revenge. Smith, upon learning of these circumstances, dismissed the charges. On another occasion, after Waller had shown a political circular to a Negro inmate named J. C. Pusey, the deputy warden tried unsuccessfully to persuade Pusey to swear that Waller was delivering unauthorized mail to the prisoners. In August, 1886, so oppressed was Waller by Higgins' machinations that he wrote to Martin threatening to resign and accept a job elsewhere. Martin, who was counting upon Waller's speechmaking ability for the forthcoming state campaign, persuaded him not to go, and then ordered Smith to interpose his authority between the deputy warden and the assistant steward. Nonetheless, Waller resigned at the end of the year.[6]

Both John Martin and John Waller anticipated that they would profit politically from the latter's appointment to the staff of the state prison. The spoils system was no less firmly rooted in Kansas than in other states during the last part of the nineteenth century. Officials from governor to mayor carefully selected their most ardent and influential supporters to fill the appointive posts under their control, and then called upon these worthies to deliver speeches, write articles, and utilize their connections throughout the state or county in behalf of the official who appointed them. Since the state's admission to the Union, those Kansas politicians who were out of office had complained bitterly if vainly about the political activities of appointed officials, especially those at the state prison. Not surprisingly, then, Martin, who even went so far as to formally name Waller as his personal representative among black Kansans, persuaded Warden Smith to release his black steward several days a week during the summer and fall of 1886 in order that he might campaign for the Republican ticket.[7] For his part Waller perceived that he could use his position at the prison—and as Martin's emissary to the black community—to enhance his own political fortunes.

In February, 1886, John M. Brown announced that he would challenge McCabe for the Republican nomination for auditor. Brown, who was called "the Colonel," made public his plans at a mass meeting of blacks held in Topeka on February 10. Brown and his lieutenants hoped the gathering would be unanimous in their support, but, unfortunately

John M. Brown

for the Colonel's cause, the McCabe people had gotten wind of Brown's plans and packed the courthouse with their supporters. Sol Watkins, a Brown man, was beaten for the chairmanship by A. J. Darnell, a McCabe supporter, by a vote of sixty-seven to sixty-five. Following a prolonged and acrimonious debate, the gathering endorsed McCabe for a third term in a close vote. Brown had thrown his hat in the ring to stay, however, and he regarded this initial setback as only the first skirmish in a much larger war.[8]

The rivalry between McCabe and Brown placed Kansas blacks in a difficult position. There was a tradition against third terms in Kansas politics—John Martin and ninety other delegates had signed a pledge opposing third terms at the state convention in 1882—and it appeared to many that McCabe's greediness was threatening the black community's representation on the state ticket. McCabe's candidacy offered Republican bigots an opportunity to conceal their Negrophobia behind a mask of opposition to a third term. On the other hand Brown was challenging a proven incumbent. McCabe had earned a reputation as an honest, industrious, and courteous public servant, and he enjoyed the support of a number of white papers, including the powerful *Topeka Daily Capital* and *Leavenworth Times*.[9]

As far as Waller was concerned, McCabe had had his day. Although he attended the Topeka meeting and made a speech in behalf of unanimity following McCabe's victory, three weeks later he wrote a long letter to P. I. Bonebrake, chairman of the Republican state central committee, lashing his former friend. Waller charged that McCabe had supported black independents in Wyandotte and Leavenworth in 1885 when they fielded a "colored men's ticket" for county offices. These renegades had cost the regular Republican nominees hundreds of votes in both cities. Now, Waller charged, McCabe was plotting with Republican rebels and with black Democrats such as William Eagleson and C. H. J. Taylor, a prominent Kansas City lawyer and politician, to foist his third-term candidacy on the Republican party and the black citizens of Kansas. The vast majority of his brethren opposed McCabe, and he, Waller, would not support the former real-estate dealer from Nicodemus even if he were nominated.[10]

As McCabe and Brown struggled throughout April, May, and June to line up delegates to the state convention scheduled for July in Topeka, the competition degenerated into a mudslinging contest. George C. Smith, a former Kansan and now a minor official in Washington, D.C., who had known Brown during his days as sheriff of Coahoma County, Mississippi, charged that the Colonel had been driven out of that state

Edward P. McCabe

not by "bulldozers" but respectable citizens enraged by his record of graft and corruption. The *Capital* at once called for Brown's withdrawal lest he prove, if nominated, to be a political millstone. Although Brown issued a public denial and filed a libel suit against Smith, the major Republican journals continued to give the story credence.[11]

When the Republicans assembled on July 7 in the capital, Martin was duly renominated and a platform adopted which advocated prohibition, protectionism, a square deal for the workingman, and, as always, "a free ballot and a fair count." The only real question was whether or not the party should renominate McCabe and Samuel T. Howe, the state treasurer, who was also running for a third term. Howe's fate was tied to McCabe's because nearly all agreed that the party could not deny the state auditor another term without rebuffing Howe. To do otherwise would be to risk appearing blatantly racist. Chief challenger for Mc-Cabe's place was General Tim McCarthy of Larned. This ebullient Irishman rolled into Topeka on the opening day of the convention complete with "the famous Coyote band" and a contingent of Pawnee Indian supporters. Although most agreed that McCabe had a majority of the delegates in his camp on the eve of the convention, his support melted quickly during the next two days. A caucus of 100 who opposed the third term met on the evening of July 7 and listened to Sol Watkins tell them that, although blacks deserved continued representation on the state ticket, they would not ask a third term for any member of the race. There were other blacks, he pointed out, who were equally competent to fill the post. The situation had deteriorated to such an extent that McCabe officially withdrew before the balloting began and half-heartedly threw his support to Brown. When the first tally was completed, Brown had received 105 votes to McCarthy's 145. In a subsequent runoff among the top three candidates, Brown polled only 85 to McCarthy's 231. The blacks' four-year "lock" on the auditorship had been broken.[12]

Waller was bitterly disillusioned; crossing McCabe had been a dangerous gamble. McCabe had lost, but so had Brown, and there was a good chance that blacks in Kansas would blame Waller and Brown for their loss of representation. Waller was doubly disappointed because he had evidently been promised a good position in the auditor's office if Brown won.

If Waller was appalled at the outcome of the Republican state convention, the Democrats were overjoyed. "Set it down that the colored vote will never again be a unit in support of the Republican ticket in Kansas," predicted the *Topeka Democrat*. "Thank God we are rid of the nigger is the exulting cry that is coming up among Republicans throughout Kansas."[13] While the Democratic party housed some of the most strident Negrophobes in the state, party leaders were sensitive to the black vote and some had even actively courted it. In 1884 Governor George Glick invited Waller to visit him at the statehouse. According to Glick, the anti-Negro feeling extant within the party was due to the "villainous and abusive articles against myself and the democrats" in the state's black newspapers. If Negroes would open their minds, the Democrats could offer them a home. On August 5, 1886, the Democratic state convention met in Leavenworth, nominated Colonel Thomas Moonlight for governor, adopted a platform calling for a tariff for revenue only, protection for the workingman, and the immediate opening up of all Indian lands.

Ignoring the Negrophobes of the party, the assembled delegates then named William D. Kelley, a black, as the Democracy's candidate for auditor.[14] The *Topeka Democrat* hailed Kelley, then turnkey at the Leavenworth county jail, as "one of the best known representatives of his race in Kansas" and noted with pride that after his nomination by acclamation he was received with open arms by Thomas Fenlon, Governor Glick, and other party luminaries. The *Democrat* claimed that the action of the Democratic convention in nominating a Negro "marked an epoch in Kansas."[15]

The Republicans at first pretended to be amused: "The whole state was laughing yesterday over the stupendous blunder of the democratic convention trying to catch the colored vote by nominating a black man for state auditor," editorialized J. K. Hudson in the *Capital*. "Such a backaction, double somersault took the breath of every old mossback."[16] This blasé attitude proved transitory, however. Rumors soon began to circulate to the effect that antiprohibition Republicans would bolt the party and fuse with the Democrats in a solid antiprohibition front. A number of the choice offices had allegedly been promised to the wets. Sobered by news of the impending merger, Republican papers began to attack Kelley and the Democrats in earnest. "The mulatto—W. D. Kelley . . . is a man of no standing either at home or abroad, and a blatherskate and blackguard who will not receive the support of a corporal's guard of the colored voters," sneered Anthony in the *Times*.[17] During the campaign Anthony, Hudson, Thacher, and other Republican editors constantly reminded black Kansans which party had been responsible for the Emancipation Proclamation. Indeed, the bloody shirt was much in evidence. "Who burned their [Negroes'] schoolhouses in southern states? Who beat and maimed their teachers? Who has disfranchised them in half a dozen states? . . . Every colored man knows it was the democrats that did these things, and not one of them ever heard a Kansas democrat denounce the outrages," thundered the *Capital*.[18] In fact, declared Hudson, the Democrats would do the same thing in Kansas were the Republicans not there to restrain them. Suddenly Republican leaders became very critical of black bloc voting. When a state convention of Negro men met in Topeka on August 5 and passed resolutions urging blacks to become a united force in politics and to support the Democratic party, which had dared to nominate a Negro, Hudson accused Kansas Negroes of drawing the color line. It was positively un-American.[19]

Given Brown's defeat and the nomination of Kelley by the Democrats, Waller's active support of the regular Republican ticket seemed to Martin and Bonebrake a matter of no small import.[20] Waller was not anxious to participate, however. "It was my hope," he wrote to Governor Martin on September 11, "that the present campaign could be run without my having to take any special part more than to cast my ballot and work at the polls."[21] Again Waller faced the Negro politician's classic dilemma; if he were ever to hold elective office, he would simultaneously have to avoid undue controversy, cultivate powerful whites, and maintain his credibility with the black community. He felt the party had let him down, and he did not relish the prospect of campaigning against a Negro. In fact, in an interview with the Kansas City *Times* on September 3, Waller expressed his dissatisfaction with Brown's rejection by the Republican party and announced his intention to sit out the '86 campaign. Waller's statement elicited angry rebukes from both Warden Smith and Martin, and subsequently another personal appeal from the governor to stump the state for the Republicans. Waller, with some misgivings, eventually decided to campaign for Martin, whom he regarded as his patron and a true friend of the race. In the end Waller perceived that the best stratagem for blacks in their pursuit of office was not to play off one party against another but to demonstrate their absolute loyalty to one organization. Then, it was hoped, the rank and file of that party— the Republicans in this case—would view black candidates for office as Republicans first and Negroes second. "We have no sympathy with that class, or element, of republicans, who mean to rule or ruin," he wrote in 1888. During the period from October 5 to October 30, Waller, on leave from his job, delivered twenty-two speeches in twenty-two towns.[22] Typical was an address he gave on October 13 in Topeka: "I stand here tonight and say that all of you will walk up to the polls and vote the straight republican ticket. . . . There may be some men on the state ticket that you do not like. . . . There may be some men on the ticket whom I do not like. Nevertheless, they are the regularly nominated candidates of the party and should receive your support and mine."[23] He steadfastly refused to attack Kelley, however, and in interviews with the *Leavenworth Times* and *Atchison Champion* chided those white Republican papers that were then raking the Democratic candidate: "This slandering of a whole race to get at Kelley is the most inexcusable thing ever resorted to. . . . Today we are 'niggers', tomorrow 'coons'. . . . The colored people have become utterly sick of that sort of rot in both Republican and democratic papers. . . . It is a blow to our manhood and tends to humiliate us. . . . The colored people are in the politics of the state and nation to stay and the sooner the papers of all parties come to a realization of that fact the better."[24]

In the end Martin swamped Moonlight, receiving a plurality of

33,000. Kelley's nomination by the Democrats did little to help the rest of the ticket; the vast majority of blacks took Waller's advice and stuck with the party of Lincoln. In fact Kelley enjoyed solid support among neither Democrats nor blacks. He received 92,284 votes to McCarthy's 161,052, running 15,000 behind Moonlight and the rest of the ticket. Of the counties with a significant black population, Kelley carried only Leavenworth.[25] As one frustrated Democrat of Howard put it: "Not a God-Damned nigger in Howard could be bought, persuaded or driven into voting the Democratic ticket."[26] At least one Negro politician came out of the election of 1886 smelling like a rose. Soon after Tim McCarthy was sworn in as auditor, he named John M. Brown to a $1,200 a year clerkship. Perhaps, as the McCabe forces had charged, Brown had in fact acted as a foil for the Irishman.[27]

Early in February, 1888, Waller moved from Leavenworth to Topeka and established a law office in partnership with another young black attorney and Republican politician named Turner W. Bell. Topeka seemed to Waller an ideal base of operations. Aside from the fact that it was the state capital, thus enabling Waller to keep in touch with the white power structure, 8,000 of Kansas' 75,000 blacks lived there. Since selling the *Western Recorder* in 1885 Waller had lacked a forum for his views and the means for keeping his name before his constituents. Consequently, in partnership with his cousin, Anthony Morton, he established the *American Citizen* on February 23, 1888.[28] Where he got the funds for such an undertaking is not clear, but given the fact that there had been no black paper in Kansas since the collapse of the *Benevolent Banner* in October, 1887, other Negro politicians and the Republican state central committee probably helped defray the cost of publication.

Waller's second newspaper was a six-column, four-page weekly, with the first and fourth pages containing original matter, and the second and third, syndicated national and state news. A single copy was five cents while a year's subscription was $1.50. Subscription sales received a boost when a week before the first number appeared J. K. Hudson ran a very favorable article on Waller and his plans for the *Citizen*.[29] "It shall be our aim to bend every effort in an honorable way," Waller informed his readers in the initial issue, "to protect the material, intellectual, and political interests of the colored people of Kansas." But, he added significantly, "while we are republicans, we shall . . . place the citizen before the state, and adhere to the party only as a means to attain the greatest good to our great country."[30]

Topeka in 1888 was a thriving community of some 40,000 people. Situated in the center of the city were the extensive repair shops of the

Rock Island, the Union Pacific, and the Atchison, Topeka, and Santa Fe railroads. There were in addition stockyards, several packing houses, a soap factory, pickling plant, and vinegar works. The letting of numerous state contracts kept the construction industry booming, and real estate prices increased geometrically in the late 1880s and early 1890s. Retail business flourished. North Topeka, separated from the rest of the city by the Kaw River, offered nearly every economic opportunity that was available south of the river. In short, Topeka in 1888 was a western boom town, proud, self-confident, optimistic.[31]

Black Topekans lived primarily downtown near the capitol and central business district, in the western portion of the city in Tennessee-town, and in a large enclave in North Topeka called Redmonsville. There were in Topeka, as of 1889, twenty-five colored churches, eight black schools (public or private), thirteen Negro policemen, nine black firemen, and one black justice of the peace. Most Negroes worked for the packing plants, railroad shops, construction companies, the city, or the state. A number of women found employment as domestic servants for the city's sizable white middle class. Like Leavenworth, Lawrence, and Kansas City, black Topeka had its wealthy elite. John Brown; W. I. Jamison, the justice of the peace; William Harris, a dry goods merchant; and saloon-keeper Nick Chiles were allegedly worth from $20,000 to $30,000 each. In addition the black community could boast several groceries, over a dozen restaurants, two barber shops, several lawyers, and two doctors. "Culture" enthusiasts were proud of the fact that Topeka contained more literary societies and women's auxiliaries than any other town in Kansas. Among the largest were the Pleasant Hour and Inter-state Literary clubs; Waller belonged to both. Situated in North Topeka was Garfield Park, a beautiful, wooded area that served as the site of emancipation celebrations and excursions which annually drew blacks from all over the state. In August of 1888 and 1890, for example, Waller addressed emancipation crowds in Garfield Park that exceeded 10,000 persons. Blacks from all over eastern Kansas would arrive early by rail and spend the day consuming tons of barbecue and gallons of punch, listening to speeches, and playing baseball.[32] All in all, for an educated, sophisticated Negro with a rather compelling political ambition, Topeka seemed the place to be in 1888.

Unfortunately for black Republicans in Topeka and throughout the state, the Brown-McCabe split did not end in 1886. In September, 1887, for example, McCabe supporters, responding to a call in the *New York Age* by T. Thomas Fortune for the establishment of a national Afro-American League, convened a meeting of black men in Salina. Although the league was promoted as a nonpartisan civil rights organization, Brown, Sol Watkins, and other supporters of the Colonel denounced the Salina meeting as a political rally and unsuccessfully tried to persuade state race leaders to attend a separate convention. In the end, the Colonel was forced to abandon his scheme and attend the Salina gathering, which did in fact avoid politics and merely established a state league.[33]

Waller chose to deal with the McCabe-Brown problem by posing publicly as a compromise, unifying figure who could put an end to the "factionalism" that had so long plagued black Republicans, while simultaneously working to undermine his two rivals within the party. During the preceding four years, Waller wrote in the *Citizen* in 1888, the race had been weakened by a divided leadership. Factionalism had diverted the attention of Negro spokesmen from such pressing problems as an increase in school segregation, exclusion from public facilities, and prejudice in general. Petty quarrels, moreover, had enabled the state's white politicians to put off black demands for representation on the state ticket. Time and time again members of the central committee had told Negroes that nomination depended upon black Kansas' ability to unite behind one man. This, according to Waller, was exactly what blacks must do. Simultaneously, Waller began booming Brown for a seat in the state legislature and McCabe for county clerk of Shawnee County. If he could interest his rivals in these lesser posts, the way would be clear for his nomination for state office. Brown did in fact run for a seat in the House but lost in the Republican primary. McCabe disdained the county clerkship and instead sought first to be elected delegate-at-large to the Republican national convention and then clerk to the Republican state central committee. Fearing that election to either of these posts would enable McCabe to once again lay claim to being Kansas' "representative Negro," Waller worked assiduously for his defeat. McCabe, he told the state central committee, no longer represented the blacks of Kansas. They were tired of his grasping ambition and were ready for a new face. Whether or not Waller's maneuverings had any impact on the party's decision is unclear, but McCabe did not go to Chicago nor did he receive a job with the central committee.[34]

While Waller labored to undo Brown and McCabe, he sought to maximize his own visibility among blacks as a champion of civil rights and an untiring crusader for political recognition. When in early July two black men were lynched near Chetopa, Waller cried out in the *Citizen*: "It seems that Kansas is gradually drifting into the Ku Klux. . . . Mob violence must go whether in Kansas or elsewhere."[35] In April he successfully defended three Leavenworth Negroes, Walter, Joseph, and

Solomon Drake, accused of slitting the throat of one Henry Richter, a well-to-do butcher. The incident so aroused Leavenworth whites that the sheriff had to move the Drake brothers to Topeka to keep them from being lynched. On the opening day of the trial, Waller and his clients entered the district courtroom in Leavenworth to find it filled with a large crowd of armed and angry whites. The Topeka lawyer managed not only to avert a lynching but succeeded in persuading an overwhelmingly hostile jury that his clients were innocent. Several weeks after completion of the Drake trial a white farmer and his son shot and wounded Ed Ramsey, a young Topeka black man accused of raping the farmer's daughter. When the authorities elected to keep Ramsey in jail while releasing the two whites on bond, Waller pronounced equal protection under the law to be a thing of the past in Kansas. At times Waller's militant image called for public criticism of the Republican party. Particularly galling to Negroes was the defeat in early April of G. I. Currin for police judge of Topeka. Currin was the regular nominee of the Shawnee County Republicans, and party leaders, both white and black, campaigned hard for his election. Nonetheless, rumors to the effect that Currin was illiterate and that election of a Negro police judge would retard immigration to Topeka induced hundreds of Republicans to scratch him.[36] Waller was furious. In a series of editorials he denied charges by the *Topeka Capital* and other white papers that blacks had deserted Currin; his demise was due, he said, to ungrateful and prejudiced white "mugwumps." "We are at a loss," he subsequently wrote in disgust, "to discover a distinction between North Carolina sentiment and that of Topeka touching the Negro."[37]

The problem of appealing to two potentially antagonistic constituencies was hardly new to Waller; the solution to this perennial dilemma was implicit in his political philosophy. He continued to regard the Republican party as the political organization most likely to advance his interests and those of the race. Throughout 1888 he emphasized in his speeches and editorials the party's traditional commitment to human rights. In an address to the Shawnee County Republican League Waller declared, "I am for John Sherman [for the Republican presidential nomination] because he belongs to the Abraham Lincoln school of republicanism. . . . We want a statesman, a man with a backbone for president . . . one-half of the voters of this union are virtually disfranchised and we seem helpless to stop it. I believe in a government that is able to protect its citizens everywhere, and that is the principle upon which the Republican party is based: protection to our homes, protection to our industries, and to the citizens of this country."[38] This approach allowed

Waller to remain a party loyalist and yet avoid appearing to his black constituents as a cringing sycophant. It also provided him with frequent opportunities to wave the bloody shirt. Waller rarely missed an opportunity to link Kansas Democrats with their southern brethren who were then allegedly lynching, burning, disfranchising, and exploiting the black man. This in turn served to deflect somewhat the ire of white Republicans aroused by his criticism of the party and the state.

The Republican delegates who gathered in Wichita on July 25, 1888, for the state convention were fairly optimistic. The Democrats were badly split by the prohibition issue. Indeed, when that party held its convention in June, Governor Glick and other party members who favored repeal of the prohibition amendment had lost control to the drys, headed by Judge John Martin of Topeka. The liquor forces were disconsolate. "To hell with John Martin," declared an irate former saloon-keeper, "I would rather vote for William D. Kelley, the damn black nigger!"[39] A few Republicans were apprehensive about the Union Labor party, which had gained considerable support among the depression-ridden farmers of southern Kansas, but most were sanguine about the party's chances to recapture the state house. Although they proved unwilling to nominate a black to run on the Republican state ticket with Lyman Humphrey, the convention's gubernatorial nominee, the Republicans did select Waller as a presidential elector and as an alternate delegate to the national convention slated to meet in Chicago later in the month.[40]

The campaign of '88 was bitterly contested. The Democrats denounced Humphrey and other Republican nominees as a coterie of loan sharks and usurious bankers totally out of touch with the common man. The Republicans, both white and black, relied on the "bloody shirt." No decent, freedom-loving citizen, they proclaimed, could vote for a party that systematically exploited millions of defenseless blacks and then murdered them when they resisted. Following his return from the Chicago convention, Waller threw himself into the state campaign, making some fifty speeches from August through October. In an address delivered in Osage City he attracted state-wide attention when he observed that it was ironic that the Democracy should be advocating separation of the races. True, white Democrats had always kept their distance from black males, but they had proven inordinately fond of black females.[41]

Democratic divisions and Republican unity spelled disaster for the Democracy in 1888, and the Union Labor threat never materialized. Humphrey won in a landslide, the party of Lincoln captured 123 out of 126 seats in the Kansas House, and Kansas delivered proportionately the largest plurality for Benjamin Harrison of any state in the Union.[42] It was Waller's finest hour. "John L. Waller, republican elector at large from Kansas is the only colored man in the electoral college," trumpeted Joe Hudson in the *Topeka Capital*. "He represents the banner republican state, resides in the banner republican county as well as the banner republican precinct in Kansas."[43] The Republicans celebrated their victory with a mammoth torchlight parade through downtown Topeka. From 7:00 P.M. until midnight the city was filled with a continuous roar from drums, cowbells, brass bands, and tin horns. The parade began with a volley from company B of the state militia. The revelers, headed by the Lawrence Cyclone Club with drum corps, closely followed by various Republican flambeau clubs (drill teams), 200 school children on horses, and various colored political organizations, proceeded north on Kansas Avenue to North Topeka and then countermarched back into the heart of the city. Various floats featured, among other things, workers tending a smelting furnace and a replica of a giant log cabin. Fireworks followed and then speeches by Republican dignitaries delivered from the balconies of the Copeland House and Windsor Hotels. Waller followed the lieutenant-governor-elect:

> The Republican party has demonstrated the fact that when it lays aside its petty divisions, it is invincible. I am a black Republican. The time has come for a free ballot and a fair count. The leaders of the south claim they are afraid of Negro domination, and when the colored man attempts to use his legal right to cast one full ballot, he is refused the privilege, and if he protests the least is given the alternative of making himself scarce at the polls or being shot down in cold blood. . . . Grover Cleveland who found himself to be an expert fisherman, will soon have an opportunity to fish or cut bait. . . . His veto record has been vetoed by the voice of the people. I have the distinguished honor of being the only colored man who will sit in the electoral college and I shall vote for Harrison and Morton.[44]

Having one of their number chosen presidential elector and alternate to the Republican convention in Chicago brought Kansas blacks a degree of national notice, but it did little to improve their image or power within the state. Waller's positions were largely honorary and certainly temporary; what they needed was a permanent power base within the state hierarchy. Thus, no sooner had the campaign of 1888 ended than the black Republican leadership of Kansas renewed its efforts to capture the party's 1890 nomination for state auditor.[45] Maneuvering for the auditorship had become an annual rite among Negro Republicans by

1890, but they were particularly anxious to secure recognition from the party in that year because of a challenge to their hegemony within the Negro community by a clique of black Democrats and Populists.

Kansas Democrats made a serious effort to attract the black vote as early as 1884. The Democracy had been able to take advantage of a split within the Republican party to capture the state house. In their drive to retain power, party leaders proved willing to court the growing black electorate. Accordingly, in 1884, the Democratic state convention selected Charles H. J. Taylor, an aspiring black lawyer-politician, as a delegate to the party's national meeting. As Democratic leaders had hoped, Taylor's election, as well as his subsequent appointment by the Cleveland administration as minister to Liberia, attracted the attention of blacks throughout the state and nation.[46] W. D. Kelley's nomination for state auditor two years later made an even greater impression. Although Kelley was defeated in the general election, many blacks remembered that the Democrats had nominated a Negro for state auditor when the party of Lincoln had been unwilling to do so.

The recognition accorded black voters by Taylor's appointment and Kelley's nomination was only one of a number of factors impelling Kansas Negroes to "give the Democrats a chance" in 1890. Rumors that President Harrison planned to resurrect Chester Arthur's policy toward the South antagonized many blacks.[47] Others were swayed by the Democratic rhetoric which insisted that the high tariff, sound money, probusiness doctrines of the Republicans had nothing to offer the vast majority of black Kansans who were either farmers, day-laborers, mechanics, or small businessmen. Continued affiliation with the party of Blaine and Harrison would inevitably isolate the black leadership from the masses.[48] Still others were rebelling against the tactics of intimidation frequently used by white Republican bosses. "Only blacks seem to lack the freedom to choose between parties, to scratch or boost as they please," H. W. Rolfe wrote Waller in May, 1888. "If a fellow seeks to remove the republican plack [sic] from the back of the Negro, he will be branded a traitor, a hypocrite, a fool, and a renegade by his own race and the bosses will tell him he can no longer haul dirt or clean the streets under a republican administration. Colored men have been dismissed from common labor on the streets simply because they refused to tell how they voted."[49] But above all there was the hope of office and the recognition that it implied. Warner T. McGuinn, who took over the helm of the *American Citizen* in 1888, proclaimed in dedicating his editorial page to political independence that "one of the aims of the *Citizen* will be to lift the leaders of the race in Kansas especially from the dish pans of the state prison and tenth rate county offices to political positions more commensurate with their abilities."[50]

Although there were black Democrats in Kansas well before Charles H. J. Taylor's arrival, it was this well-to-do Georgia immigrant who acted as Democratic pied piper to disgruntled black Republicans from 1887 through 1899. Historians such as August Meier have labeled him an unqualified accommodationist. And in fact Taylor's book *Whites and Blacks*, written after his return from Liberia in 1887, did breathe "a spirit of conciliation toward the white South." He was highly critical of Radical Reconstruction in this work and urged blacks to seek the friendship of southern whites whenever possible. Accommodation, however, was for Taylor a matter of style, a rhetorical device to deflect the initiatives of radical white supremacists. He was never willing to overlook lynching, discrimination, and disfranchisement in the name of racial harmony. From the editorial pages of the *Wyandotte World* and later the *American Citizen*, Taylor showed himself to be a staunch defender of the race against all forms of injustice. Indeed, he appealed to blacks to defect to the Democrats in order that they might gain political leverage, which in turn could be translated into equality of economic opportunity and full citizenship.[51]

Taylor, perhaps more than Waller, realized that the black politician's ability to satisfy the demands of Negro voters was severely limited because he must serve the political machines supported by the propertied classes in the white community. Taylor argued that the average Negro shared a greater community of interest with the large landowners, small entrepreneurs, and international businessmen who dominated the Democratic party than with the financiers and industrialists who guided the Republican party. "The race has no interest in manufactures," he asserted in 1891. "They are not even employed in them. . . . Why should we want the necessities of life to help the home producers with whom we have no part."[52] Thus, he reasoned, adherence to Democratic doctrine would enable the black politician to reconcile the two constituencies with which he had to deal far more easily than he could through continued membership in the Republican party.

In late May, 1888, black Democrats and "independents" met to discuss race problems in Kansas and to establish an organization that would disseminate their views. Taylor was elected chairman of the convention. Prominent black Republicans such as Turner Bell and Charles Langston not only attended but agreed to serve as members of a state central committee.[53] The *American Citizen*, which Waller and Morton had sold in August to George A. Dudley and H. H. Johnson, two prosperous Kansas City real-estate dealers, subsequently became the Democracy's spokesman within the black community.[54] As election day approached, a number of other journals became willing to advocate desertion of the Republicans, if only on a temporary basis. "The negro's place is not in the front, nor in the rear of this political battle, but halfway," advised the *Topeka Benevolent Banner*. "He has tried everything in politics, but the right thing, and that is the division of his vote as a man."[55] The Democrats even went so far as to test Waller's loyalty, but he rebuffed them, declaring that "in our soul we are a republican."[56]

No less alarming to Waller and other Republican leaders than the Democratic resurgence among blacks was the challenge from the Populists. Kansas Populism was rooted in the deterioration of the farmer's economic position during the decade that began in 1885. In the early 1880s the state had entered a period of exceptional prosperity based primarily on high prices for both corn and wheat. From 1880 to 1885 population increased by 37 percent, or more than 300,000, and the value of property more than doubled. This led to speculation, grossly inflated land prices, and credit purchasing by immigrants. The boom collapsed in the winter of 1887–1888 and mushroomed into a major depression as drought and crop failures during succeeding years further eroded the farmer's purchasing power. In 1890 the total mortgage debt of Kansas was 27 percent of the actual value of all Kansas real estate.[57] When Kansas farmers, in an effort to end farm mortgage foreclosures, establish effective state regulation of railroads, and put an end to monopolistic practices by bankers and businessmen, founded the people's party in 1889, they decided to attempt a political alliance with the Negroes of the state.[58] As their emissary to the black community, the Populists chose Benjamin Foster, who was a Topeka minister, a militant, and a former Republican.[59] Foster was born a slave in 1856 but rose from that humble beginning to attend Trinity School and Emerson Institute in Alabama during Reconstruction, and subsequently to obtain a degree from Chicago Theological Seminary. He served throughout the late 1880s and 1890s as pastor of the Lincoln Street Congregational Church. In 1890 he stumped the state in behalf of the new party, and in the process established a Negro Populist league. As a reward for his efforts and as part of its bid for the black vote, the party convention which met in August selected Foster as Populist nominee for state auditor.[60]

Initially, black Republicans reacted to the activities of Taylor, Foster, and their supporters with a good deal of anxiety. Not only did they feel that their own position within the black community was threatened, but they also feared that these mavericks would alienate white

Republicans, thereby paving the way for the triumph of those who favored keeping the Negro's role in party affairs to a minimum. Waller, McCabe, and others well remembered that, when they had warned the 1884 Republican state convention that failure to send a Negro to the national convention would result in mass defection, they had bluntly been told by a spokesman for the white majority, "If the colored men, after we, the Republican party, have freed them want to vote the Democratic ticket, because they were not given a representative to Chicago, let them go and be damned."[61]

Waller's successes in 1888 convinced most black Republican leaders that he was the party's best hope for heading off the Democratic-Populist rebellion among blacks. In the spring of 1889 W. B. Townsend and Blanche K. Bruce began touting Waller for minister to Haiti. These two Republican loyalists, then co-editors of the *Leavenworth Advocate*, believed that the threat posed by Taylor, Eagleson, Foster, and company was so pressing that the white leadership within the Republican party must demonstrate its good faith immediately. Even E. P. McCabe, then in Washington, agreed to recognize Waller's ascendancy among black Republicans and campaign for his appointment to the Haitian post. Not so John Brown. In December, 1888, he launched yet another attempt to establish an organization that would allow him to control black political life in Kansas, or at least to claim to do so. Brown and his chief lieutenants, Sol Watkins and S. W. Winn, joined with Judge Stephen A. Hackworth, who had appeared suddenly in Topeka in the mid-1880s, and another white Radical refugee from the South, W. H. Dinkgraves, to call a meeting of all southern Republicans who had been forced by the "ku-kluxing" Democrats to leave their homes and flee to Kansas. The stated objective of the organization was to apply pressure on the incoming Harrison administration to take whatever action was necessary to ensure a free ballot and a fair count in the South. Hackworth and Dinkgraves, however, hoped to use the association to obtain federal appointive positions in the South, while Brown wanted to be recognized by the new administration as spokesman for the black community in Kansas. The first state convention of southern expatriates was held in Topeka on February 15. Delegates from Leavenworth and other cities attempted to persuade the meeting to endorse Waller for the Haitian position, but the majority, most of whom were from Shawnee, hooted them down.[62] Townsend, Bruce, W. A. Price, and other Waller supporters were furious. Townsend angrily charged that the meeting was "activated by the wishes of a clique in and about Topeka that have concerted themselves together to sit heavily not only upon the aspirations of Mr. Waller but upon those of any other man who does not deem it necessary to bow to the whims and caprices of the 'gang of would-be political bosses and dictators.' "[63]

Although Brown's opposition to Waller had little to do with the outcome of the situation, the Haitian mission eventually went to Frederick Douglass. The "Wallerites," the name given Waller and his supporters by the Brown faction, then appealed to General Harrison Kelley, a prominent Negrophile and a member of the state Board of Charities. As a result of Kelley's influence and a recommendation from Governor Humphrey, the board appointed Waller steward at the Osawatomie insane asylum in July, 1889. But this and his ensuing selection as deputy county attorney for Shawnee County, only earned him the ridicule of the Democrats and Populists.[64] Denouncing Waller as a lackey of the white Republican power structure, the *American Citizen* observed that being named "head-waiter" at a "little one-horse asylum" was small reward for a presidential elector. "We cannot but regret," wrote McGuinn, "that he has not the backbone to decline such positions with thanks."[65]

Waller himself was not happy in his new post. The insane asylum, a huge Y-shaped three story structure situated atop a ridge overlooking the town of Osawatomie, was far removed from the state's population centers and from Susan and the children, who remained in Leavenworth. Few of the denizens were black and none could talk politics. In September, 1889, Waller applied for and received a transfer to the state school for the blind in Kansas City, where he was to be superintendent of industrial arts—that is, overseer of the school's broom manufactory. The Board of Charities reasoned that Waller's political effectiveness would be much greater in Kansas City than Osawatomie.[66]

Conditions at the Kansas City institution proved even less tolerable than those prevailing at the insane asylum. The white director, Colonel Alan Buckner, was a prominent figure within the Kansas Republican party and had at one time in 1888 been touted for the post of attorney general. Though a clergyman, minister, Union veteran, and a Republican, Buckner was also a rabid racist. Upon Waller's arrival, he informed the students that a "nigger" had come to teach them. He subsequently assigned the entire Waller family to two tiny rooms above the institution's dispensary and ordered the cooks not to cook for them unless they sat at a separate table in the cafeteria. At one point, the "Reverend Colonel," as Waller referred to him, denied the Wallers use of the institute's washrooms, and then offered John a sum of money if he would leave. Never one to suffer abuse quietly, Waller described his treatment in a series of letters to Humphrey, the Board of Charities, the *American Citizen*, and the *Leavenworth Advocate*. The upshot was an unannounced visit by the board to the institute in July, 1890, and, following a hearing, an official reprimand for Buckner. Despite his victory over the colonel, Waller left the institute for the blind in mid-summer, 1890. Nearly a year earlier he had decided to make an all-out effort to capture the Republican nomination for auditor.[67]

From feeling threatened by the activities of Negro Democrats and Populists, the Republican faithful had gradually moved to the position that, despite past evidence to the contrary, the political revolt could be used to advantage against the white supremacists within the party. Waller said as much in a document he issued calling a state convention of Negro men for August 11, 1890, to meet in Salina. The notice that appeared in the *Advocate* and *Citizen* on July 26 bearing his signature admitted that the Republicans, "fortified by a tremendous majority in this state," had been able "to deny to the colored voters the representation . . . commensurate with our numerical strength."[68] Nonetheless, Waller advised prospective delegates, the means of redemption were at hand: "Because of the altered condition and threatened revolts, the colored voters are now in a position by a united effort to obtain some representation from the party whom they have loyally supported."[69] This mood of optimism was prompted by several developments that had taken place in 1889–1890. President Harrison's failure to appoint an acceptable number of blacks and persistent rumors concerning his "southern policy" had galvanized black Republicans in Kansas and throughout the nation, and produced a storm of protest that the white leadership in the G.O.P. could not afford to ignore. The Wallerites believed that Republicans in Kansas would prove particularly sensitive to black demands because of the common front established by the Populists, Farmers' Alliance, and Knights of Labor. In early January, 1890, the Alliance and the Knights formally agreed to cooperate in all matters business or political, and promised to work for currency inflation, passage of stay laws, enactment of antitrust legislation, a graduated income tax, and other reforms which black Republicans were sure would frighten their white counterparts into recognizing them. They reasoned that if conservative white Democrats in the South were willing to distribute political plums to black Republicans in order to enlist their aid against the rising tide of agrarian radicalism, why should not white Republicans in Kansas do the same. Finally, Negro Republicans were heartened by the election in the fall of 1889 of Colonel John Brown as Shawnee County clerk. Because blacks regarded it as a test of the party's current attitude toward the "black and tan" faction, Brown's campaign had attracted state-wide attention. Wallerites, Democrats, and Populists joined with the "Brown machine" to work for the

Colonel's election. Major white dailies such as the *Capital*, the *Lawrence Journal*, and the *Leavenworth Times* stood by the Colonel and managed to sway enough white voters to secure his election. Unfortunately, Brown's victory was not indicative of a new determination among white Republicans to accord Negroes the recognition for which they were clamoring. Brown won, but ran from 1,000 to 1,500 votes behind the rest of the ticket. The *American Citizen*, admittedly an independent sheet, estimated that no more than 12 percent of the white Republicans in Shawnee voted for the black candidate.[70] Thus, the optimism that stemmed from Brown's victory was ill-founded.

Because of the uncertain political situation, the convention of Negro men that met at Salina on August 11, 1890, attracted state-wide attention among whites as well as blacks.[71] A number of white Republicans objected to the meeting and accused the "black and tans" of drawing the color line. Nevertheless, the Wallerites pressed ahead, convinced that their success at the state Republican convention depended in no small part upon the black community's ability to avoid both the appearance and reality of factionalism. "The colored republicans of this state," wrote Townsend in the *Advocate*, "are forced to take such steps as this because the colored element only is ignored by the party and because we desire to avoid the stereotype argument or (subterfuge) . . . that 'you colored people are divided; one faction wants M and the other wants B; when you are united upon one man we will grant you your request.' "[72] During the two days prior to the opening session, dozens of prominent Negroes representing every political viewpoint and every section of the state streamed into central Kansas. When Townsend was elected permanent chairman, it was clear that Waller and his supporters would control the meeting. Although there were several aspirants from northwest and southeast Kansas for the position of auditor-designate, Waller was the first choice of the convention by an overwhelming margin. His long service to the party, close contacts with the white power structure, and growing stature within the national black elite made him seem the best possible choice.[73] Indeed, the convention reacted as if his election were tantamount to nomination by the Republican convention. "For four or five minutes [after Waller's nomination]," one observer reported, "there was the greatest rejoicing—hats were waved, ladies shook their handkerchiefs, men shouted themselves hoarse."[74] Resolutions were passed expressing "cold indifference" and "supreme contempt" for all measures of forced expatriation of black Americans to a foreign land, which a number of southern white racists were then advocating, and declaring that "all discrimination of a public character founded on accident of race or color are [sic] irritating, impolitic, and repugnant to the nature and spirit of the popular form of government."[75] In an attempt to reassure Republican leaders as to their loyalty, the convention specifically repudiated the Farmers' Alliance.[76]

The Republican convention that met at the Copeland House in Topeka on September 2, 1890, manifested considerable concern over the challenge posed by the Populists and Democrats; but their anxiety did not, as Waller and his associates had hoped, make them more solicitous of the black community. To appease laborers and farmers, the delegates constructed a platform that advocated such radical reforms as free textbooks, a popularly elected railroad commission, and the abolition of child labor, but they refused to come out in support of the black man's civil rights or denounce the racial violence that was then sweeping the nation. The only positions that were contested were state treasurer and state auditor. Humphrey and the rest of the ticket, all of whom were running for second terms, were unopposed. By the opening gavel no less than fifteen men had announced for auditor. Everyone acknowledged that C. M. Hovey, a farmer from Thomas County, and Waller were the leading candidates; but many predicted a deadlock, in which case the convention would have to turn to a compromise figure. Waller, whose name was placed in nomination by W. B. Townsend, actually led on the first ballot, 104 to 103 for Hovey. The next nearest candidate polled 49. On the second ballot Waller's total jumped to 128 but Hovey's increased to 169. During the third and decisive poll, the convention stampeded for Hovey, and all other candidates except Waller withdrew. The final vote was 450 to 99. Although the Salina convention had endorsed Waller by acclamation and white newspapers such as the *Abilene Reflector* and *Leavenworth Times* had boomed him for auditor throughout 1889–1890, the convention had chosen a white. According to one account, the extreme anti-Negro faction within the party delayed the third ballot for auditor for several hours while it convinced the majority that nomination of a "nigger" would drive white Republicans into the Democratic fold. Others insisted that Waller's downfall was the work of John Brown who, as a delegate to both the Salina meeting and the Republican convention, had secretly lobbied against Waller's election. Still others argued that vocation rather than skin color determined the outcome of the contest. According to the *Topeka Capital*, 370 of the 567 delegates to the convention were farmers and they were determined to elect a farmer.[77] Historian William Chafe probably identified the principal reason for Waller's defeat when he noted that both party leaders and the rank and file, remembering the landslide of 1888, were suffering from an acute case of overconfidence.

The Republican party in Kansas cannot be said to have caved in to a "lily-white" faction in 1890 or at any time during this crucial decade. There were no calls among Republicans during this period for disfranchisement of the black man or even for his exclusion from city and county office. In fact, in 1894 the party was to nominate Blanche K. Bruce for state auditor. The Republican party in Kansas did not, moreover, perceive itself as threatened by white supremacist Democratic and/or Populist parties, as did so many southern Republican organizations during this same period. Indeed, the Populists who nominated Foster for auditor and the Demo-Pops (the two parties fused in Wyandotte and several other counties) who nominated C. H. J. Taylor for a seat in the state legislature could hardly pose as racial purists. Nonetheless, there was a good deal of residual prejudice among the Republican rank and file. In addition, some party leaders such as J. K. Hudson felt that the Salina meeting constituted a dangerous precedent, and decided that it would be just as well if Waller were defeated in order to forestall future attempts by the "black and tans" to dictate to the party.[78] Finally, most Republicans believed in 1890, as they had since the Civil War, that blacks had no alternative but to vote Republican. After all, Republicans "fought, bled, and died" to emancipate the Negro, while the Democratic party consisted primarily of former slave-owners, and the Populists were mostly poor whites who were even more virulently anti-Negro than the old slaveocracy.[79] "The address of Candidate Foster to the colored voters will have very little effect on colored men who are accustomed to vote the republican ticket because it is the ticket of their friends on a platform of justice which knows no color or 'previous condition,'" predicted one Republican editor.[80] In sum, Republicans simply did not feel that the black vote was necessary for victory, and they thus proved unwilling to placate the Wallerites by awarding them a place on the state ticket.

Waller was deeply disappointed and frustrated at his rejection by the Republican convention. His selection by the Salina gathering as the black community's choice for a place on the Republican state ticket represented ten years of patient work. At some financial risk to himself, he had established two newspapers in the interests of the race. His editorials and speeches had won for him, he believed, a reputation as an uncompromising yet thoughtful advocate of full civil rights and equality of economic opportunity for the black man. There were, moreover, no apparent tactical flaws in his decade-long push for state office. He had waited McCabe and Brown out, not making his move until the majority of black Kansans, convinced that each of these leaders had had their chance, had tired of their bickering. Waller had been just as careful in cultivating the proper image among whites as among blacks. He had passed through the "severe American crucible," to anticipate a phrase, and made something of himself. He was an educated, law-abiding, responsible, self-made man—a Negro whom John P. St. John, Daniel Votaw, Mary E. Griffith, Harrison Kelley, and John Martin could be proud of. His economic views were rigidly orthodox, and he had been faithful to his superiors in the party. Why, then, had he been denied at the threshold?

The answer was obvious, even to such an incurable optimist as Waller. He had been refused access to the inner councils of the Republican party and election to state office simply because he was black. Waller concluded in the wake of his defeat that the tendency within the Republican party to ignore the Negro in general, and himself in particular, was part of a deteriorating racial climate in Kansas and in the nation as a whole. Indeed, as early as 1888, Waller's speeches and writings began to reflect a sense of deep foreboding. Reacting to G. I. Currin's defeat for police judge, specifically, and to the lynchings and discrimination that seemed to be sweeping America, the editor of the *American Citizen* complained: "What with every work shop door slammed in the Negro's face, every hotel, every restaurant, aye, every church in this city, why foster hope? . . . Shall we ever reach the end? Are we ever to be able to proclaim that the American flag is indeed the emblem of Liberty?"[81] During the course of an address delivered in 1889 at the dedication services of the A.M.E. Church in Leavenworth, he warned:

> A conspiracy is forming against the Negro in this country which has reached a larger and more gigantic proportion than many of us imagine. Race prejudice is on the increase . . . a cloud is gathering and increasing in size and unless averted by the Negro, will burst. . . . We are educating our children but when they are through with their schooling, what have they to do? The colored societies are a success in everything except protecting the race. . . . There is a conspiracy all over the North to drive the Negro from all the important marts of labor, and force him to hold on to the minimal occupations. . . . The anarchist who places a bomb under the spacious courthouse and blows it to pieces and who marches through the street with a red flag, can find a place for his boy in [the white man's] business house, manufactory or machine shop, immediately after his return from the destruction of private property, while the law abiding Negro will be refused every time.[82]

108

Such expressions of disillusionment by no means meant that Waller rejected the American creed of material betterment through self-reliance and enterprise. Despite disappointment at his own misfortune and his anxiety concerning the overall status of the Afro-American, Waller simply could not bring himself to reject the system. Nor could he purge his philosophy of the Social Darwinism and materialism that had become deeply rooted during the preceding decade. Waller had not espoused high tariff policies, paid daily homage to free enterprise, and held up the Gospel of Wealth as the pathway to salvation for blacks simply to ingratiate himself with the white power structure. Given the environment from which he had come, his attitudes, and his still rising level of expectations, the black Kansan could not accept separatism, socialism, Populism, or apathy as reasonable alternatives. Accordingly, instead of rejecting the Horatio Alger myth following his rebuff at the hands of the Republicans in 1890, Waller merely sought to act it out in a different milieu, one that would free him from the restrictions imposed by the color bar and at the same time would allow him to retain his American citizenship and work for the advancement of his people.

CHAPTER SEVEN

A New Frontier

John Waller's answer to his repudiation by the Kansas Republican party and to the ultraracism of the 1890s was a decision to participate in the development of America's New Empire. Specifically, he looked forward to establishing a vast plantation in some underdeveloped area of the world, an enterprise that he believed would inevitably benefit his race, his country, his party, and himself. Such a scheme, moreover, would not do violence to his long-cherished faith in individual and racial progress. In looking abroad for the key to realization of his personal destiny and that of his race, Waller reflected the growing interest among Afro-Americans in opportunities overseas, particularly in Africa.

Confronted during the 1890s by a rising tide of institutionalized racism, a substantial segment of the Negro community in the United States looked to the underdeveloped, nonwhite regions of the world as havens from prejudice and exploitation. Of this group, the most publicized were black nationalists like Henry McNeil Turner and Edward Blyden—men who argued throughout the closing years of the nineteenth century that the only alternatives to lynching, disfranchisement, and segregation were emigration, colonization, and the development of a unique black identity. For these men, as for others in the back-to-Africa movement, the primary purpose of emigration was separation. Convinced that America had nothing to offer the black man, they urged Negroes to seek a totally new environment. Only in a foreign land—-Africa for Turner and Blyden—would the Negro be able to pursue his destiny and exercise his genius free from

111

the blighting impact of race prejudice.[1] Once in Africa, black Americans could use the only two things of value they had acquired in the New World—Christianity and Western technology—to uplift and civilize the "dark continent."[2] Together, emigrant and native would build a strong, united Africa able to demand and obtain respect for black men the world over.

There was another group, however, that cast its gaze beyond America's shores but refused to reject American society, continuing to believe that the democratic premises of the Constitution and Declaration of Independence, together with the free enterprise system, would eventually lead to equality and full citizenship for Afro-Americans.[3] Contending that the markets and raw materials of Asia, Latin America, and especially Africa offered an opportunity for group and individual advancement for blacks as well as whites, these individuals came to advocate a unique version of the New Manifest Destiny.

Despite a lull in formal diplomatic activity between 1865 and 1890, expansionism remained an important if latent force in American society during the last quarter of the nineteenth century. Most citizens still believed that it was their duty to carry the blessings of democracy, Christianity, and capitalism to less fortunate peoples. With the coming of the Industrial Revolution—the value of manufactured goods exported from the United States exceeded that of raw materials for the first time in 1895—the economic impetus to expansion became particularly important. After Alfred Thayer Mahan laid down the ground rules which enabled the United States to convert from continental to overseas expansion, contemporary economic and psychological factors merged with traditional Manifest Destiny to stimulate American economic growth abroad and to produce a brief but vigorous adventure in formal empire-building. As a result of the New Manifest Destiny, the United States acquired between 1889 and 1899 the Samoas, Hawaii, Puerto Rico, Guam, and the Philippines.[4]

Prominent Afro-Americans such as T. Thomas Fortune, editor of the *New York Age*, H. C. Smith of the *Cleveland Gazette*, Monroe Dorsey of the *Parsons Weekly Blade*, and T. McCants Stewart, a prominent New York attorney (who eventually settled in Honolulu in 1898), insisted that the New Empire presented a special opportunity for blacks to establish plantations, acquire mining concessions, and found profitable trading enterprises.[5] As early as 1884, Fortune was urging blacks to take advantage of Africa's seemingly exhaustless resources. Later, in 1902, Theodore Roosevelt appointed the editor of the *Age* a special commissioner to study labor and race conditions in the Philippines and Hawaii and to report on

the possibility of colonizing black Americans in the nation's Pacific poses-
sions. Upon his return to the United States, Fortune advised the White
House that "under proper arrangements" 5,000 blacks could be settled on
the island of Luzon alone. Fortune urged the government to give the Negro American "a proper chance to enjoy life, liberty, and the pursuit of
happiness" in America's insular possessions.[6] In arguing for retention of
the Philippines in 1898 and acquisition of other "tropical or semi-tropical
countries," the *Coffeyville* (Kansas) *American* asserted that "the black
American has the same necessities imposed on him that fall upon the
white. . . . He must move. . . . He must explore. . . . He must promote
and establish. . . . The white American finds for himself new fields
readily enough. . . . May not the black American find his in the new
territories of the United States?"[7] By 1895 Smith was predicting in the
Gazette that "the Afro-American will inevitably find employment for his
increasing wealth in foreign enterprises."[8] Typical of those Negroes who
urged black participation in the New Empire was the Reverend Dennis
Jones, who declared in a speech delivered before the national convention
of Negro Masons that from the very beginning of the republic "expansion
has animated our most progressive statesmen, and we might as well
attempt to stop the flow of Niagara as to try to stop the growth, grandeur,
and mighty forces of America." He went on to praise the Republican
party for opening the markets of the world to all men, black as well as
white.[9]

Black disciples of the New Manifest Destiny were reacting to many
of the same historic impulses that impelled the white majority to endorse
overseas adventure. As Charles Campbell and others have pointed out, a
basic assumption of the founding fathers was that America would need
an expanding economic and political marketplace to survive and grow.
Such expansion, they argued, would provide the underpinnings for general material prosperity, sublimate domestic differences, and bind the
nation together in a great common effort. Black leaders like T. McCants
Stewart and Benjamin Arnett, no less than Albert Beveridge or Whitelaw
Reid, accepted these as self-evident truths. In addition, blacks no less
than whites supported overseas adventure in an effort to find diversion
from the monotony of the factory system, the anxiety of labor-manage-
ment disputes, and the political polarization of the 1890s. Indeed, the
Afro-Americans' status as an oppressed minority made them even more
vulnerable than whites to the seductive appeal of empire-building. Finally, a number of prominent blacks subscribed to the theory of the
disappearing frontier. As evidenced by the marked interest within the
black community in migration to Colorado, Minnesota, and Oklahoma

in the post–Civil War period, many Negro leaders had looked to the American West during the nineteenth century as the answer to the problems of a closed society.[10] By the 1890s, however, these same men were convinced either that the continental frontier was disappearing or that it was not the answer to America's social and economic problems.[11] As a result, they began to look abroad for new regions to exploit.

Those Negroes urging their brethren to take part in the competition for overseas concessions and commercial advantages, or who participated themselves, were actuated by more than a desire for personal gain or by concern over America's status as a great power. They believed that the New Empire offered well-to-do enterprising Afro-Americans the opportunity to improve not only their own status but that of the community as a whole. Indeed, men such as Stewart, Fred Jeltz, and even Henry M. Turner argued that black business enterprises in other countries could redound to the benefit of the entire race.[12] By enhancing the prestige of the United States, thus eliciting the approval of white America, and by adding to the community's collective wealth, expansion would augment the Afro-American's economic and political power base at home. This resulting increase in wealth, power, and prestige could be enlisted in the struggle for justice and equality in the United States.[13]

Moreover, exponents of commercial expansion believed the New Empire offered a unique opportunity for black American concessionaires to demonstrate that Negroes could compete as successfully for the world's markets and raw materials as whites, that they no less than other Americans possessed superior energy and skill. Many expansionists believed that Negroes would prove more successful than Caucasians as agents of civilization because they would be physically better able to endure the rigors of a tropical climate and their black skins would facilitate relations with the natives. Even such an outspoken antiimperialist as Booker T. Washington believed that Afro-Americans had a duty to carry the blessings of democracy and capitalism to their less fortunate brethren in Africa and that they were best suited to do so. By 1905 Washington and other Tuskegeeans were actively involved in Togo, Sudan, South Africa, the Congo, Free State, and Liberia, uplifting and civilizing.[14]

Some Afro-American expansionists like Kansas' F. L. Jeltz of the *American* and Monroe Dorsey of the *Parsons Weekly Blade* strongly supported the annexation of both Cuba and Hawaii. "We want these and other places as outposts of commerce and maritime power. . . . We want them for the development of our national energies, for extension of our trade and support of our flag."[15] Jeltz, writing in the *American* in 1898, declared: "The Philippine Islands will offer an excellent opportunity for Negro colonization, not colonization for the purpose of getting out of this country, but for the same purpose for which the white man colonizes, for the purpose of making money."[16] Others, more sensitive to the anticolonial struggles of nonwhite peoples around the globe and the implications of this struggle for the Afro-American, rejected overt colonization and instead supported an informal imperialism, that is, economic penetration without political annexation.[17] Whether they were overt imperialists or commercial expansionists, it is safe to say that a significant number of educated black Americans believed that economically underdeveloped, nonwhite regions of the world constituted an environment where the Negro could avoid the blighting impact of proscription and discrimination, enhance their own and the race's power and prestige, and at the same time remain within the American milieu.

John Waller was particularly susceptible to the lure of overseas empire because he had spent much of his adult life in the midst of a community of people who had succumbed to the myth of a "promised land," who were convinced that the Negro would be best able to realize his potential in economically underdeveloped regions not yet exploited and controlled by the white man. The immigrationist impulse in Kansas, moreover, did not end with the Great Exodus of 1879–1882. In September, 1886, a group of Topeka blacks headed by George Charles and his son Charles Charles established an African Emigration Association "for the purpose of accumulating means to help that part of our people who wish to obtain homes on African soil." Expressing the conviction that slavery had so retarded the Negro's development that he could never hope to compete with his white fellow citizens on an equal basis, the Charleses called upon the persecuted blacks of the South and the unemployed Negroes of the North to join with them in establishing a haven for Afro-Americans in the land of their origin. As of January, 1887, the association claimed 500 members, with full-fledged chapters in Wyandotte, Wamego, Manhattan, and Osage City. Repeated appeals in the late 1880s and early 1890s to both state and federal governments for funds went for naught, however, and the A.E.A. was never able to finance transportation to Africa. Then, early in 1888, none other than Colonel John Brown and several other black Kansas "entrepreneurs" launched a scheme to colonize blacks in Brazil and the Argentine Republic. When several prominent Negroes stepped forward to denounce the South American project as purely a money-making scheme designed to enrich its creators, the "movement" collapsed.[18] By far the most important of the post-exodus immigration movements launched by black Kansans involved a scheme to colonize the Cherokee Strip in Oklahoma.

The Indian Territory—that is, the lands that were to comprise the state of Oklahoma—was sold to the United States by the Creeks and Seminoles in 1866. It was clear from the language of the treaties that the region was to be used for Indian and Negro reservations. The Cherokees, Choctaws, and Chickasaws, as well as the Creeks and Seminoles, had living among them at that time several thousand blacks, former slaves of Indians. The federal government anticipated that these individuals plus many newly emancipated southern blacks would want to take advantage of their freedom and establish homesteads in the West. In the years that followed, however, few blacks moved to the Indian Territory, and pressure from land-hungry whites halted the settlement of additional Indians on the treaty lands. These same whites demanded that a portion of the I.T., a forty-mile wide band of territory along the southern boundary of Kansas known as the Cherokee Strip, be opened to white settlement. The federal government procrastinated, for, under terms of the treaty with the Cherokees, the strip was to be reserved for friendly Indians. Nonetheless, federal troops proved unable to stanch the flow of white squatters that moved into the area during the late 1880s, and in 1889 Washington officially opened the strip. A number of black Kansans had long looked at the band of territory simultaneously as a potential haven for the oppressed blacks of the South and as an area which they themselves could exploit through farming or real-estate dealing. In July, 1889, W. I. Jamison, D. B. Garrett, H. W. Rolfe, and Bill Eagleson established the Oklahoma Immigration Association. The corporation proposed to establish immigration bureaus in several southern cities and all the principal towns of Kansas. The initiators of the scheme had little luck in attracting southern Negroes, but by February, 1890, more than 2,000 Kansas blacks had crossed into the strip. Traveling via the Rock Island and Santa Fe railroads or by buckboard, the colonists preempted some 145,000 acres of public land and laid out the all-black township of Lincoln, the center of the projected colony.[19] According to the *Capital*, many of those who went were not destitute but were "worthy citizens prosperous in business beyond expectations."[20] By early 1890 the prospect of creating a black utopia in Oklahoma had captured the imagination of blacks throughout the state. Negroes envisioned the establishment of a full range of black-controlled institutions—churches, schools, hospitals, orphanages, and asylums, as well as a government controlled by Negroes for Negroes. Indeed, during the opening weeks of 1890, Edward P. McCabe, who had been in Washington since 1889, actively campaigned for territorial governor of Oklahoma. The dream of a black homeland in Oklahoma was never realized, however. As the number of blacks moving into the Cherokee Strip increased, so did the hostility of white "sooners" living in the area. Stories involving the shooting and beating of black squatters began to drift northward, discouraging would-be immigrants. Moreover, the Oklahoma Immigration Association became involved in a scandal when one of the directors sold land which the company did not actually own. Finally, McCabe lost out to a white in his bid for the governorship.[21] The Oklahoma fever had served, however, to rekindle interest in Afro-American colonization among black Kansans generally and in John Lewis Waller particularly.

Given the milieu from which Waller came, his status as an upwardly mobile member of the black community, his anxiety over mounting racial tensions, and his commitment to the precepts of American society and to Social Darwinism and individualism, it was natural for him to turn to the New Empire as the solution to his quest for security and progress. Although he was responding to the immediate situation in Kansas and to contemporary events influencing other proponents of black empire, Waller's conversion to overseas expansion was also a product of his own experience and thought. He had, for example, always believed that the relatively open environment of the frontier offered the best opportunity for blacks to advance materially and intellectually, to gain confidence, and to improve the image of the race as a whole. In 1879, at the height of the Kansas exodus, he had urged Congress to appropriate one million dollars for the colonization of enterprising blacks in Nebraska, Colorado, Minnesota, New Mexico, and Kansas. There the oppressed and exploited former slaves of the South, free from the restraints imposed by racial prejudice, could achieve economic independence and gain experience in self-government. "I hope no man will quiet himself on the theory that the 'exodus' is over," he wrote. "It is not nor will it be unless the most implicit assurances can be given on the part of the law-making powers that we shall immediately be secured in all our rights."[22] In the late 1880s Waller became caught up in the Oklahoma fever. Arguing that black pioneers would be able to "establish themselves so firmly that they could hold their own from the start," he recommended settlement of the Oklahoma territory by 100,000 Negroes.[23] Waller adhered to the theory that the migration and colonization of a substantial number of southern Negroes would improve their lot and the condition of those who remained behind. A new exodus would create a labor shortage in Dixie and dramatically increase the economic leverage of the farm and industrial laborers who chose to stay.[24]

During most of the 1880s Waller was opposed to schemes aimed at colonizing abroad because he associated them with the ongoing efforts of white supremacists to expatriate blacks and because he believed over-seas colonization would involve loss of citizenship. "I insist that we, the descendents of that band of black people who came to Jamestown in 1620, have no more right to be exported to our mother country than the descendents of those who came over on the *Mayflower* the same year," he wrote in the *Topeka Capital*. "In the face of anarchy, socialism, and all sorts of dangers threatening the perpetuity of our institutions," Negroes, some living "in the most distressing and squalid poverty," had remained loyal to the flag, and they would never voluntarily relinquish their citizenship.[25] By 1891, however, it had become apparent that land-hungry whites were not going to allow blacks to exploit an acre of western terri-tory if they could prevent it. During the 1880s Waller had joined his fellow Republicans in accepting overseas expansion by the United States as beneficial to the economy and the party. It eventually occurred to him that the answer to his problems and those of his race lay in temporary exploitation, *à la* E. H. Harriman and Cornelius Vanderbilt, of some vir-gin wilderness overseas. Blacks would be free to mine, farm, and develop without having to worry about the "bulldozing" tactics of land-crazed whites. Conditioned by various assumptions about the value of frontier life and the need of blacks to acquire wealth, devoted to a social system based on competition and material achievement, stung by his personal misfortune, and depressed by the deteriorating racial climate in America, Waller decided sometime in the early 1890s that colonization and ex-ploitation of a commercial empire, which had brought power and prestige to many white Americans, could do the same for blacks.

The opportunity for Waller to implement his schemes was made possible by a bizarre combination of white Republican anxiety over Negro voting trends in 1890 and aid rendered by a prominent black Democrat. Between August and November, 1890, the Democrats and Populists blitzed the Republicans with hundreds of speakers, rallies, and parades. As part of their massive election campaign, the Demo-Pops redoubled their efforts to win over the black vote. No less than fifty Democratic newspapers ran editorials detailing Waller's untiring labors in behalf of the G.O.P. and blasting the Republicans for rejecting him. Foster appealed to Negroes to vote for the party of the common man—the only party which had chosen to recognize the Negro by placing one of his number on the state ticket. Meanwhile, Taylor and Eagleson cam-paigned tirelessly for Charles Robinson, the Democratic gubernatorial candidate. Belatedly, white Republican leaders recognized the threat. Republican editorials became increasingly shrill. Joe Hudson accused John F. Willets, the Populist gubernatorial nominee, of swindling his widowed sister. Republicans frantically tried to persuade Negroes that if they voted Democratic and/or Populist they would be voting for L. L. Polk and Ben Tillman, two of the most irascible white supremacists who ever lived.[26] The counteroffensive was too little, too late. Townsend, who stuck with the party of Lincoln, noted in mid-October that "the prospects are that there will be a strong falling off in the solid Negro vote." The Democrats, he noted, were quietly but steadily "working at the blacks to become full-fledged 'Johnnies' [Democrats] or to cast their vote with the Farmer's ticket." Townsend predicted that as a result "many of our prominent colored men were going to vote for either Foster or Robinson."[27] November's election returns proved the editor of the *Advocate* to be a prophet. The Republican majority of 82,000 in the gubernatorial contest of 1888 was reduced to 15,000 in 1890. Moreover, the Populists and Democrats captured control of the House of Representatives. Desertion of the Republicans at the polls by black Kansans was clearly a significant factor in the party's declining fortunes. The Populist candidate for auditor, although not elected, captured 120,000 votes and ran as well as or better than other Populists. For example, Robinson carried the predominantly black first ward in Topeka, an area that had gone Republican in every previous election.[28]

Some prominent white Republicans, anticipating disaster, began pressing the Harrison administration immediately after the state convention to provide a diplomatic post for Waller. United States Senator Preston B. Plumb wrote to Secretary of State Blaine in June that "it is exceedingly important that he [Waller] should be provided for right away."[29] Praising the black Kansan as "a bright man, a man of good habits and unquestioned integrity," and calling him "the representative colored man of Kansas," Congressman B. W. Perkins urged President Harrison to appoint Waller to a consular position as soon as possible.[30] J. H. Robertson, proprietor of the Commercial House Hotel in Seneca and a leading figure in the Kansas Republican party, was more explicit. "There was disappointment and consequent disaffection among the colored people because Waller failed of nomination on the State ticket," he wrote to Harrison in October, 1890. "His appointment would therefore have a good impact on the party's chances in November."[31]

Adding his voice to those of Plumb, Perkins, and Robertson was C. H. J. Taylor, the prominent black politician and former minister to Liberia who had taken over the revolving editorship of the *American Citizen* in early November, 1890. Events had done nothing to alter Taylor's devotion to political independence. Both he and W. H. Eagleson had campaigned actively for Democrat Charles Robinson in the November, 1890, governor's race, and Taylor had run unsuccessfully as the Democrat-Populist fusion candidate for the House of Representatives from Wyandotte County.[32] Taylor saw in Waller's frustration and subsequent desire for a position overseas an opportunity to enhance the prestige of the "Popocrats" among Kansas Negroes. At this point Waller was more than willing to serve Taylor's purposes. Despite the fact that only two years earlier he had referred to Taylor as "a low, scheming, unscrupulous ward politician," Waller late in 1890 joined the staff of the *American Citizen*.[33] Taylor immediately began booming his new employee for a consular position. In return, Waller wrote a series of editorials criticizing the Harrison administration and, implicitly, the Republican party, for the president's refusal to appoint a significant number of blacks to patronage jobs. On February 5, 1891, Waller was named United States consul to Madagascar. Whether Taylor played a direct role through his contacts with the State Department and the black establishment in Washington, or an indirect part by hiring Waller and thus alarming Republicans at both the state and national levels, he clearly had a hand in the appointment. Both the *Leavenworth Advocate* (black) and *Leavenworth Times* (white) credited Taylor for securing Waller's new position.[34]

Just precisely when John Waller began to formulate plans for the establishment of a plantation-colony in Madagascar is unclear. Such a course of action may have started taking shape in his mind immediately after his failure to obtain the Republican nomination for auditor in 1890, or he may not have conceived of himself as a foreign concessionaire until near the end of his tenure as consul in 1894. Whatever the case—the timing was not important—Waller bade farewell to Susan and the children on April 8, 1891, and departed Topeka for New York. He remained in New York for more than two weeks making the acquaintance of T. Thomas Fortune, T. McCants Stewart, and other prominent Negroes. Departing for London on May 16, 1891, the consul-designate made the eleven-day trans-Atlantic passage aboard the British steamship *Etruria*.[35] One can only wonder if he drew any comparisons between his trip, made in a comfortable second-class cabin, and the notorious two-and-a-half month middle passage by which his ancestors were transported across the same ocean to their "homes" in the New World. Although Waller's travails consisted merely of a couple of rude Irishmen and temporary seasickness, his knowledge of history must have enabled him to empathize with his forefathers. Perhaps, though, he was too preoccupied with the future to dwell on the past. Among the passengers on board the *Etruria* was Commodore Cornelius Vanderbilt, one of America's most active commercial expansionists. If Waller had begun to develop plans for a plantation-colony, he must have regarded Vanderbilt's presence as a favorable omen. During the voyage the black diplomat made friends with C. H. Cuppy, "a young humorist from Indianapolis," who subsequently showed him about London.[36] After an extended stay in England—he was much impressed, he wrote, with the beauty of the English countryside— Waller left for Madagascar, arriving there on July 24, 1891. He officially assumed the duties of United States consul on August 1.[37] Unfortunately for the black diplomat, Africa at the close of the nineteenth century was the scene of an intense Anglo-French colonial rivalry. Nowhere was this competition any keener than in Madagascar.

In 1890 Madagascar was a vast, underdeveloped land whose untapped resources beckoned to the great colonial powers. An island exceeded in size only by Greenland, Borneo, and New Guinea, Madagascar possessed what seemed to many international businessmen an unlimited potential. The land contained 30,000 square miles of virgin timber, and an unmeasured amount of rubber, mahogany, and ebony; rich mineral deposits; and thousands of acres of fertile land suitable for the cultivation of sugar, tea, coffee, and vanilla. Its two principal cities, Tananarive, a thriving metropolis of some 100,000 in the center of the island, and Tamatave, a busy port on the east coast, were bustling centers of trade. The Hovas, an olive-skinned people rumored to have come to Madagascar from Polynesia some 2,000 years before, governed its six million inhabitants with an iron hand. Though numbering only several hundred thousand, the Hovas used their control of the strategic central plateau, together with superior weapons, to dominate the other tribes. The political system under which the Malagasies lived was in theory an absolute monarchy, but the matrilineal dynasty was in reality a front for the prime minister, who was *ex officio* husband of six successive queens. His power, in turn, depended upon the support of the nobility. The Malagasy social structure was feudalistic, with rigid gradations from nobles to slaves. One curious aspect was the absence of private property; the monarch owned all the land. The Hovas were an intensely proud people. Although they had accepted Christianity, they remained determined to resist the political intervention and economic exploitation that so often followed in the wake of missionary activity.[38]

The preeminent threat to Malagasy independence was France. French explorers claimed the island for Louis XIII in 1642. Shortly thereafter Cardinal Richelieu granted a trade monopoly to the Compagnie d'Indes Orientales. In succeeding years few nationals emigrated, and by the 1880s France could boast only a small colony and naval base at Fort

Dauphin, located on the southeastern coast. Commercial activity was restricted to one mercantile house, and total French investment amounted to no more than a hundred million francs. From this modest stake French citizens realized little more than a hundred thousand francs per annum. Although Paris always hoped that the huge island would become an important component in France's mercantilist system, the nation's deep and abiding interest there was not primarily economic.[39] The Jesuits were extremely active in Madagascar and, by the end of the nineteenth century, claimed over 100,000 converts. The missionaries had long clamored for the establishment of a protectorate which would enable them to proselyte without competition from Christians of other nations or regulation by the native government. The editor of the *Revue Bleue* (Paris) in an article appearing in November, 1894, deprecated the lack of government support being shown French Catholic missionaries and proclaimed that the only alternative to submission to the Protestants was "to take possession of Madagascar by force, as we have done in Tonkin and Tunis."[40] Even more important in determining French attitudes was the widespread conviction that it was the nation's "destiny" to hold sway over Madagascar. Gabriel Hanotaux, the foreign minister who ultimately presided over annexation, aptly summed up the reasons for France's acquisitive posture toward the island: "A colony is not a farm given to the mother country for exploitation, and which has no value unless it earns a rent by the end of the year. . . . Carrying and perpetuating its name, language, and thought to new countries, a civilized nation already accomplishes a good deal if it thereby prolongs its own existence in space and time."[41]

No less than in Egypt, North Africa, or Southeast Asia, the chief obstacle to French pretensions was Great Britain. Englishmen in Madagascar contested the French in virtually every field of human endeavor. Methodist missionaries arrived on the island in the middle of the nineteenth century, and by 1894 the London Missionary Society counted over 1,300 churches in this "the most fruitful field of English endeavor."[42] A story on Madagascar appearing in a January, 1895, issue of the *New York Times* emphasized the degree of Methodist commitment to the Hovas and their subjects: "France might annex all the rest of the African continent and not stir these English mission-loving folk so violently as by a single armed attempt to advance the pretensions of Catholicism in Madagascar."[43] Scarcely less important than British concern for Madagascar's spiritual welfare were the interests of numerous English merchants operating throughout the eastern half of the island. Because French colonial rule inevitably meant high tariff barriers, they were no more anxious than the missionaries to see the establishment of a French protectorate. In their continuing battle to restrict French influence in the island, British colonists had by the latter part of the nineteenth century established close ties with the Hova power structure. In fact, most members of the Hova nobility were Methodist, the commander in chief of the Hova military was an Englishman, and, prior to 1890 at least, the prime minister was ardently pro-British.[44]

Even though British investments and influence in Madagascar transcended those of France, Whitehall decided in 1882 to relinquish all claim to the island in order to persuade France to recognize British dominance in Egypt. Therefore, in December, 1885, when the French resident general forced the queen of Madagascar to surrender control of foreign affairs to his office, the British made no attempt to block the move. Paris was unwilling to grant Britain a free hand in Cairo, however, unless Whitehall explicitly recognized French dominion in east Africa. Accordingly, in August, 1890, Lord Salisbury and William Waddington, the French ambassador in London, signed a joint declaration on Africa in which France recognized the British protectorate over Zanzibar and Pemba (and tacitly over Egypt), and in return Britain acquiesced in French control of Madagascar and all of the central and western Sudan.[45]

Despite the Salisbury-Waddington Pact of 1890, opposition to French authority in Madagascar continued unabated both from Britons residing there and from the Hova monarchy.[46] The *Madagascar News*, mouthpiece of British missionaries in the island, blasted London for its act of appeasement and announced that Englishmen in Madagascar would recognize the French protectorate only as it concerned treaties the Hovas might make with foreign powers. The Methodist archbishop of Madagascar, Robert Cornish, begged the home government in vain for protection from the Catholic onslaught he believed was sure to follow unchecked French rule. Even more apprehensive than the English were the Hovas themselves. The monarchy, correctly perceiving France to be the primary threat to Malagasy independence, had scoured the international community between 1860 and 1880 in search of allies against France. Unable to find a European ally willing to enter into an anti-French pact that would at the same time leave the nation's independence intact, the Hovas concentrated on building up their military establishment. With the enthusiastic aid of British *colons*, they had succeeded by 1890 in fashioning a force capable of making the French pay dearly for any forcible attempt at annexation.[47] In an address to the throne delivered in September, 1890, the prime minister issued an unmistakable warning to the Quai d'Orsay: "This kingdom is a bed for only one person and you are the sole Sovereign," he declared to the queen. "If anyone dare to touch this kingdom or any portion of it, even of the size of a grain of rice, we shall never suffer it."[48] Thus, although discouraged by the Salisbury-Waddington Pact, the Malagasies were determined to resist to the end. Another local British paper, the *Madagascar Mail*, aptly summed up the sentiments of both the government and its English friends: "The Hovas look upon Lord Salisbury's actions as a betrayal of their interests and we English here are completely dumbfounded at the idea that we are now at the mercy of the French."[49] Deserted by White-hall, the Hovas and their British friends turned for aid to the diplomatic representative of the only other power with a significant interest in Madagascar—the United States.[50] In doing so they provoked a confrontation between French imperialism and black America's version of the New Manifest Destiny, an encounter that ironically led to total absorption of Madagascar by France in 1895 and ultimately, if incidentally, to the thwarting of Waller's plans for a plantation and colony.

The United States consulate in Madagascar was located in Tamatave. Situated on a low, flat promontory jutting out into the Indian Ocean, behind a grassy and often swampy plain stretching inland, Tamatave was the island's chief port. The town's approximately 4,000 inhabitants lived in wooden homes along one narrow main street and a number of still narrower sandy lanes. Eight to ten miles inland a range of wooded hills rose steadily in height, forming a series of natural terraces. The hills culminated in a massive plateau in the center of the island, in the middle of which rested the capital city of Tananarive.[51]

No sooner had Waller settled in the small but comfortable consulate than he was summoned to Tananarive to be officially received by Queen Ranavalona. The ceremony, certainly one of the most memorable events in Waller's life, was held at Ranavalona's palace. After resting overnight, the American consul was summoned to a huge inner courtyard. Presently the gates of the yard swung open and a grand procession entered. Rank after rank of Malagasy infantry paraded past the bedazzled American. The royal bodyguard of spearmen followed and then Queen Ranavalona and the prime minister. Behind her majesty and his excellency came the court singers and then, bringing up the rear, a body of Saklahava head-men in the picturesque costumes of their tribe. The royal pavilion which housed the throne was of Oriental architecture. A canopy of crimson and gold surmounted gold-lined pillars, whose corners were adorned with two crossed spearheads. From the summit of the canopy there rose a crown-shaped dome of gold and deep purple velvet. Silk curtains, green and gold in color, draped the eastern, southern, and northern sides of the pavilion. From the queen's shoulders a magnificent train of crimson velvet flowed over a dress of white silk, whose skirt was decorated with panels of embroidered velvet. Atop the olive-skinned monarch's head was a golden crown and around her neck a diamond necklace.[52]

Once Ranavalona was seated, she and her consort received Waller in a brief but gracious ceremony. Two oxen, six sheep, and innumerable chickens were slaughtered for the feast that followed.[53]

Unfortunately, Susan Waller arrived too late to partake of the festivities. She, Minnie, John, Jr., Helen, Jennie, and Paul Bray left Kansas in August, 1891, but did not arrive until December of that year.[54] There were few conveniences in Tamatave, but, as was her wont, Susan made the most of the situation. When she was not accompanying John to Tananarive for some social function, she tutored the younger children in math, English literature, and French.

The elaborate festivities staged by the Hovas upon Waller's arrival reflected their hope that he would serve as a counterweight to French power, that somehow he would be able to protect Madagascar from complete absorption. No doubt the government believed that as an American and a man of color the new consul would sympathize with Madagascar's struggle to retain its independence in the face of European imperialism. Waller would surely view the Malagasies as nonwhite people threatened by the racism which inevitably accompanied colonialism. Predictably, he was equally well-received by the British colony. Prominent Englishmen such as H. Andrew and E. Underwood Harvey, editors of the *Madagascar News*, and Archbishop Cornish cultivated Waller, seeing in him a potential bastion against French Catholicism and mercantilism.[55] It soon became apparent that the black Kansan was more than willing to serve Anglo-Hova interests, primarily because they happened to coincide with his own.

Shortly after his arrival in Madagascar, Waller became involved in a Hova-French dispute that went to the heart of the issue of Madagascar's independence. One of the concessions that France demanded but did not obtain when she negotiated the 1885 treaty with the Hovas was the right to grant *exequatur*—official authorization to operate, given to consular agents by the country in which they are stationed—to all foreign consuls assigned to Madagascar. According to A. A. Heggoy, a historian of French colonial policy in East Africa, the Quai d'Orsay was convinced that "should foreign consuls and other diplomatic officials receive *exequatur* from the Malagasy Queen or prime minister, the French protectorate would be but a fiction."[56] The Hovas certainly shared this view. In 1887 the prime minister notified Secretary of State Thomas F. Bayard that "if consul of any nation having treaty rights with Madagascar applies for *exequatur* through the French Resident General, this government will consider it a breach of treaty."[57] To the delight of the Hovas and the outrage of the French *colons*, Waller applied directly to the queen for his commission. Subsequently, French Foreign Minister Alexandre Ribot issued an official protest to the State Department, intimating that the consul's action could be considered a deliberately unfriendly act on the part of the United States.[58]

Waller's action in challenging France's right to grant *exequatur* was in accord with past American policy toward Madagascar. Though Washington was hardly prepared to go to war to prevent French hegemony, American diplomats, for a variety of reasons, made strenuous efforts during the last quarter of the nineteenth century to preserve Malagasy independence.[59] In fact, by the mid-1890s America was generally recognized as the only member of the international community willing to challenge French imperialism in Madagascar. "They [the Malagasies] have no reason to be grateful to any European nation," observed the *Manchester Guardian* in August, 1895, "for the only country which has shown a disposition to favor their cause is the United States."[60]

Probably the most important motive behind the State Department's policy of resistance was a desire to maintain an economic open door. As Walter LaFeber has pointed out, the search for foreign markets dominated the foreign policy of the Harrison administration. Both the president and Secretary of State James G. Blaine were convinced that one of the "highest duties" of the United States was to enlarge the area of foreign trade. Commercial empire would inevitably enhance the power and prestige of the nation. More tangibly, underdeveloped regions would simultaneously furnish the raw materials necessary to fuel America's giant industrial complex and the markets to absorb its surplus. By the latter part of the nineteenth century, Africa no less than Latin America and the Far East had come to be regarded by United States diplomats and businessmen as a legitimate field of endeavor. Initially, the most important force pushing the United States into involvement in Africa was the fear within commercial and missionary circles that the continent would soon fall under foreign domination.[61] The first steps toward a more aggressive African policy were taken during the administration of Chester A. Arthur. In his annual message to Congress in 1883 he argued that America could not afford to remain indifferent to the potentials of African commerce. He suggested that the United States cooperate with other interested powers in maintaining freedom of trade and residence in central Africa.[62] By the 1890s American merchants were translating President

Arthur's suggestions into action. "The American people are beginning to recognize the fact that Africa offers a large and profitable market for the commerce of the World," noted the *Lagos* (Nigeria) *Weekly Record* in 1892, "and that it will be to the commercial interest of America if her merchants will endeavor to participate with England and France in the large trade carried on with this [continent]."[63] Commercial statistics bear out the *Record*'s claim. Between 1890 and 1900 United States trade with Africa increased at a faster rate than with any other area. By the turn of the century it constituted approximately 20 percent of America's commerce with nonindustrialized regions. Reflecting this surge of interest in Africa by the United States business community, American diplomats attempted to commit the European powers to an economic open door in Africa. The American delegate who attended the Conference of Berlin on Africa (1884–1885) persuaded the European powers to endorse the "American Project," which called for the continued neutrality and independence of the Congo Basin. Five years later, at the Congo Conference of Brussels, the Great Powers acknowledged the United States' interest in Africa by pledging to notify Washington at once of any changes, contemplated or actual, in the map of the Dark Continent. Somewhat to their surprise, the American representatives responded by declaring that the United States reserved the right to pass judgment on all changes, in light of its national interest.[64] "What a field for enterprise is here," proclaimed an article entitled "American Interests in Africa" appearing in the spring, 1890, issue of *The Forum*. "What an opening for our manufacturers among its fifty million of unclad inhabitants thirsting for trade; what an opportunity for exerting civilizing and christianizing influence."[65]

While those Americans concerned with the African market had focused their attention on the Congo region in the 1880s, by 1890 a number had shifted their interest to Madagascar. The Malagasy market was more than just a myth. United States exports to the island amounted to $584,770 in 1892, while imports in that year reached $271,108. United States–Madagascar trade constituted more than 30 percent of the total trade of the island, a figure made all the more important by the fact that France controlled but 10 percent. There were in 1891 two large American commercial houses in Tamatave doing a brisk business in cotton goods, rubber, and hides. In fact, American cotton merchants had for many years enjoyed a virtual monopoly on trade with the interior. With total investments in Madagascar amounting to well over a million dollars, Yankee entrepreneurs felt quite as threatened by a total French takeover as did their British counterparts. They labored under no illusions about the economic repercussions of annexation. The consul at Tamatave notified the State Department in July, 1895, that customs regulations which would accompany the establishment of a French protectorate would mean a loss to American cotton trade of 25 percent on cost price and 40 percent on profits. It is hardly surprising, then, that as the French posture toward the Hova regime became more menacing a number of American business journals, including the influential *Commercial and Financial Chronicle*, called upon the State Department to take whatever action necessary to protect United States interests in Madagascar.[66]

The fact that in Madagascar, as in so many other outposts of United States' commercial empire, there was a community of interest between America's business and diplomatic representatives enhanced the importance of economic factors in United States–Malagasy affairs. The vice-consul in 1892, for example, was also the Madagascar representative of Ropes, Emmerton, and Company of Boston, a large commercial house. Moreover, the most persistent and effective advocate of those with an economic stake in Madagascar was John Campbell, Waller's predecessor at Tamatave. Throughout his tenure he had urged Washington to take every measure possible to block a French takeover. "Our commercial interests in Madagascar," he wrote Assistant Secretary William H. Wharton in September, 1890, "are larger and more important than those of either France or England, or indeed of any of the other treaty powers represented here. . . . Hence, I hope the Department will at once see the necessity of permanently settling these questions with the powers . . . which may lead to a requisition for a share in the Protectorate by our government."[67]

Also contributing to Washington's continuing concern over the fate of Madagascar was the bipartisan desire to attract the sizable black electorate still functioning in America during the last decade of the nineteenth century. As C. Vann Woodward has noted: "As a voter, the Negro was both hated and cajoled, both intimidated and courted, but he could never be ignored so long as he voted."[68] Black ballots had been quite important to Harrison's election not only in Kansas but in other states as well, a fact not lost on either the Republicans or the Democrats. Both for political and ideological reasons, Harrison displayed a keen sensitivity to the opinions of the black electorate throughout his term in office. According to historian Richard Welch, "Harrison stood with such old time Republican senators as Hoar and Chandler in refusing to admit that the aims and ideals of Radical Reconstruction had been disproved or that the Republican Party had outgrown its concern for the Negro."[69] Over the enraged protests of white supremacists, he appointed Norris

Wright Cuney, a black and a prominent Texas Republican, as collector of customs at Galveston.[70] In June, 1889, he promised a delegation of black Alabamans that he would work unceasingly to secure for the Negro "protection of life and property, and the right to vote and have it honestly counted."[71] In response to Harrison's call in 1889 for federal legislation to protect Negroes in their voting rights in federal elections, the Federal Elections Bill was introduced in Congress in 1890. Although it did not pass, Harrison gave it his fullest support.[72] Perceptive Republican politicians could not help but be aware that many black Americans identified with the Hovas as a nonwhite people threatened by European colonialism, and they perceived that the black community would respond favorably to any government that dared to challenge French efforts to establish a protectorate.[73]

Finally, the decision to challenge the French in Madagascar was at least in part a reflection of the State Department's irritation over the efforts of the Quai d'Orsay to extend French control over areas long regarded by Americans as their private preserve. In 1888, for example, a Franco-American confrontation in regard to Haiti threatened to disrupt relations between the two nations. The Harrison administration was extremely desirous of acquiring a naval base in the Caribbean. A revolution in Haiti provided the opportunity. The nation had divided into a northern faction headed by the forces of Hippolyte, and the southern group led by Légitime. As European, especially French, influence began favoring Légitime, Washington began to tilt perceptibly toward the northern faction. Hippolyte, who finally gained control of the nation in 1899, at first promised the United States a base at Mole St. Nicholas but later reneged. The State Department and especially Secretary Blaine were convinced that France was responsible for the dictator's intransigence and that Paris was intent on converting Haiti into a protectorate.[74]

No less alarming to American policy-makers were the attempts of the French Foreign Office to establish a protectorate over various tribes in Liberia. This west African republic, colonized by American ex-slaves, was sandwiched between the British colony of Sierra Leone and the French-controlled Ivory Coast.[75] A number of factors rendered Liberia vulnerable to its imperial neighbors: boundaries of the black republic were ill-defined; Monrovia was unable to prevent Liberian natives from conducting raids against their neighbors in Sierra Leone and the Ivory Coast; and, finally, the central government had borrowed heavily from European financiers. Even though the State Department warned the Great Powers as early as 1879 that the United States had special interests in Liberia and would take whatever steps necessary to preserve the nation's independence, European entrepreneurs and soldier-diplomats continued to violate Liberian sovereignty throughout the last quarter of the century. By the early 1890s Whitehall was busily engaged in implementing a rapprochement with the United States, and as a result British activity in Liberia decreased sharply. Détente with the United States did not rank high on the Quai d'Orsay's list of priorities. Ignoring warnings from both Republican and Democratic administrations, Paris continued to plot a Liberian protectorate.[76] When the French in 1893 compelled Monrovia to cede a strip of territory lying between the San Pedro River and Cavalla, Franco-American relations were strained to the breaking point.[77] It is reasonable to assume that State Department officials believed that a firm challenge to French pretensions in Madagascar could not help but lessen pressure on Liberia and dampen French ambition in the Caribbean.

Nevertheless, the Salisbury-Waddington Pact and France's obvious determination to control Malagasy affairs caused a momentary weakening of the State Department's resolve. By 1891, however, those with a stake in Madagascar, particularly the black consul at Tamatave, had managed to persuade United States policy-makers that the national interest would be best served by continued resistance to French aggression. As previously noted, every party with an interest in Madagascar recognized the right to grant *exequatur* as the symbol of Hova sovereignty. After receiving the sharp note from the Quai d'Orsay on September 30, 1891, which demanded, among other things, that Washington order its representative to reapply through the French resident general and to communicate in the future with the Hovas only through French authorities, the State Department briefly considered pulling out of Madagascar. Waller pointed out that this would be interpreted by the monarchy as a gross insult, and that the United States could, by refusing to recognize French control over consular credentials, become the dominant force in the island. He repeatedly requested permission to go Tananarive and mediate between the French and the Hovas. Such authorization was never forthcoming, but Washington once again decided to resist a French takeover.[78] Until the Chamber of Deputies voted in 1896 to formally annex Madagascar, the State Department took the position that because no consul who had applied through the resident general had yet received his *exequatur*, the United States could not acknowledge French authority.[79]

Though Waller's position was sanctioned by the State Department, France—and particularly Frenchmen in Madagascar—chose to believe that America's refusal to acquiesce in their protectorate was primarily due to the black consul at Tamatave. Further alienating the French were

Waller's unceasing efforts to halt a projected "free labor system" whereby France would enslave the Malagasies and members of other tribes, and export them to various parts of the empire. The United States consul's frequent and vociferous public denunciation of this trade embarrassed French authorities and caused them to delay implementation. French authorities concluded that Waller was at worst an official agent of Anglo-American imperialism and at best a tool of the Hova prime minister.[80] By the end of 1891, no matter which role they attributed to him, the French colony viewed the American as a threat to their interests.

The altercation over granting of *exequatur* was the first but not the most important episode in what quickly became an undeclared war between Waller and the French.[81] The second bore directly on the Kansan's scheme for establishing a black colony in the island and ultimately helped to convince the French that annexation was the only solution to the Madagascar problem.

In June, 1893, Waller learned that he would be replaced by a white Democrat from Georgia, under the new administration of Grover Cleveland. The Kansan welcomed his dismissal because, relieved of official duties, he was free to negotiate with the Hovas for a land concession. As indicated by a letter he wrote to James Ruff of Coffeyville in June, 1892, Waller had found Madagascar eminently suitable as a field for black development and investment:

> We are much pleased with this country and we are surprised at the high state of civilization of the colored people here. It is true that the country is only partially developed, but it is also true that there is a great awakening among the people and I think ere long the whistle of the steam locomotive will be heard in this part of Africa, even as it is heard at Capetown, Natal, and Mauritius. . . . You would be astounded at the thrift of the colored people in this "dark" continent, as it is called by the highly civilized portion of the world. Here the colored man is found in all the different mechanical avocations of life. There are carpenters, blacksmiths, printers, lawyers, doctors, and merchants. The Queen is a colored lady of rare culture and beauty. . . . Madagascar is a beautiful country and when it becomes known to the world and her capabilities are shown [they] will place her among the great countries of the world. The resources, both agricultural and mineral, are inexhaustible. An abundance of living water is everywhere to be seen. Millions of good beef cattle roam the beautiful valleys and feed upon the many mountains.[82]

In January, 1894, the new consul arrived in Tamatave and Waller abandoned the consulate that had been his home for the past two and a half years. He, Susan, Helen, Minnie, Jennie, and the boys moved to Tananarive where Waller, in partnership with an Englishman named George Tessier, opened a large grocery store. The ex-consul became a grocer merely to keep food on the table, so to speak; this vocation, like barbering, was to be a means to an end. In January and February Waller obtained a series of audiences with the queen and prime minister and harangued them on the wisdom of drawing American investment capital to the island. American commerce was already dominant in Madagascar; the more the Hova government could increase this economic stake, the greater the likelihood that the United States would interpose its authority between the Malagasies and the French.[83]

In March, 1894, two months after Waller officially stepped down as United States consul, the French were stunned by news that the queen had granted the ex-diplomat a 150,000-acre concession in the rubber-rich south.[84] The land grant, only the third ever made to an individual by the monarchy, was for a period of thirty years and subject to renewal.[85] Waller's emphasis on the political benefits to be derived from the granting of concessions to Americans had paid off.

As far as the Hovas were concerned, the Waller concession was part of the government's continuing effort to sidetrack French imperialism, which by 1894 appeared bent on nothing less than outright annexation. In 1893 the Hovas, encouraged by Grover Cleveland's actions in connection with the Hawaiian revolution, had appealed to the new chief executive to block a French takeover and thus further enhance his reputation as champion of the downtrodden. When Washington refused to go on record as the guarantor of Malagasy independence, Tananarive turned to Waller's projected plantation as an alternative method for involving the United States in Madagascar's problems. The Hovas were well aware that the ex-consul intended eventually to establish an Afro-American colony on the concession. They reasoned that Washington would be as willing to protect black Americans in Madagascar as in Liberia. The prime minister hoped that the United States, in defending the rights of Waller and his colonists, would simultaneously preserve Malagasy independence. The fact that the boundary of the Waller concession overlapped that of Fort Dauphin, the site of a projected French military installation, was further indication that Tananarive's prime motive in making a grant to Waller was a desire to use American power as a counterweight to French ambitions.[86]

English *colons* were, needless to say, enthusiastic supporters of the

132

projected plantation. Significantly, the Reverend James Richardson of the London Missionary Society had witnessed the transaction. The British-owned *Madagascar News* praised Waller as one of the most progressive agriculturalists in the island and hailed the concession as an unqualified blessing.[87]

The French did not agree. Announcement of the Waller grant was made just as the Franco-Malagasy conflict was coming to a head. Relations between Paris and Tananarive had deteriorated steadily after 1891. Throughout the summer and fall of 1893 the resident general reported to the Foreign Office that the Hovas were importing large quantities of arms and ammunition. In early 1894 news that roving bands of Malagasies were attacking French *colons* and destroying their property aroused public ire in both Madagascar and France.[88] On January 26 the Chamber of Deputies voted unanimously to "sustain the government in whatever it undertakes to maintain our situation and rights in Madagascar, to restore order, to protect our nationals and to make our flag respected there."[89] At the time there was an intense debate within the cabinet concerning Madagascar. The leading military men and their representatives argued for direct control to "prevent past abuses and misunderstandings," while moderates argued that direct rule would be cumbersome, expensive, and offensive to the other powers. For many Frenchmen, the Waller concession was the last straw.[90]

France's decision to force the Treaty of 1885 on the Hovas had been prompted not only by a desire to cut all formal diplomatic ties between the Great Powers and Madagascar, but to force the queen to make long-term land grants to French citizens. Although the Hova monarch had agreed in principle, she had refused to do so in practice.[91] Not surprisingly, French authorities viewed the Waller concession as a "slap in the face."[92] Terming it an unmistakable challenge to French hegemony, as indeed it was, the resident general declared the land grant "null and void."[93] The semi-official French newspaper *Le Madagascar* demanded that the "colored gentleman" and his Hova patrons be put in their place. "The future American colony," declared the editor, "will be most detrimental to us. . . . Even suppose that this little Republic should desire to have the honorable Mr. Waller for President, we doubt indeed that it would constitute for the future of Madagascar an element of peace and very *bona fide* progress."[94] Frenchmen throughout the island demanded that the home government take action.

Meanwhile, in the spring and summer of 1894 Waller had launched a multiphased development program designed to convert his concession into a profit-making operation, to provide Afro-Americans with a new field of investment, and to shield the enterprise from possible intervention by the French authorities. Although the land grant was made to Waller alone, his silent partner in the "Wallerland" venture, as the black entrepreneur chose to dub his concession, was E. Underwood Harvey, editor of the *Madagascar Mail*. Harvey, who was acting partly out of an urge for personal profit and partly out of a desire to thwart the French, was to serve Waller as an intermediary with English financial interests, a minor investor, and a very effective propagandist. The black Kansan and white Englishman agreed that the first priority, for both economic and political reasons, should be to interest as many influential Anglo-Americans as possible in the operation. To this end, on March 17 Harvey sent a circular entitled "Important Rubber Concession to an American Citizen"[95] to the editors of over a hundred newspapers in the United States and Great Britain. The response was gratifying. The *New York World* published a lengthy article on the grant and expressed a desire to be kept conversant with political developments on the island. The June 20 edition of the *Baltimore Sun* included a similar piece, under the caption "American Enterprise Abroad." Notices of the concession subsequently appeared in newspapers and magazines ranging from the *Muscatine* (Iowa) *Journal* to the *British Manufacturer*.[96]

Although the ex-consul envisioned Wallerland as a haven for oppressed American Negroes and an investment field for Afro-American capital, he believed that in view of the diplomatic situation it was imperative to have settlers, whatever their origin, present and actually working their leaseholds as quickly as possible. With the venture in progress, he reasoned, it would be much more difficult for the French to interfere. On May 2, 1894, Waller and Harvey dispatched Paul Bray, Waller's stepson, to the nearby British colony of Mauritius.

When Paul Bray chose to accompany his mother and siblings to Madagascar in the fall of 1891, he was twenty-one years of age. He had moved to Kansas in 1884 from Ohio. While living with his mother and stepfather he attended and graduated from the Leavenworth public school system. Following graduation he worked in succession as a traveling salesman for the *American Citizen, Leavenworth Advocate,* and *Indianapolis Freeman*. Something of a dandy, the handsome young man cut a wide swath through black society as he moved from town to town in eastern Kansas.[97] As had been true in Kansas, Bray lived in Madagascar only intermittently with the Wallers. Like Waller, he managed to ingratiate himself with the Hova government. When Waller received his concession, he offered his stepson a position as traveling agent and junior partner, and Bray accepted.

Bray, equipped with Wallerland calling cards, begin recruiting settlers from the large colony of blacks on Mauritius. Suffering from competition from Asiatic "coolie" labor and from the cyclones that periodically swept the area, ravaging their farms, the Mauritians proved quite receptive to Bray's sales pitch. The terms for a piece of Wallerland were liberal enough. Leases were to run for twenty years, with options for two renewals. Rent for the initial two years was to be free. Upon expiration of the grace period, the lessee would pay a twenty-five cent increment per acre annually up to the eleventh year, and $1.50 per acre per annum thereafter. Wallerland Enterprises could afford such terms because the contract that the ex-consul had signed with the Hovas required merely that he make a $500 payment after the fifth year and then remit 10 percent of his income annually.[98]

With Bray buttonholing Mauritians and Harvey bombarding the Anglo-American press, Waller turned his attention to long-range planning. On March 30, 1894, he wrote to John Mercer Langston, prominent black politician and civil rights leader, informing him of the grant and describing in elaborate and tempting detail the economic opportunities in Madagascar.[99] After Langston expressed interest, Waller wrote again on May 12, describing the progress of his enterprise and asking the former congressman to contact Negroes who might be willing to invest: "I am in correspondence with financial houses both in England and America who are very much interested in my concession," he reported, "and one Chicago firm has offered to furnish the Saw Milling and other machinery and $10,000 in funds to commence the development of the concession. . . . An English firm offers to furnish whatever I may need in the way of farming utensils and all manner of merchandise." Asserting that it was his desire "to be able to keep my concession within the control of colored men," he asked Langston to organize an Afro-American syndicate capable of providing the capital for long-range development. In closing, Waller announced his intention to name Langston and Warner T. McGuinn, then practicing law in Baltimore, as legal representatives for Wallerland.[100]

French hostility toward the Wallerland scheme, together with a steady deterioration in Franco-Malagasy relations, convinced Waller and Harvey that the United States must be persuaded to fill the power void created by the Salisbury-Waddington Pact. As soon as the French authorities got wind of the concession, they utilized a variety of techniques designed to either reduce its size or subvert the scheme altogether. Sometime early in 1894 an emissary from the resident general approached Waller and tried to persuade him to accept 20 square miles instead of

225. The black Kansan refused. The French next indicated that if Waller would agree to be "guided" by them in developing his concession, the money for cultivation and improvement would be provided. Again he demurred. Upon learning of Bray's trip to Mauritius, the French authorities in Madagascar sent word to the French consular representative there to obstruct his activities. *Le Madagascar* subsequently printed articles denouncing Waller and pronouncing his concession invalid, and then distributed copies in Mauritius. Those Mauritians who chose to ignore this warning and take up residence in Wallerland were systematically harassed by lieutenants of the resident general.[101] On August 10, in an attempt to compel Washington to take a more visible position in support of Wallerland and the Hovas, Waller instructed Langston and McGuinn to put two questions to the State Department: (1) did the Malagasy government have the right under existing treaty arrangements with the United States to grant concessions to American citizens, and (2) were such grants in violation of the treaty then in existence between France and the United States? In addition, the two black lawyers were instructed to seek the aid of Senator John Sherman "who from his large knowledge of foreign affairs can be of great service to you and who in case the Secretary of State decides adversely [refuses to recognize the validity of the claim] can bring the matter before the committee of Foreign Affairs."[102]

As Waller sought official sanction for his land grant, he also initiated a publicity campaign to inform American opinion about the "rape of Madagascar." The effort had actually begun in mid-March with Harvey's circular to the American press. "Aside from the big concession being of great importance to America," he wrote, "it should attract the attention of the American Press to the efforts the young, progressive Malagasy nation are making to maintain their independence and resist foreign encroachments."[103] By the fall of 1894 Langston and McGuinn were spending far more time in bringing the Hova's plight to the attention of the American people than in clearing legal obstacles from Wallerland's path. In early October, for example, McGuinn persuaded the *New York Sun*, whose editor, Charles Dana, was an outspoken expansionist, to publish an article condemning "French transgressions" in Madagascar and asserting that any interference by France with the Waller concession would constitute a violation of the United States–Malagasy Treaty.[104]

By the fall of 1894 the Wallerland scheme had progressed to the point where Waller felt able to make plans for a recruiting and fund-raising trip to the United States.[105] He was prevented from leaving, however, by State Department procrastination in regard to the recognition of his claim and by the machinations of Edward Telfair Wetter, the white Democrat who had replaced him as United States consul. The delay was to have a decisive impact on Waller's fortunes.

Although determined to protect American trading interests in Madagascar, the State Department hoped to avoid a direct Franco-American confrontation over Wallerland. In spite of the fact that the French resident general in May, 1894, made public the fact that he was under orders to block the Waller concession, American officials refused to publicly recognize the validity of Waller's claim. On October 10, for example, Acting Secretary of State Edwin Uhl told Langston and McGuinn that, in the absence of a specific infringement of Waller's rights by French authorities, the administration was "hesitant to express an opinion."[106]

Three days later, though, the French forced the Cleveland government to make clear its position. "The government of the Republic does not recognize the existence of concessions accorded by the Malagasy Government to private individuals," read an official proclamation issued by the resident general. "The French Government regards as null and void any concession which has not been approved by the French Resident General at Tannarive [sic]."[107] The State Department responded by notifying Waller's lawyers that it recognized the right of the Hova government to lease land to American citizens and thus regarded Wallerland as a legitimate enterprise eligible for the same protection from the United States government as any other American overseas concern. In a November 2 letter to Susan Waller, then in Tananarive, Waller expressed satisfaction with Washington's position but at the same time voiced concern over another, more pressing problem. "Oh, Sue," he exclaimed, "if you can only get friends to help me, I will teach Wetter a better lesson, if I can only get out of his hands and get hence. . . . You don't know how this man has wronged me."[108]

From the moment in January, 1894, that Wetter assumed his duties as United States consul at Tamatave until Waller's departure from Madagascar in the spring of 1895, the white Georgian went out of his way to make trouble for his black predecessor. Evidently, Wetter's natural racism was exacerbated by the fact that his father, a prominent slaveholder, had been ruined by the Civil War and Reconstruction. In his very first dispatch to the State Department, Wetter accused Waller of mishandling the estate of one W. F. Crockett, an American businessman who had died in Madagascar in June, 1892, and announced his intention to prevent Waller from leaving the island.[109] Unable to gather any convincing evidence of Waller's guilt, the new consul put off bringing his predecessor to trial until October 1, 1894, the very eve of Waller's departure.[110] In consular court—Wetter was judge and jury—Waller was found guilty, given forty-five days to come up with $1,964 (the sum allegedly owed the Crockett estate), and confined to the island. The question of the Kansan's guilt in this matter is obscured by Wetter's prejudice and impatience. It is clear only that Waller had permission from Mrs. Crockett to invest the estate and pay 5 percent interest to the family. At the time of the trial Waller had loaned all cash from the estate to private individuals. The promissory notes were then in his possession but were later seized by the French.[111] In his report to the department, Wetter indicated that he had decided not to transmit the evidence in the case as "the postage would be quite heavy." The importance of the incident lay in the fact that it delayed Waller's departure from the island. As a result, instead of being safely abroad, peddling shares on his concession, he was caught squarely in the middle of the Franco-Hova dispute.

On October 8, 1894, the French resident general, Le Myer de Vilers, delivered an ultimatum to the Hova government demanding unqualified recognition of French control over both foreign relations and internal affairs. At the same time, French *colons* began spreading rumors throughout the island of a Hova uprising that would engulf all foreigners in a blood bath.[112]

On October 24, the queen presented the resident general with the draft of a new treaty that would give France partial control over Malagasy foreign affairs but would leave the queen unquestioned sovereign over internal matters. Terming it "un ridicule contre-projet," de Vilers rejected the proposal out of hand and ordered the immediate evacuation of all French civilians. On November 27 the Chamber of Deputies voted a credit of sixty-five million francs to finance annexation of the island. The French navy quickly invested Tamatave, and in December, 1894, a French army of 15,000 men landed on the east coast. In January, 1895, the French began their assault on Tananarive. In the army's ascent from the swampy coasts of eastern Madagascar to the central plateau where the capital was located, well over a third of the expeditionary force would succumb either to Hova spears or to yellow fever.[113]

Meanwhile, in Tamatave, which had been placed under martial law in December, occupation troops were venting their wrath against Americans living there. Waller became a special target. Wetter, like Waller, had not applied to the French resident general for his *exequatur*. Ironically, French authorities blamed the black Kansan for his successor's actions; indeed, they continued to blame him for the entire "obstructionist" attitude of the United States. Consequently, Waller found himself the object of a carefully orchestrated campaign of harassment, which had begun even before formal occupation of Tamatave. On the night of November 16, for example, a group of French sailors broke into the residence of John Dublin, a black American citizen with whom Waller was staying, and attacked the ex-consul with fists and pikes. Wielding a chair, Waller managed to drive the invaders out and bolt the door, avoiding serious injury. By January, 1895, Waller could not venture onto the streets without being assaulted verbally or physically. Then, just before dawn on March 5, 1895, Waller was arrested at Dublin's house by French military police and charged with being a Hova spy.[114]

According to a number of observers, the resident general and the Hanotaux government believed that in arresting Waller they had at last removed the chief symbol of resistance to French domination on the island. Even Wetter, who was wont to underestimate Waller, was of this opinion. On April 20, 1895, he wrote Assistant Secretary Uhl: "Waller has a concession-grant which created more bitter feelings, more animosities in France than anything that has happened here in five years so I understand. . . . Waller in prison is harmless, Waller abroad may found an American Negro colony in Madagascar and ultimately overthrow French supremacy."[115]

The basis for the arrest and charges were letters Waller had written to his wife, to George Tessier, and to the son of a Hova official who was in the employ of Wallerland Enterprises. All three were then residing in Tananarive, Susan Waller being a houseguest of the Tessiers. The correspondence, mailed collectively on January 20, 1895, in violation of French postal regulations, described the French bombardment of Tamatave that had taken place in October, 1894, and the atrocities subsequently committed against the natives by occupation troops. Waller dwelt especially on a number of brutal rapes he had witnessed. One passage contained a promise to Waller's Hova employee that while abroad he would purchase Colt revolvers for him and his family. Finally, the ex-consul had warned his wife to beware of two individuals referred to simply as D. and P., who, he claimed, had been hired by the French to spy on the Waller family. Unbeknownst to the black Kansan, the French had two days previously imposed absolute censorship of the mails, prohibiting letters to Tananarive that were not first cleared through the censor. As a result, Waller's mail was impounded and read. The military authorities in Tamatave charged that these letters proved that Waller was inciting the Hovas to all sorts of "horrible crimes against the French," that he had given the government important information about the condition and movement of the French garrison at Tananarive, that he was running guns to France's enemies, and that he was deliberately endangering the lives of John Poupard and Robert Duder, two Americans living in Madagascar with whom Waller had quarreled.[116]

Charged under military law, Waller was interrogated, imprisoned, and held without counsel until his preliminary hearing on March 14, 1895. The arraignment proceedings were held *in camera*. The court ruled that there was sufficient evidence for an indictment and scheduled trial for March 20. French authorities finally assigned Waller a lawyer but permitted the prisoner to consult with him for the first time only two days before the trial. During the course of the proceedings, the five-man military court appeared far more concerned with speed than justice. The officers in charge limited the defense to one witness, refused to have all of the evidence read in court, and closed the proceedings after two and a half hours. Except for Waller and Bray's testimony, the trial was conducted entirely in French, a language which neither of the Americans had mastered. The court found the accused guilty as charged and sentenced him to twenty years at hard labor.[117]

Waller had appealed to Wetter for aid throughout the pretrial period, but to no avail.[118] Wetter claimed in a March 11 dispatch to the State Department to have protested vigorously to the resident general and to have engaged legal counsel for the accused. He explained that his efforts had come to naught, however, because of the intense feeling against Waller: "The French have been anxious to get at Waller for a long time, and are, I feel sure, desirous of making the most of this opportunity, whether they have a case made or not."[119] Other evidence indicates that the factor most responsible for Wetter's inability to help the imprisoned Kansan was not France, but his animosity toward Waller. Wetter had indeed found a lawyer for Waller, but he had then refused to use consular funds to pay him. On March 20 he had written Waller in jail that "in view of consular regulations prohibiting interference in behalf of any who had been guilty of infraction of local laws," there was nothing he could do.[120] Significantly, in the same letter in which he pronounced Waller guilty, the consul denounced the Kansan for unkind remarks he had made about Wetter in the correspondence (copies of which had been given to Wetter) that had been seized by the French. Indeed, despite his later protestations to the contrary, Wetter apparently did not even mention the Waller case to the French authorities until March 22. In his reply to Wetter's note of that date, the French commandant expressed surprise that the chief United States official in Madagascar would take so long to involve himself in the case. "I am led to conclude," he wrote to Wetter, "that it was intentionally that you kept aloof of the suit."[121]

140

On March 23 the French authorities denied Waller's frantic appeal, based on his contention that the French had no jurisdiction in Madagascar, and ordered implementation of the sentence. That same day, the military commandant ordered Paul Bray permanently expelled from the island. Unlike Waller, there was little doubt about Bray's complicity in the rebellion; he had already been arrested once as a Hova spy, and at the time of his banishment he was negotiating with Tananarive for a commission in the Hova army. On the twenty-third Waller was placed aboard the French steamer *Dejeune* and chained to the deck in the hold of the ship. After enduring the taunts and spittle of "the rabble of Tamatave," he set sail late that afternoon for France and twenty years at hard labor.[122]

CHAPTER EIGHT

Politics, Chauvinism, and Civil Rights: Popular Opinion and the Waller Affair

The French at first believed that because of his color they could deal with Waller as they pleased. As one American businessman in Madagascar put it: "They thought he was a nigger, had no money, and that we white Americans, like Wetter and myself would not bother our heads about him."[1] The French were badly mistaken. Despite the fact that a Democratic administration was in office and America's ambassador to France was a former Confederate brigadier and Louisiana plantation-owner, Washington labored frantically to secure the ex-consul's release, even at one point threatening an open break with France unless the Quai d'Orsay met American demands.

In taking an aggressive stance in the Waller affair, the Cleveland administration was reacting to pressure from a variety of groups who saw in the ex-consul's predicament a chance to advance their own interests. Of these, the most vocal was the black press. Whether imperialists or pacifists, nationalists or internationalists, black observers of foreign affairs implicitly or explicitly judged diplomatic developments on the basis of their anticipated impact on the plight of the Negro American. In no case was this truer than in the attitudes of the black press toward Waller's imprisonment. Negro journalists, perhaps at their most influential in the 1890s, saw in the incident an opportunity not only to help a fellow black in trouble but also a chance to draw attention to the plight of all Afro-Americans and to blunt the drive then being mounted by John T.

143

Morgan, Benjamin Tillman, and other outspoken racists to exclude the Negro from the mainstream of American life.

The Waller affair attracted the attention of many Negro editors in the United States simply because they were proud of the fact that an American Negro had become the center of a dispute between two great nations.[2] The press repeatedly contended that the affair would rank in history with the other major diplomatic incidents of the nineteenth century. George Knox of the *Indianapolis Freeman* put Waller on a level with no less a figure than "that greatest of blacks, Toussaint l'Ouverture."[3] Shortly before Waller's arrest in March, 1895, the *American Citizen* declared that the ex-consul had "become something of a potentate and bids fair to rival the triumphs of Cecil Rhodes."[4]

The Waller affair was particularly tempting editorial fare for those who sought to draw America's attention to the condition of the domestic black community by underscoring the nation's tradition of anticolonialism and urging Washington to aid exploited, nonwhite peoples overseas. In analyzing the Cuban revolution, the Hawaiian imbroglio, and the Venezuelan boundary dispute, a large number of editors first assumed a community of racial identity with the native population and then voiced vigorous support for their efforts to fend off white colonialism. Emphasizing the fact that "97 percent of the Venezuelan population was Mulattoe, Indian, and Negro," the *St. Louis American Eagle* called upon the Cleveland administration in January, 1896, to do everything within its power to protect that embattled republic from British imperialism.[5] The *Broad Ax* of Salt Lake City not only urged Washington to spread the mantle of the Monroe Doctrine around the Venezuelans but called upon the nation to lend all possible aid to Cuba, another black society fighting against colonialism and racism. Cuba, it asserted, "is engaged in a struggle today of republicanism and democracy against monarchy and plutocracy. . . . In many respects it is a similar struggle to our own Revolution, to escape the grinding heel of despotic power."[6] The Malagasies, no less than the Cubans or Venezuelans, elicited widespread sympathy among American Negroes. The *Cleveland Gazette*, which frequently ran front-page portraits of the Hova queen, Ranavalona III, praised Madagascar as a "progressive, Christian nation," and in March, 1895, denounced the French assault on Madagascar as an uncivilized attack on a powerless nation of liberty-loving people.[7] Waller's arrest provided black spokesmen with a double irony: John Waller, despite the racism he had encountered in his native land, was risking his life to bring the blessings of liberty and democracy to the beleaguered Hovas; he was a black man taking up the white man's burden. Proclaimed the *Parsons*

Weekly Blade: "The French have no more right in Madagascar than a burglar has in a man's parlor. . . . They are attempting to force on the people of the island a protectorate that is of all things the most hateful and detestable. . . . he [Waller] is paying heavily for his sympathy with an outraged people."[8]

The same longing for social justice that caused many blacks to identify with nonwhite societies threatened by European imperialism also prompted them to rally around the flag whenever America faced an external threat. Just as Negroes had rallied during the American Revolution, the War of 1812, and the Civil War, a large segment of the black community rushed to defend the nation's prerogatives during the crises of the 1890s, hoping that the diplomatic incident in question, by unifying the nation and providing an opportunity for black Americans to prove their patriotism, would facilitate the drive for full citizenship.[9] In the Waller affair, the black press perceived a twofold opportunity to turn American chauvinism to their advantage. First, by striking an aggressive pose toward France, blacks believed they could win the respect of the increasingly jingoistic white majority. In an outburst that would have done the *New York World* justice, the *Parsons Weekly Blade* exclaimed: "If war must come, let both England and France let loose their dogs of war at the same time and they will see how quick we can slap them into the long sleep which has no ending."[10] Second, Negro spokesmen, by stressing Waller's American citizenship, sought to establish him as a symbol of the national sovereignty. In that way they might induce the white power structure to view all black Americans as full-fledged citizens deserving equal protection under the law. "Mr. Waller," the *Cleveland Gazette* averred, "is the exponent of our national existence, and the man outraged in his rights is as grave a matter as though the head of a nation had been arrested and imprisoned."[11] Declaring that Waller was "an American citizen—period," the *Kansas City Journal* called for "the taking of whatever steps are demanded to preserve the dignity of the American name, to avenge this insult to American honor, and to right the wrong that has been done."[12]

A number of editors, particularly those who advocated racial self-help and solidarity, saw in the New Empire an unparalleled opportunity for blacks to make their personal fortune and in the process augment the power and influence of black America as a whole. For these men Waller was a model and, more, a harbinger of things to come. H. C. Smith of the *Cleveland Gazette*, who campaigned tirelessly in behalf of Waller's release, lauded the Kansan as "the first man who has identified himself with a large industrial interest outside the country," and he predicted that "with better education and larger opportunities offered in America, the Afro-American will find employment for his increasing wealth in foreign enterprises."[13] Naturally, these black disciples of economic expansion were extremely desirous that the State Department show the same willingness to protect black entrepreneurs and their property as they had in looking after white businessmen and their interests overseas. Declaring that Waller's imprisonment was the work of French trading companies "bent on thwarting a rival entrepreneur," John Mitchell of the *Richmond Planet* demanded that Washington protect the ex-consul just as it would any other American businessman.[14]

In diplomatic incidents involving black Americans, whether in an official or private capacity, the black press invariably viewed the posture of the federal government as a measure of the nation's willingness to grant full and equal citizenship to the Negro American. This tendency to test the system and, when it failed, to confront the white power structure with evidence of its ingrained racism found an ample outlet in the Waller affair. Less than two weeks after Waller's imprisonment, T. McCants Stewart, an influential black lawyer, editor, and politician, notified the administration that he and his brethren were watching carefully: "Afro-Americans throughout the country feel that the cause of American citizenship appeals through this case to our Government as well as to patriotic Americans everywhere, and we feel sure that this Government will allow no harm to be done to Mr. Waller, but will make clear that an American citizen is as safe to do business abroad as he is under the capitol at Washington."[15] Monroe Dorsey of the *Parsons Weekly Blade* also saw the incident as a test of the white power structure's position toward full citizenship for blacks. According to this militant editor, the lines were clearly drawn. Waller was a black American citizen who had been wronged by another nation. Given the State Department's past efforts to protect United States nationals in similar straits, his failure to obtain Waller's release and indemnification would constitute irrefutable proof that blacks could never expect equal justice under American law.[16]

As the months passed, with no apparent progress in the Franco-American negotiations, the black press proclaimed that Waller had become another casualty of the ever-present American caste system. Blacks could expect no more protection abroad than they received at home. In April, 1895, George L. Knox's *Indianapolis Freeman* concluded bitterly, "The Greatest Republic on earth in the presence of a government of the first class, especially if the rights of a black American citizen abroad are to be looked into, is also the greatest flunky among the governments of the earth, and never deserved one drop of the sea of blood that has been shed by the Negro in her defense."[17] In September W. Calvin Chase, the outspoken editor of the *Washington Bee*, stated flatly: "Had Mr. Waller been a white man the matter with France would have been settled long ago."[18] The *Cleveland World* was willing to take the case against the American color line one step further. It argued that institutionalized racism was responsible not only for the State Department's mishandling of the affair but for Waller's arrest as well: "The French government has kept close watch upon the feeble and paltry behavior of this government toward the Americans in Hawaii and naturally concluded that if it would overlook the claims of those united in the dominant white population of this country, the wrongs inflicted upon the representative of the colored race—the consul to Madagascar—would be even more exposed to slights and neglect."[19]

The Cleveland administration proved remarkably sensitive to black opinion in the Waller affair because the president had been laboring since the beginning of his second term to attract as many Negro votes as possible.[20] Blacks were by the late 1880s becoming increasingly dissatisfied with the party of Lincoln. "There is a new generation of people now ready to become a factor in politics," declared the *Marquette Monitor* in 1888. "It is a generation of educated, intelligent colored American citizens, with all the ambition and political instinct peculiar to Americans. . . . They prefer to remain loyal to the party that gave their fathers freedom but they justly expect a fair recognition for their continued allegiance to the party."[21] Shortly after Cleveland's first inauguration, W. Calvin Chase urged southern Negroes to be independent in the body politic.[22] In 1890 T. Thomas Fortune of the *New York Age* warned that if the Republicans did not produce for the Negro there would be no support for them at the polls. Part of the problem, he declared, was that the party had fallen into the hands of "autocrats and bloated corporationists."[23]

By 1895 Cleveland, through his willingness to appoint black officeholders, had established a reputation for fairness within the black community. According to H. C. C. Astwood and George Downing, both active black Democrats, Cleveland's decision to appoint Negroes to the posts of minister to Haiti, minister to Liberia, recorder of deeds, and consul at Santo Domingo, as well as a number of lesser posts, had swelled the ranks of Afro-American independents and Democrats, and had badly frightened black Republicans. This, plus growing black dissatisfaction with the G.O.P. and the subtle efforts of Cleveland's political organizers, resulted in the creation of a number of black Democratic organizations in the late eighties and early nineties which worked assiduously in behalf of Cleveland's 1892 campaign. Among the best known were the National Colored Tariff Reform Association organized in Washington, D.C., in March, 1890, the Young Afro-American Democrats established in New York in 1891, and the John M. Palmer Democratic Club, founded by Jerome Riley in September, 1891. According to C. H. J. Taylor of Kansas, as of 1894, there were black Democratic organizations in seventeen states. By far the most important of these was the Negro National Democratic League, which included among its leaders H. C. C. Astwood of Louisiana, Peter H. Clark of Chicago, J. Milton Turner of Missouri, and Taylor.[24]

Although Cleveland named even more blacks to appointive office during his second term than he had during the first, his inability to obtain Senate approval for many of them threatened the president's hard-earned gains among black voters. Southern Democratic senators, led by the Louisiana delegation, rejected Cleveland's Negro nominees for diplomatic posts in Haiti, Madagascar, Santo Domingo, and Sierra Leone, and for the offices of register of the Land Office and fourth auditor, forcing him to name whites to these positions. Astwood, whose appointment as consul to Calais was also rejected by the Senate, wrote Cleveland on April 15, 1896: "I must deplore the meagre representation given to us from an administration that promised such large possibilities for us. . . . The Negro vote which was practically divided is becomeing consolidated against the Democratic Party." Blacks held the political balance of power in many of the largest states, he warned, and time was running out.[25] Undoubtedly, the mounting rebellion among black Democrats worked to Waller's advantage by forcing Cleveland and Olney to take as aggressive a position as possible.

As president of the Negro National Democratic League, recorder of deeds, and one of the few black Cleveland appointees to survive the Senate gauntlet, C. H. J. Taylor was in an ideal position to advise the president on how best to improve his standing among black voters. By the fall of 1895 he was warning the White House that if it did not act vigorously in the Waller matter everything the administration had done in the past to ease the Afro-American's suspicions of the Democratic party would have been for nothing.[26]

Black opinion was unusually important to the decision-making process within the administration as it related to the Waller affair because for once there was a community rather than a conflict of interest between the black and white press. To be sure, white Americans did not see in the Waller affair an opportunity to elevate the status of the Afro-

American; they were, however, willing for a variety of reasons to overlook the fact that Waller was black. Among the most important of these was the widespread popular conviction that America had a mission in world affairs to defend the weaker races against European colonialism and to ensure that all peoples had the opportunity to emulate the American example.

Indeed, sympathy for the Malagasies and a tendency to see Waller as their protector were no less widespread among the whites than among blacks. "It is a thousand pities that so brave and patriotic a nation as the Malagasy should be despoiled of its rights and its country as it surely will be by the French," editorialized the *Chicago Tribune* in June, 1895.[27] The *New York Times* was more outspoken. When the Hova capital fell to the French in October, 1895, the *Times* proclaimed, "A more flagrant, unjustified, and outrageous project of national robbery and spoliation is not recorded in history."[28] Many believed that the Hovas, like the Cubans, were innately liberty-loving, that they were deliberately seeking to duplicate America's experience, and that it was the government's duty to come to their rescue. An aged New Englander named Charles Booth wrote to the State Department in late April urging immediate action to secure Waller's release and forestall French annexation of Madagascar: "I have witnessed the wonderful growth of our country," he declared, "and in my day we have passed into the most influential people in the world . . . . I cannot but think we have a right and duty to discharge toward peoples struggling to follow our example."[29] The Reverend James M. Whiton fully agreed. Writing in *Outlook* in September, 1895, he called on Washington to put an end to the "unrighteous war of conquest" then raging in Madagascar. "American interests," he advised his readers, "are those of an unprejudiced sympathy with the oppressed and wronged the world over."[30] Whiton, Booth, and the editorial pages of newspapers as diverse as the *New York Herald-Tribune, New York Sun, New Orleans Times-Picayune, Chicago Tribune,* and *New York Times* had no problem in viewing Waller, despite his color, as a legitimate agent of American civilization. Had he not challenged French hegemony in the *exequatur* matter, and was not his concession the occasion for French invasion? In fact, those who believed in America's mission abroad were willing not only to grant Waller full citizenship but to convert him into a symbol of the national sovereignty.[31] There is no indication, however, that as a result they became willing to accord Waller's black brethren in the United States those rights guaranteed to all citizens in the Declaration of Independence and the Constitution.

Undoubtedly, the most important factor behind white concern for Waller was the public's determination to see that the "rights" of American citizens living abroad were respected. For a number of reasons, the nation's feeling of inadequacy and desire for respect were reaching a peak in 1895.[32] Because of America's inferiority complex in regard to Europe, the question of the protection of individual rights often proved more compelling than did European violation of the Monroe Doctrine and acquisition of foreign territory. Whether imperialists or antiimperialists, virtually all Americans could agree that the nation must protect the life and property of its citizens in foreign lands. It was a matter of honor. "If they [the French] persist in refusing to accord to a citizen of our Government that protection, which they themselves are so careful in exacting," wrote W. A. Tetrick to Secretary of State Richard Olney in behalf of the 2,200 residents of Kingman, Kansas, "we demand that it be secured if it takes every Gun-boat, Gatling gun, torpedo, and sword in this country to do it . . . . The Honorable Mr. Waller is an American Citizen, and as such is entitled to the protection of our flag."[33] Pointing up the importance of nationalism in shaping white attitudes on the Waller affair was the fact that to American whites the question of Waller's guilt or innocence was less important than France's refusal to meet the State Department's demands to see the evidence by which the ex-consul had been convicted. When France declined to allow American diplomats to examine the Waller letters, the *Memphis Commercial-Appeal* wrote: "Whether or not Waller did actually conspire against the French is one thing, but the practical refusal of the French to permit . . . United States Government to inspect the record is quite another. . . . the American people cannot endure the idea that their ministers at foreign capitals must kneel and beg that they may obtain the most ordinary consideration."[34] Whitelaw Reid's *New York Tribune* was convinced that America's lack of vigor in the Waller case was a sure sign of moral decay. "Americanism meant something grand with 3,000,000 honest hearts back of it," said the paper in an editorial; "with 70,000,000 it appears to be a synonym for sycophancy and National cowardice."[35]

There was more than simple nationalism or sympathy for a downtrodden people in the widespread show of support for Waller among whites. Quite a number viewed the Kansan as a legitimate entrepreneur and, more importantly, as a symbol of the "open door" in east Africa. Those preoccupied with United States economic expansion were well aware that, under the United States–Malagasy treaties of 1867 and 1881, the right of American citizens to apply for and receive concessions had been clearly stated.[36] Convinced that the French had arrested and imprisoned Waller at the behest of French concessionaires jealous of the Kansan's good fortune, white exponents of commercial empire were fearful that, if the United States gave in, American investors and traders would be gradually squeezed out of foreign markets around the world. After extolling the economic potential of Madagascar, the *Chicago Tribune* observed in March, 1895, that "the right of the Hovas to make concessions of this kind [Wallerland] has never before been questioned and as the French protectorate over Madagascar is limited to the regulation of foreign intercourse, it will . . . be the duty of Secretary [of State Walter] Gresham to make a vigorous protest."[37] Americans interested in the Malagasy rubber trade wrote to the State Department urging that it take whatever measures were necessary to preserve Waller's civil and property rights.[38] As time wore on, some observers displayed greater concern over the fate of Waller's concession than over his imprisonment. By late August the *New York Tribune*—Whitelaw Reid was an aggressive proponent of United States economic penetration of underdeveloped areas—was insisting that the Cleveland administration protect Waller and his concession at all costs.[39] If all else failed, the State Department could invoke sanctity of contract.[40]

Finally, Grover Cleveland's political enemies, who were legion by 1895, saw in the Waller affair another chance to attack the president. Despite the efforts of C. H. J. Taylor and other black Democrats, a large majority of black citizens in the 1890s were convinced that the Republican party still offered the best hope for implementing the pledges made to the freedmen during the Civil War and Reconstruction. A number of editors saw in the Waller incident an opportunity to damage the Democrats in general and the Cleveland administration in particular. The *Cleveland Gazette* wasted no time in utilizing the State Department's inability to secure the Kansan's release to make unflattering comparisons: "When there was a misunderstanding between the United States and Chile, Mr. [James G.] Blaine demanded that our terms be met within the next twenty-four hours, but this Democratic administration has been juggling with Mr. Waller's case for over a year and are no nearer a settlement now than when it was beginning . . . . Mr. Cleveland could send troops to Chicago to protect the interests of George B. Pullman, but he is too busy catching fish and rocking babies to give this matter the attention it deserves."[41] The staunchly Republican *Leavenworth Herald* asserted that "the actions of the Cleveland administration in regards to the Monroe Doctrine, the firing upon American ships, the imprisonment of American citizens, are enough to make every citizen of this republic, regardless of politics, blush with shame."[42] Edward Wetter proved an especially tempting target for black Republicans. "Georgia Democrats as a rule," observed Robert Porter of the *Cleveland World*, "are apter at tearing down the flag as [William] Blount did at Honolulu than unfurling it to the breeze when the rights of American citizens are in danger."[43]

White Republicans eagerly joined in this partisan tirade. The Waller case was an ideal issue because it allowed Republican spokesmen to attack the Democrats on two of their most vulnerable points: a passive foreign policy, and proscription of the Negro's civil rights.[44] Only a week after Waller's arrest, Reid's *New York Tribune* charged the administration with gross neglect and attributed its apathy to racism: "Aversion to act in this case is due to the fact that Waller, although an ex-Consul of the United States, is only a Negro."[45] According to the highly partisan Republican *Kansas City Journal*, cowardice rather than Negrophobia was the guiding force behind Cleveland's "inactivity": "This is the crowning act of an Administration which has been distinguished for its abject submission to foreign insult . . . . Every American ought to blush for shame at the spectacle."[46]

By the summer of 1895 Americans representing various segments of public opinion saw in Waller's predicament an opportunity for advancing their respective interests. Blacks, reflecting a persistent inclination to judge foreign policy in terms of its implications for Afro-Americans, viewed the incident as a means of forcing the white majority to recognize the inconsistency between the nation's treatment of its black and white citizens. Waller was touted as a symbol of national sovereignty and American capitalism who just happened to be black. As a Negro Republican, he was portrayed as the victim of a white Democratic administration that sacrificed national honor and interest on the altar of racism. In these ways, it was hoped, Waller's predicament could be used to combat the rising tide of violence and discrimination threatening black Americans at home.

Support for the ex-consul was not limited to Negroes. White nationalists saw in the incident a chance to force the State Department to take a more active role in world affairs, to assert the nation's prerogatives as a great power. In addition, commercial expansionists, fearful that the markets of the world were being closed to the United States just as American businessmen were poised to take advantage of them, demanded that Washington protect Waller and his concession in order that all nations might understand that the United States intended to keep the door open. And white Republicans utilized the Waller case to attack the Democrats on their two most vulnerable points—passivity in the international arena, and racism in the domestic sphere.

CHAPTER NINE

A Matter of Expediency

The eleven day passage from Madagascar through the Suez Canal to France left a lasting impression on John Waller. Chained in the hold of the *Dejeune*, he was given two blankets on which to sleep and two meals a day consisting of boiled rice and water. The iron bar securing his manacles was located directly below the main hatch, which was kept open throughout the trip. During its first night out, the *Dejeune* encountered a tropical storm and Waller was soaked to the skin. Awaking the next morning with chills and fever, he grew increasingly ill during the remainder of the voyage. While the French vessel made its way through the Suez, members of the crew twice awakened the ex-consul, threatening to murder him. Finally, mercifully, the ship arrived at Marseilles, and Waller was transferred to the French military prison there.[1]

Initially, Waller was utterly demoralized over his arrest and imprisonment. So swiftly had he been tried and convicted that he did not even have time to make arrangements for the return of his family to America. There appeared little chance that he could secure his freedom, and none at all that he could salvage his dream of commercial empire. With the passage of time, however, and the knowledge that a variety of groups, black and white, Democratic and Republican, were agitating in his behalf, Waller began to see his misfortune as a potential blessing. Because his imprisonment was causing a furor in the American press, and in the process focusing public attention on the Franco-Malagasy conflict, the incident might ultimately lead Washington to interpose its authority between France and the Hovas. In turn, Hova independence would mean the survival of Wallerland. It was also possible that in the course of securing his freedom the State Department would be able to force the French to pay a large indemnity as well. Unfortunately, the only thing the black Kansan salvaged from his ten-month stay in the Maison Clairvaux, his French prison, was a degree of national and international notoriety.

It was not that the Cleveland administration was unwilling to defend Waller's rights. Public outrage, directed first against France and then at the government's handling of the case, coupled with Cleveland's continuing attempt to build a following among black Americans, and Secretary of State Olney's jingoism, ensured that the State Department would exert considerable effort in Waller's behalf.[2] The ex-consul's hopes were disappointed because France was determined to use the "Waller affair," as it came to be called, to end American influence in Madagascar. After overcoming its surprise at the uproar in the United States created by Waller's imprisonment, the Quai d'Orsay decided to release Waller only in return for American acquiescence in the French protectorate over Madagascar. The State Department attempted to keep America's position in east Africa and the question of the validity of the Wallerland concession separate from the issue of Waller's release, but to no avail. France refused to discuss release of the black entrepreneur, or even to allow American representatives to examine the evidence in his trial, until French dominance in Madagascar was uncontested.

By March 25, American newspapers were full of reports concerning the ex-consul's arrest and imprisonment. The *New York Times, New York Tribune, Chicago Tribune,* and a number of other white journals, as well as virtually every black paper, ran front-page stories on the Waller incident. Even the *Washington Post,* renowned for its Negrophobia, was up in arms. "From all that can be learned to the contrary," declared the *Post,* "Waller has quite as valid a title to every acre of ground that had been granted him as any Frenchman in Madagascar, and deserves the immediate intercession of the American government."[3]

Public notice given to Waller's situation, coming as it did in the midst of criticism over Cleveland's handling of the Hawaiian issue and the Cuban situation, made it imperative that the administration take a stand as quickly as possible. The man who was to preside over the Waller case from March to May was Secretary of State Walter Q. Gresham. Although he was fully aware of the political ramifications, Gresham's view of the Waller affair was dominated by a desire to maintain America's economic position in Madagascar. Civil War hero, distinguished lawyer, and former Republican, Gresham was, according to historian Walter LaFeber, "the purest example of economic expansionist."[4] Gresham blamed the economic depression following the Panic of 1893, and the violent strikes and other manifestations of social unrest that accompanied it, on the inability of the domestic market to absorb the goods produced by America's burgeoning industrial plant.[5] America's problems would be solved, he declared on several occasions, if overseas markets could be found to absorb the nation's industrial surplus.[6] The secretary assumed from the very beginning that not only Waller's arrest but the French invasion of Madagascar was due to the potentially lucrative concession granted to the ex-consul by the Hova monarchy. Thus, in his dispatches to James B. Eustis, the United States minister to France, Gresham repeatedly emphasized the fact that Waller was a native American citizen and an ex-consul who had remained in Madagascar "with a view to establishing relations of trade between that country and the United States."[7] As an economic emissary of the nation, he should and would be fully protected in his rights.

Washington could not, of course, base its demand for Waller's release on public outrage or on the open door. As in the past, American policy-makers couched their demands for the protection of American rights in terms of international law. From the beginning the State Department took the position that in arresting and imprisoning Waller France had clearly exceeded its authority under international law and existing treaties. Washington argued that in the first place the ex-consul had been tried in the wrong court. In a March 24 press conference, State Department officials pointed out that Franco-American treaties then in effect provided that a citizen of the United States arrested for complicity in insurrection would be tried by a civil court unless captured with arms in hand. As everyone knew, Waller had not been apprehended under these conditions. The Cleveland administration insisted, secondly, that Waller's arrest and imprisonment had violated the 1881 treaty between the United States and Madagascar. Because the treaty clearly granted the United States rights of extraterritoriality in Madagascar, Waller could only be tried for his alleged offenses against France by a mixed court, with the United States consul presiding.[8] In pursuing this line, the Cleveland administration clearly linked Waller with America's stake in the island. For if the State Department brought up the point concerning extraterritoriality and then conceded France's right to try Waller, it would at the same time recognize French hegemony in Madagascar. The State Department was no more willing to do this in the spring of 1895 than it had been in 1891. American officials could not at this point anticipate that the French Foreign Office would be able to exploit the popular clamor in America for Waller's release and indemnification to compel the Cleveland administration to acquiesce in French annexation of Madagascar.

Unfortunately for the United States and Waller, the incident was no less a *cause célèbre* in France than in the United States. One American diplomat remarked that the concession to the ex-consul and his challenge to French hegemony had created "more bitter feelings, more animosity in France than anything that has happened in five years."[9] On March 25 the semiofficial *Le Courier des Etats-Unis* applauded the "exemplary chastisement" applied to Waller and rejected American protests out of hand. The editor argued that if the United States had acquiesced in the French protectorate over Madagascar Washington might have more cause for complaint. Since the United States was insisting on treating the Hovas as an independent people, then they must admit that a state of war did in fact exist between France and Madagascar and that Waller was subject to being tried as a spy. Either way, the Cleveland administration would have to recognize French hegemony to get him out of jail.[10] *Le Figaro* declared that Waller was not worth a Franco-American confrontation and then self-contradictorily threw down the gauntlet: "Formal complaints should come from France and not from America, which is entirely in the wrong."[11] *Estafette* was no less sure of the righteousness of the French position. "Our line of conduct is clearly marked out," declared this widely read Paris journal, "and we need pay no attention to idle complaints. . . . Indeed, Mr. Waller ought to have been immediately shot for his glaring treachery."[12]

Despite the bellicosity of the French press, Gresham decided to formally request permission to examine the charges, evidence, and sentence in the Waller case, and he so instructed Eustis on April 10. In so doing, the administration was obviously insisting that the United States and the United States alone had the right to judge the merits of the case. France's initial response was procrastination. Foreign Minister Gabriel Hanotaux assured Eustis that Waller had indeed conveyed vital military information to the Hovas and that he had been fairly tried and convicted. As soon as the pertinent papers arrived in Paris, all necessary information would be provided to the United States embassy.[13]

In the meantime, John Mercer Langston had made the transition from legal representative for Wallerland Enterprises to Waller's personal counsel. Langston already had considerable experience in representing American citizens who claimed to have been wronged by foreign governments. While minister to Haiti in 1883 the black Virginian had secured a $10,000 indemnity for Charles Morrell, an African Methodist Episcopal missionary assaulted by a band of natives. To help with the case Langston, on his own authority, hired the famed international lawyer and former abolitionist Crammond Kennedy.[14] During the next ten months Langston and Kennedy would serve Waller both as propagandists, at opportune times releasing sensational tidbits concerning the ex-consul's treatment, and as lawyers, pressing their client's claim that he had the right to trade with whomever he wished and travel wherever he wanted.[15]

On yet another front, Paul Bray, Waller's stepson and partner in the Wallerland venture, was working frantically to elude the French authorities, keep the concession afloat, and get his stepfather out of jail. Although the French court-martial had ordered Bray exiled when it convicted Waller, he had been allowed to stay on in Madagascar. Knowing that Bray had testified at the trial and had been present throughout the proceedings, the resident general hoped to persuade him to sign a statement to the effect that the court-martial had been conducted in a proper manner and that the accused had been treated fairly. After Bray repeatedly refused to cooperate, the French on April 20 ejected him from Madagascar. From Tamatave he traveled to London where he attempted to whip up financial support for Wallerland and political support for the Malagasies. He soon ran out of money, however, and was forced to journey to Paris and appeal at the embassy for the funds necessary to pay for his return to the United States. Eustis, at Gresham's direction, agreed, but only on the condition that Bray report immediately to the State Department and tell the full story of the Waller affair. Bray readily consented, and on May 9, 1895, he departed for America aboard the Dutch steamer *Veendam*. As soon as the vessel was sighted off Fire Island some ten days later, the Coast Guard cutter *Hudson*, with a State Department official aboard, was dispatched to remove him. Later in the week, in company with Langston and Kennedy, Bray called at the department and described how he and Waller had suffered at the hands of French imperialism. Every official he encountered, from Eustis to Acting Secretary of State Edwin F. Uhl, warned him to speak to no one. Further public pressure would only hamper the department's efforts to secure Waller's release.[16]

During Bray's sojourn in Europe, the Cleveland administration had not been idle. In mid-May Washington decided that the Waller case was of sufficient importance to warrant resorting to the time-honored tactic of showing the flag. Consequently, on May 15, the Navy Department ordered Commodore Thomas Perry of the U.S.S. *Castine*, then at Mozambique, to call at Tamatave and investigate the Waller affair. The navy accepted the Waller assignment enthusiastically because it had for a number of years been in the forefront of those arguing in favor of an active policy in Madagascar. America's admirals had long been cognizant of the fact that there were at least two sites for coaling stations on the east African island, possession of which by the United States would allow the navy and merchant marine to operate freely in the Indian Ocean. Naval officials were also mindful of the economic possibilities in Madagascar. Commander Purcell Harrington, who had visited Tamatave in September, 1885, and refused to salute the French flag, insisted that America must strengthen its economic ties with the island. Predicting that Madagascar would emerge as "one of the great nations of the world," he argued that it was manifestly in America's interest to help the Hovas retain their independence.[17] The commander of the *Castine* fully shared this view. Although he had received no specific instructions, Perry advised Washington that he did not intend to salute the French flag. To do so would be to recognize French dominance in the island, something he was sure his country would not approve. After all, the United States–Malagasy Treaty was still in effect, and "the sincerity of a treaty with the weak is equal to that of a treaty with the strong."[18]

The *Castine*'s visit infuriated the French both in Tamatave and in Paris. They correctly interpreted the presence of the gunboat as a peremptory demand for Waller's release and a direct challenge to French authority in the island. Indeed, the *Castine*'s mission led to an incident that, although not directly related to the Waller case, served to further strain Franco-American relations. As was the custom, Consul Wetter boarded the *Castine* soon after its arrival and paid his respects to Commodore Perry. When Wetter attempted to return to shore, he was stopped by a party of French soldiers, verbally abused, and arrested. A potentially dangerous situation was averted when the port commander hurriedly ordered Wetter's release and compelled the offending officer to apologize. The *Castine* incident, as it came to be called by the American press, clearly indicated that the Waller affair and the Franco-American confrontation over Madagascar, with which it had become identified, had reached a dangerous state.[19]

At the height of the excitement surrounding the *Castine*'s visit to Tamatave, Walter Gresham died. His successor as secretary of state was the belligerent, ambitious Richard Olney. Cleveland, smarting over charges that he was conducting a spineless foreign policy, had selected Olney in hopes he would establish a reputation for vigor and courage in protecting America's interests. The new secretary, like the old, was an outspoken exponent of commercial empire. Moreover, he was determined that the world should accord the United States the great power status he believed it deserved.[20] As a result, during his term in office Olney proved to be a relentless advocate of those Americans abroad whose rights had been violated by a foreign power. Waller was no exception.

Shortly after Olney's appointment, the Quai d'Orsay gave the first indication that it intended to use Waller's imprisonment, and the domestic pressure it was exerting on the Cleveland administration, to force Washington to recognize France's preeminent position in Madagascar. On May 31, Ambassador Eustis once again asked that all papers relating to the Waller affair be made available for the embassy's inspection. "The case of Mr. Waller has been much commented upon in the United States," he told Hanotaux, "and as it was specially recommended to me by my government . . . I shall feel obliged if a reply could reach me at an early date."[21] In the course of their interview, Hanotaux remarked that the French government would hold invalid all such concessions as the Hovas had made to Waller. Eustis declared that he was not at liberty to discuss the matter and insisted that the only issue in question was whether or not Waller, an American citizen, had been justly treated by the French authorities in Madagascar. Hanotaux did not answer, but the following day he presented the ambassador with copies of the charges and sentence in the Waller trial. The evidence was not provided; that, he advised Eustis, was still somewhere in east Africa. Three days later the Quai d'Orsay instructed French authorities in Madagascar to let it be known that henceforth all cases involving foreigners, even those in which American was contesting with American, were to be tried under French law and in French courts. Though the State Department continued to insist to France that there was no connection between America's political and economic position in Madagascar and the Waller trial, it was obvious that the Foreign Office had decided not to release the ex-consul until it had obtained satisfaction on "other matters." Time was on France's side, for with every passing day the demands from both blacks and whites for Waller's release grew more shrill.[22]

While Eustis was sparring with Hanotaux in Paris, news that Waller's health was deteriorating, coupled with reports that his destitute family was stranded somewhere in the Indian Ocean, increased pressure on the Cleveland administration to free Waller from prison and secure a generous indemnity from the French. When Waller was arrested in late March, his wife and four children were in Tananarive. It was imperative, Susan Waller believed, that the family make its escape before the French expeditionary force reached the Hova capital. The task appeared impossible until a former acquaintance of Waller's appeared and offered his services. Mrs. Waller's would-be rescuer was Ethelbert G. Woodford, a white, an American, an influential member of the Democratic party, and an international businessman who had long been interested in the numerous banking and rail opportunities in Madagascar. Woodford had first met Waller on a trip to the island in 1891. The two men became immediate friends and subsequently whiled away many an hour fantasizing about the profits to be reaped in Madagascar by enterprising concessionaires. Woodford had left later in the year but then returned to Tamatave in 1895 after Waller had been arrested. After doing all he could in Waller's behalf, Woodford journeyed to Tananarive in early April where he met the "destitue Mrs. Waller." Shortly thereafter Woodford booked passage for himself, Susan, Minnie, John, Jennie, and Helen on the *Pembroke Castle*, the last vessel to leave the island prior to the French takeover. The *Pembroke Castle* sailed from the northern port of Vatomandry, which was guarded by a huge sand bar. The "terrible surf" threatened to overturn the vessel, but it made it through. The Wallers, according to Woodford, bore the ordeal with singular courage. The *Pembroke Castle* arrived in Maritius on June 14. Woodford remained in Port Louis until July 12 when he departed for Europe, leaving the Wallers behind. At this point Mrs. Waller sent a request to the State Department through the United States consul for money to return to America. While waiting for a reply from the State Department, she wrote to her imprisoned husband describing her harrowing experiences. The letter was subsequently cabled over State Department lines to Washington and then to France. After recounting various episodes in which she had been harrassed by French colonists and soldiers, she expressed the hope that America would rescue the Waller family from the "cold and merciless" forces that had imprisoned her husband and left her in such an ignoble predicament.[23] Bray and Langston managed to obtain a copy, which they immediately turned over to the press. Her story, they believed, would touch the hearts of even the most hardened racists. The press was properly sympathetic. Upon hearing of Mrs. Waller's plight, George Knox of the *Freeman* announced that "as far as the case has gone . . . Uncle Sam has simply clinched his hold upon the reputation he has always had, viz., of being an overgrown booby and flunky in the presence of great power."[24]

Hard upon the heels of Mrs. Waller's pitiful story came news that the ex-consul was coughing his life away in a dank cell in the Maison Clairvaux. Actually, Waller was not harshly treated in prison. Following a three-week stay in the military prison at Marseilles, he was transferred to the Maison Centrale de Clairvaux near Nimes. Evidently he was given a private cell and kept separate from the other prisoners. Meals were simple but adequate, and he was allowed to exercise in the central courtyard two hours after dinner. Had he had the money, he could have purchased reading materials and extra food; but not until August, 1895, did his friends and family produce any funds. Indeed, prison officials refused to allow him any mail whatever until late summer, although thereafter he received letters and newspaper clippings almost daily from Susan, Paul Bray, and Laura Martin, Waller's sole surviving sibling, who was then living in Cedar Rapids.[25] The black Kansan did suffer intensely during his months of isolation because of his ignorance of the whereabouts and well-being of his family. For all he knew, until he was informed otherwise in August, Susan and the children were trapped in war-ravaged Madagascar. "I am almost crazy about my wife and the children from whom I have not received a line, or even a word since I was arrested. . . . If I know that they are still alive and safe from the accidents of war, then I could suffer . . . the burden of my most unjust and too hasty imprisonment," he wrote to his sister in early August.[26] Although not allowed to read his mail for the first six months of his imprisonment, by early summer Waller was regularly smuggling out several letters a week to friends in the United States. In early July one of these reached Senator J. H. Gallinger of New Hampshire. In it, Waller complained that he had had two severe attacks of "congestive chills."[27] Because the French insisted that he "furnish his own medical attendance," there was nothing he could do to arrest his physical deterioration. Waller clearly implied that death was inevitable if the United States did not come to his rescue. Gallinger sent a copy to the State Department on July 2 and, in conjunction with Senator Daniel Voorhees of Indiana, demanded that the State Department protect Waller. Shortly thereafter, Kansas congressman Charles Curtis informed the department that in response to reports of Waller's "grave illness" a mass meeting had been held in Topeka and that the assemblage had appointed a special committee consisting of ex-governor Thomas Osborne, Lieutenant Governor J. A. Troutman, and Albert M. Thomas to go to Washington for the purpose of inquiring into the status of the former consul.[28] Still later in the month, Governor Morrill of Kansas wrote a public letter to Grover Cleveland: "The people of our state feel that a great outrage has been perpetrated upon one of its citizens. . . . It is not a question of race or color; it is a question of American citizenship."[29] Significantly, the *New York Times* attributed Waller's "lamentable condition" only secondarily to French perfidy. The chief culprit was the cowardly Cleveland administration.[30]

News of the ex-consul's declining health alarmed the State Department far more than reports concerning Mrs. Waller's predicament. The family's situation was simple to remedy. Olney merely ordered Assistant Secretary Alvey Adee to authorize Consul Campbell to pay their way home immediately. Waller, however, could not be helped so easily. The Kansan's death in prison, American officials warned, would make a break in relations between France and the United States inevitable. By mid-July, negotiations regarding his release had reached an impasse. Hanotaux had told Eustis repeatedly that he could not furnish the American embassy with copies of the evidence because the material was still in Tamatave.[31] When on July 10 Wetter asked the French commandant for a transcript of the proceedings, complete with evidence, however, he was told that this would be impossible, as the whole record had been sent to France. "The time for tender treatment of the matter has gone by," fumed Adee.[32] After conferring with Olney in regard to the "provoking dilatoriness" of the French,[33] Adee cabled Eustis on July 31: "You will immediately and urgently represent to the Government of France that delay in furnishing official evidence and denial of access by you to Waller appears not only unjust and oppressive to the latter, but discourteous to this Government."[34]

The French, of course, had no intention of allowing embassy officials to examine the evidence in Waller's case so that they might determine if the ex-consul had been treated justly. To have done so would constitute an admission by the Quai d'Orsay that America's right of extraterritoriality was still in effect in Madagascar. Nor at this point could the Foreign Office discuss the possibility of Waller's release, even in return for a total United States pullout in Madagascar. The campaign against the Hovas was going very badly—eight to ten French soldiers were dying daily on the island, and by mid-summer expenditures had already matched those of the costly Siam adventure. As a result, the government of Alexandre Ribot was in danger of political extinction. With Waller identified in the French public's mind with both American expansionism and Hova resistance, acceptance of the Cleveland administration's demands would have been political suicide. On the other hand the Quai d'Orsay recognized that America was a strong and impetuous young republic. Had not the United States nearly gone to war over an issue as insignificant as partial control over the Samoan Islands? Consequently, Hanotaux decided to continue to procrastinate on turning over the evidence, but in hopes of placating American jingoes he did allow Waller mail and restricted visitation rights. On August 5 he informed Eustis that documents relating to the Waller case would possibly reach France by the end of the month. Meanwhile, the minister of the interior had "granted permission" for a visit to Waller by embassy officials.[35]

Ever since the beginning of the Waller incident, Langston, Kennedy, and Bray had refused to criticize the Cleveland administration's handling of the case and had frequently alluded to the sincerity with which all concerned were laboring in the ex-consul's behalf. The inability of American officials to budge the Quai d'Orsay, however, caused Waller's advocates to break the truce and launch an attack on the two most vulnerable officials involved—-Edward T. Wetter and James B. Eustis, both white southerners and known Negrophobes. On August 2 Kennedy wrote Olney that the whole incident could have been avoided if Wetter had provided Waller with proper counsel. Moreover, it had come to light during the attorney's examination of State Department records that Wetter had at one time had in his possession a complete copy of the trial transcript, including evidence, but had surrendered it to the French upon demand. Kennedy's charges were later leaked to the *New York Sun* and the *New York Tribune* where they were reported as undisputed fact. The *Tribune* remarked that one had simply to look at Wetter's dispatches, which continually referred to Waller as "that coon," to see that he was thoroughly imbued with the prejudices of Georgia Democrats.[36]

Eustis even more than Wetter came in for attack from Waller's supporters.[37] Bray had established contact with a number of papers, black and white, and was by July orchestrating a relentless attack on the ex-Confederate in Paris. On July 13 the *Cleveland Gazette*, whose editor, H. C. Smith, had been acquainted with Bray for a number of years, chastized Eustis for being "disgracefully slow" in the Waller case.[38] "It wouldn't be a bad idea," Smith remarked sarcastically, "to recall him and send an American as our rerpresentative to France."[39] The *Chicago Tribune* agreed. To have expected the ambassador to put forth a sincere effort in Waller's behalf was folly in view of the fact that "Eustis . . . is a Southern white Democrat and ex-consul Waller is a Northern black Republican." There was only one solution: "If Secretary Olney is the American he is reputed to be, he will instruct Mr. Ambassador Eustis to attend to his duty. . . . Failing that, the President should remove him."[40]

Washington was not so sure that Bray and his journalistic allies did not have a point. As early as August 5, Olney had instructed Adee to prod Eustis for his slowness and reticence in dealing with the case. By August 17 the department had still not received a reply in regard to Adee's instruction of July 31. With the newspapers proclaiming that Waller was "dying of consumption," and with editors all over the country attacking the Cleveland administration as the most cowardly in the history of the nation, Olney ordered Adee to track down Eustis and find out what had been delaying his response.[41] The ambassador finally reported on the twenty-third. He had for the past two weeks been vacationing in the French countryside, he wrote, because his health had "completely given out." Olney and Adee were something less than sympathetic: "The obvious urgency and importance of the instruction cabled you on the 31st ultimo," Adee declared, "warranted the Department in looking for immediate telegraphic report of your action. . . . Your reticence and tardiness is much regretted."[42] Adee let Eustis know in no uncertain terms that the president was considering recalling him. Not even the news, received in Washington on the twenty-third, that the ambassador had obtained permission for members of the embassy staff to visit Waller was sufficient to placate his superiors. That Grover Cleveland would censure Eustis, a former United States senator and an important figure in the Democratic party, for his inattentiveness to a case involving a black Republican ex-consul was somewhat remarkable. The reprimand was in part deserved, but it was also a response to, and an indication of, the intense pressure on Cleveland and Olney.[43] "No other civilized nation would allow one of its people to be treated as Mr. Waller has been," declared the *Chicago Tribune* the day after the Eustis-Adee exchange. "The plea of ordinary justice and humanity to an individual, if not the considerations of national respect and honor, is of sufficient seriousness to induce Mr. Cleveland to omit fishing for a few days and Mr. Olney to abandon the fatiguing pleasures of tennis, and the two to put their heads together to see what can be done."[44]

After an initial press conference in March, the administration had remained fairly closemouthed about its handling of the Waller matter. But Cleveland and Olney agreed during the last week in August that the public temper required a statement. Accordingly, Adee held a press conference on the twenty-second and went over the government's handling of the matter from beginning to end. "The President and Secretary Olney are now thoroughly satisfied that Waller's military trial was not conducted in a proper manner," the assistant secretary reported, "and that his conviction of the crime of treason was based on the flimsiest evidence." The department, he said, could long since have obtained Waller's release, but it did not want to relinquish his rights in Madagascar, nor his claim to indemnity, which could go as high as a million dollars. The United States would hold to the view that it had every right to examine the evidence by which the ex-consul was convicted and to judge the case on its merits. Adee assured reporters that Eustis would make a "peremptory demand" for Waller's release and a satisfactory indemnity, and would push for the creation of a commission to determine Waller's rights in Madagascar.[45] In the wake of Adee's press conference, a number of Democratic sheets praised the administration's "forthright stand." Declaring France's treatment of Waller a "national disgrace," the *New Orleans Times-Picayune* was of the opinion that if Olney continued to stand up for American rights abroad as he had in the ex-consul's case, "he will become the most popular man in the country."[46] Republican papers, particularly those owned by blacks, remained skeptical. "If France had been this insolent to England or any other respectable nation," editorialized the *Omaha Enterprise*, "war preparations would have speedily brought her to her senses."[47]

Meanwhile, Langston and Kennedy, who had been allowed by the State Department to see all diplomatic correspondence relating to the incident, had prepared their case against France. They would maintain that the United States–Malagasy treaties of 1867 and 1881 had repeatedly recognized the sovereignty of the Hova queen and that Waller was bound to respect those treaties while residing in Madagascar. The French protectorate had never been acknowledged either by the Hovas or the United States, and yet Waller's trial had been justified under this pretended protectorate. In addition, France's efforts to compel the Hovas to cancel the Wallerland concession constituted gross interference in United States–Malagasy relations. Finally, and most importantly, Waller's trial constituted "a violation of the civil rights and liberties of an American citizen as cannot safely or honorably be tolerated by the United States Government."[48] Kennedy, who was primarily responsible for developing the arguments in Waller's behalf, was certain that under international law Washington had a right to inspect the evidence in the trial. He and Langston did not fail to point out that the United States had granted similar requests made by the French government in connection with the arbitrary arrest of French citizens during the Civil War. Precedent indicated, moreover, that failure within a reasonable time to produce a copy of the evidence in such cases could be considered as proof positive that an injustice had been done. To the administration's dismay, Kennedy chose to outline his case to the department not by confidential communique but by way of an interview with the *New York Sun*, a copy of which Kennedy sent to Adee on September 6.[49]

Olney and Adee were restrained from pressing too hard, for fear that if they humiliated the Ribot government it would fall. Eustis had repeatedly warned that if the present government lost its majority in the Chamber of Deputies "the military sentiment so strong in France with regard to the Waller case" would ensure that the Ribot regime would give way to a ministry even more difficult to deal with. Thus, the State Department contented itself with badgering the Quai d'Orsay for a specific time when the evidence would be made available.[50]

In the meantime, the administration believed that the French government's decision to allow members of the United States embassy to visit Waller could be used to stem the tide of public criticism in the United States. As it turned out, however, access proved much more of a liability than an asset, for, in a deposition which he subsequently gave to the counselor of the American embassy, Waller related in lurid detail how he was treated aboard the *Dejeune* during his trip from Tamatave to Marseilles. The State Department realized the potential political impact of Waller's story in the United States and went to great pain to suppress it. On August 30 Eustis wrote to Olney that he and Assistant Secretary Edwin Uhl, a Virginian and close friend of Eustis, had decided not to mention Waller's "outrageous treatment" except in a confidential communique, lest the revelations provide advantage to the administration's political enemies in Congress and exacerbate the war then raging between the American and French press.[51] Despite the State Department's best efforts, American papers had by September 9 obtained copies of the ex-consul's description of his version of the middle passage. News that Waller had been "chained to the deck by his arms and legs . . . and kept in that position for eleven days and exposed to gross indignities" produced a fresh round of outraged editorials.[52]

While the American press was fuming and fretting over Waller's treatment at the hands of the French, in Madagascar the Franco-Hova conflict was fast approaching a conclusion. On October 1 the French resident general compelled Queen Ranavalona to sign a treaty recognizing French hegemony in the island. In this "agreement" the Hovas recognized France as their sole representative in all external matters. All foreigners in Madagascar were to deal with the native regime through the resident only. Most importantly, at least from Waller's point of view, the French explicitly repudiated all debts or concessions contracted prior to the signing of the treaty. Seven days later Tananarive fell to the French, and shortly thereafter formal resistance ceased, though France was forced to deal with intermittent guerilla activity for years to come. Impending victory in Madagascar persuaded the Ribot government that it was now politically feasible to at least discuss Waller's release with the United States. On October 5 Hanotaux notified Eustis that at long last the record of the Waller trial had arrived in Paris and was being studied by the cabinet. On the sixteenth the foreign minister informed Eustis that the evidence proved Waller's guilt beyond a shadow of a doubt and the proceedings of the trial indicated that the ex-consul had been treated more than fairly. Hanotaux declared that in accordance with the widely recognized principle in international law that the decision of a legally constituted court can in no way be the subject of communication between two governments, he could not turn over the evidence to the United States. Strictly off the record, however, because the Ribot government was extremely anxious to settle the Waller matter, it was prepared to offer the following compromise: on France's part, release of Waller; on America's part, acceptance of this as a "final solution" to the matter. Eustis replied that he had no authority to make any deals but that he would consult his government.[53] The ambassador, whose position and reputation had been threatened by the Waller incident, was indecently anxious to accept the proposal. "The refusal to communicate . . . the Waller papers I consider final," he wrote to Olney on October 21. Washington should accept the French terms at once because "it is impossible to say how long Waller's increasing feebleness of health will resist close confinement."[54] This reversal came from a man who had previously termed stories of Waller's illness as "greatly exaggerated."

Hanotaux's proposition posed something of a dilemma for the Cleveland administration. It had committed itself to securing Waller's release, to compelling France to pay a large indemnity, and, at the same time, to maintaining America's special position in Madagascar. Indeed, as late as September 13, Adee had informed his subordinates in the State Department that "the United States will tolerate no weakening of exclusive consular jurisdiction as set forth in the United States–Malagasy treaties."[55] And yet the Quai d'Orsay had made it abundantly clear that it would never agree to free the imprisoned Kansan unless the United States agreed (1) to give up all claim of indemnity for Waller; (2) to not press for validation of his concession; (3) to relinquish the right of extraterritoriality; and (4) to acknowledge French supremacy in Madagascar. Adding to the problems confronting Cleveland and Olney was the certainty that the Fifty-Fourth Congress, scheduled to open on December 1, would launch a full-scale investigation into the Waller affair if the administration had not achieved a satisfactory settlement.

Nonetheless, the diplomatic situation made a confrontation with France out of the question. In September Olney had delivered a virtual ultimatum to the British concerning the Venezuelan affair, and he now needed all the friends in the international community he could get.[56] As a result, those in charge of Waller's fate decided that the only feasible solution was to agree to his unconditional release and at the same time discredit him. This approach would satisfy the black community, it was hoped, and simultaneously deflate those white jingoes who had been criticizing the Cleveland administration for not standing up for the rights of American citizens traveling abroad. In addition, if everything went well, the fact that the United States had tacitly recognized the French protectorate over Madagascar would be lost in the shuffle.

Before Washington could act, however, the Ribot government fell. Some American observers argued that the uproar over the handling of the Waller affair had contributed to Ribot and Hanotaux's ouster. This is highly unlikely, for there was little in their management of the matter that could possibly give offense to French nationalists. Whatever the cause of the regime's downfall, by the time the new foreign minister, Marcelin Berthelot, was ready to grant audiences to members of the diplomatic corps, Olney, Adee, and Eustis had decided that the United States would first assert its right to see the record and then, if this was rebuffed, as expected, attempt to determine if the new government was willing to follow through on the Hanotaux compromise.[57]

Accordingly, on November 7, Eustis renewed his request to see the evidence, arguing to Berthelot that Hanotaux's assertion of principle seemed somewhat after the fact, as he had never invoked it before. Indeed, his use of the definite decision concept had come only after examination of the evidence, which left the suspicion that the evidence did not justify the verdict. Berthelot, who was no less tied to the colonial party in France than his predecessor, rejected the ambassador's demand. Eustis then declared that he would "agree to anything" if it would result in Waller's freedom. Berthelot replied that his government would, he believed, be prepared by the end of the month to propose Waller's release as a matter of grace.[58]

There was still an imposing obstacle in the path of Franco-American rapprochement. Waller's family, as well as the prisoner himself, refused release under the terms of the Hanotaux compromise. Following a harrowing journey that covered half the globe, Susan Waller had arrived in the United States on October 18 and had immediately joined Bray, Langston, and Kennedy in their efforts to keep her husband's case in the public eye. Upon her arrival in Port Louis, Mauritius, on June 14, 1895, Susan and the children had applied for aid to the United States consul, John Campbell. Campbell was not sympathetic; he had never forgiven John Waller for replacing him as America's representative to Madagascar. He refused to furnish Susan with even enough money for clothing and shelter, claiming that he was given no "appropriation" for that purpose. Fortunately, she and the children found temporary lodging with some relatives of George Tessier.[59] Instead of cabling, Campbell wrote to the

State Department for authorization to pay the family's passage to France, where Susan hoped to see her imprisoned husband. Three weeks passed before the letter reached Washington. When the State Department replied—by cable—directing Campbell to care for the Wallers, he purchased third class, or steerage, tickets for them aboard a French tramp steamer. Referred to by the crew as "those niggers," Susan and the children endured a passage to Marseilles that was only slightly less trying than John's. Once in France, Susan found Eustis cold but civil. When the French categorically refused to allow her to see John, she and the children departed for New York, arriving October 21, 1895. The day of her arrival she charged that her husband would never have been arrested had he not been detained in Tamatave by Consul Wetter. Everyone in Madagascar knew that Wetter was in league with the French. She revealed in an interview with the *New York Tribune* on October 30 that she had just received a most pitiable letter from her disease-ravaged spouse in which he expressed doubt as to whether he would ever see his "beloved family" again. But when Mrs. Waller learned that the United States was negotiating with the French for Waller's release as a matter of grace, her husband's health suddenly became a matter of secondary importance. On November 10, in company with Bray, Langston, and Kennedy, she informed the *New York Times* that it would be unwise to sacrifice the chances for indemnity by agreeing to Waller's release on French terms. The French, she was convinced, would spare no expense in caring for her husband. Besides, even if he were gravely ill and were freed, he could not make the trans-Atlantic voyage and would be left alone to suffer among strangers.[60]

Waller himself noticed a sudden upturn in his health as soon as he learned of the state of Franco-American negotiations. On October 16 the imprisoned entrepreneur wrote Bray a letter, subsequently published in the *Tribune*, in which he complained of a "violent hemorrhage of the bowels" and other related maladies. "I am sure that I cannot withstand another such attack," he wrote ominously.[61] By late November, however, he felt sufficiently recovered to tell Eustis to hold out for an indemnity. "It is needless for me to state that I am ruined in all business and commercial circles," he wrote, "and that it is but fair and just that I should be reasonably indemnified." If the French wished to be rid of him, they would have to pay a minimum of $10,000 plus all legal fees.[62]

It is clear from Olney's official correspondence that he would have preferred to hold out for Waller's release as a matter of right. Nonetheless, the political and diplomatic situation simply would not allow it. Thus, during the last week in November—the week prior to the opening of Congress—the secretary ordered Eustis to obtain access to the evidence under whatever conditions the Foreign Office would grant, and to determine if there had been any legal basis at all for Waller's conviction. The French again proved unwilling to turn over the evidence, but Berthelot did agree to allow Eustis to examine the incriminating letters strictly as a matter of courtesy.[63]

By late November, both black and white newspapers were engaged in a spirited competition to see which could be most critical of the Cleveland administration and which could drum up the most sympathy for the Waller family. On November 30, 1895, the *New York Press*, a prominent white Republican newspaper, announced the establishment of a Waller relief fund. Supported by the *New York Tribune* and other Republican sheets, the *Press* launched a solicitation drive and implied that contributing to the fund was the ultimate act of patriotism. Not to be outdone, George Knox of the *Indianapolis Freeman* formed the *Freeman* Waller Fund. Knox subsequently advised blacks that contribution to the *Freeman's* subscription was not only a matter of civic duty but race pride as well.[64]

With the opening of Congress only days away and Republican newspapers alternately denouncing Grover Cleveland and France, Democrats began bombarding the administration with letters urging immediate action in the Waller case. Typical was that from one G. P. Fenlon of Kansas. "We the people are reasonably certain at this writing where Mr. [James] Corbett is at and where Mr. [James] Fitzsimmons is at," he wrote Olney, "but we are considerably worked up as to whether or not we shall prepare for battle in an effort to reach an amicable settlement of the Waller claim." The whole affair, he continued, "will enable the jingoistic Republican politicians who are without number since the last election, to further denounce the weak foreign policy of this administration. . . . As an administration, Sound Money, Tariff Reform, Third Term, Dyed in the Wool, in favor of the Restoration of Slavery Democrat, I earnestly request you to inform me whether everything has been done for Mr. Waller's benefit it is possible to do."[65] Black Democrats as well as white pressed for action. John G. Jones, wealthy Chicago lawyer and black Democratic organizer, visited the White House several times to argue Waller's cause. While he defended the administration publicly, privately he was more critical. Denouncing France's treatment of Waller as "outrageous and high-handed," he repeatedly advised the State Department to strike as aggressive a posture as possible. As previously noted, C. H. J. Taylor, whose influence had been instrumental in securing the Madagascar appointment for Waller, used his position as recorder of

170

deeds and president of the National Negro Democratic League to plead with the White House to protect Waller's rights.[66] Both Jones and Taylor made it clear that Cleveland's reputation within the black community depended upon how he managed the case. What Fenlon, Jones, Taylor, and other administration supporters hoped, above all else, was that the Waller matter could be resolved before Congress met, thus depriving the Republicans of a chance to embarrass the administration. Such was not to be.

When Congress convened during the first week in December, 1895, Republicans in both houses wasted no time in calling the administration to account. In each chamber the Kansas delegation, still conscious of the political threat posed by Kansas populism and ever-mindful of the importance of the black vote, took the lead. Under no circumstances, declared Senator Lucien Baker of Leavenworth, should Waller give up his claim for indemnity and agree to release as a matter of grace. The ex-consul and the administration should continue to demand unconditionally to see the evidence upon which Waller was convicted. It was a point of national honor, and the sovereign people of Kansas demanded nothing less. Representative Charles Curtis was no less outspoken. Complaining that the State Department had been very uncooperative in providing information on the Waller affair, Curtis proclaimed to the Washington press corps: "Rather than put him in such a position [asking Waller to accept release as an act of mercy], I would, if I had the power, send ships of war to France to back up a demand for his release, and I would take him out of that jail if it cost all the treasure and all the blood of the nation."[67] On December 6 Representative Orin Miller of Kansas introduced a resolution calling upon the president to surrender all correspondence relating to the Waller affair to the Committee on Foreign Affairs. Three days later, Senator Baker, supported by Shelby Cullom of Illinois, Daniel Voorhees of Indiana, and J. H. Gallinger of New Hampshire, submitted a similar resolution. Both measures were referred to the appropriate committee.[68] Congress had given warning.

The announced intention of the House and Senate to investigate the Waller affair, coupled with the Waller family's continued refusal to accept the ex-consul's release as a matter of grace, served to convince Olney and Cleveland that the stratagem which had been developing in their minds since early November was the only course open to them. They would have to accept Waller's release as final, even though this meant recognition of French supremacy in Madagascar and abandonment of his claim to indemnification. In the process, in order to divert criticism of their surrender of American rights, and to abort the forthcoming congressional investigation, the administration would have to discredit Waller to the point where he appeared at least partially deserving of his fate. Olney immediately set about consummating the compromise with France and tailoring the diplomatic record, which was to be turned over to Congress, to meet the exigencies of the situation. In a total reversal of his previous position, Olney wrote to Eustis on December 4: "This government cannot make itself a court of errors and appeals for the correction of mistakes of law or fact by the judicial tribunals of a foreign state. . . . This government only wants to determine whether or not there was any evidence sustaining the charges, whether there was such a total absence of proof as to make it clear that justice was denied and that the trial was a farce."[69] Eustis quickly grasped the secretary's meaning. After examining the evidence in company with Edouard Clunet, a French lawyer hired to advise the department on the finer points of French law, Eustis cabled Olney, "I have no doubt whatsoever of his guilt. . . . The evidence fully sustains the charge. . . . The whole tenor of the correspondence discloses his guilty intention and no court could have hesitated to condemn him."[70] Strangely, however, the summary of the contents of the letters which Eustis included with this comment almost exactly paralleled summaries given by Wetter in March, and by Waller and E. G. Woodford in August.[71] Each indicated that Waller had done no more than promise to purchase a pistol for one of his employees, describe French atrocities on the island, and warn his wife to beware of two men, identified only as D. and P., who were in the pay of the French. Previously the administration had maintained that on the basis of the Wetter and Waller accounts the latter had been done a grave injustice. Obviously, Cleveland and Olney now were willing to look at the matter differently. Late on the day of December 7, 1895, Cleveland released a statement announcing that the United States had been granted access to the evidence and that at this point it appeared that Waller had had a fair trial and was indeed guilty as charged. The government would continue to do all that could be done in the ex-consul's behalf, but it now seemed that the most he and his friends could expect was a simple release.[72]

In late December, Olney prepared and submitted for the president's inspection a bill of particulars against Waller. The indictment, which had little or nothing to do with Waller's relations with the French, was designed to depict him as a charlatan and a thief, a man thoroughly unworthy to be a diplomatic representative of the United States. According to the secretary's report, Waller had defrauded the widow of W. F. Crockett and had subsequently used the money to support himself in opulent style. The indictment even implied that Waller had utilized part of the estate to bribe Hova officials into granting him his concession.[73] Olney further charged that the D. and P. who Waller denounced to the Hova government as French spies in the letter to his wife were actually two law-abiding American citizens who had offended Waller by helping Consul Wetter unearth the facts in the Crockett matter. This memorandum, which was incorporated into Cleveland's final report to Congress, dealt in one sentence with the matter of the ex-consul's arrest and imprisonment: "It appears to me," Olney wrote, "that the conclusions [guilty as charged] thus arrived at by Mr. Eustis are corroborated." Both Olney and Cleveland hoped that after listening to this recitation of Waller's sins Congress would conclude that the ex-consul had received far more support from the administration than he deserved.[74]

By January the Waller family and their counsel had perceived the administration's plan. Accordingly, Mrs. Waller decided to take her husband's case directly to Congress. On the twenty-seventh Senator Baker read to the Senate her dramatic appeal. There was no doubt, she wrote, that the acts by which the French held Waller as an imprisoned felon for the last ten months were "a crime against justice." "I believe," she continued, "that had my husband been a subject of Great Britain, he would have long since been released." Having thus skillfully played upon the nation's inferiority complex, she concluded: "Therefore your petitioner, an American woman and an humble citizen of this great Republic, in behalf of my husband . . . appeals to the Congress of the United States and prays that some suitable and immediate action be taken for his release."[75] Susan Waller's frantic efforts were in vain, for the State Department had already made it clear to France that it was willing to give up its demand to review the evidence in the trial and to agree to the Kansan's release as a matter of grace. Nonetheless, Olney, chafing at the realization that the State Department's acquiescence in Waller's trial meant recognition of the French protectorate in Madagascar and abrogation of the United States–Malagasy Treaty of 1881, was determined to obtain some concession. He ordered Eustis to pressure the French into leaving some avenue open through which Waller might seek redress of his grievances. Finally, on January 26, Berthelot agreed that Waller would be permitted to bring civil suit against the French officials responsible for his alleged mistreatment aboard the *Dejeune*.[76] On February 6 the United States formally agreed to France's terms; Berthelot promised Eustis that he would immediately consult with the president and assured the ambassador that Waller would be released within the week. On February 20, Eustis cabled Olney that the president that morning had signed orders for Waller's release. On the twenty-first Eustis dashed off a long-awaited cablegram to the department which read simply, "Released."[77]

In view of the Eustis-Berthelot interview of February 6, the administration had decided by the fourteenth that it was safe to make its report to Congress and to deliver the "relevant" diplomatic correspondence in the case.[78] As Cleveland and Olney intended, the record as edited portrayed Waller as an unprincipled scoundrel who had abused his office for personal profit; he had intrigued against both the French authorities and his fellow Americans and was totally undeserving of the efforts exerted in his behalf. Although there was a good deal of grumbling from Baker, Curtis, Cullom, Voorhees, and others who had posed as Waller's champions, Congress refused to look past the report and accepted Waller's release as the best that could be obtained.[79]

Congress' willingness to drop the matter may be explained by several facts. First, both France and the Cleveland administration were determined to reveal as little as possible about the Waller affair. With Waller free, there was little Congress could do to compel either the Quai d'Orsay or the State Department to provide further information. Second, Waller's would-be defenders in Congress were restrained by the fact that Cleveland and Olney were then enjoying the plaudits of American expansionists, who were overjoyed with the secretary's bristling note to the British in regard to the Venezuelan affair and with Cleveland's rousing defense of the Monroe Doctrine in his state of the union speech.[80] Lastly, Congress declined to carry the matter further because the administration's attempt to discredit Waller before the bar of public opinion proved relatively successful.

To be sure, a number of papers, both black and white, continued to support him. "Only one side of the Waller case has been examined," complained the *Kansas City Journal* (white), "and that is the French side, presented in a record made up with a view to justifying the action of the French court-martial."[81] No less outraged was the *Indianapolis Journal* (white): "From the beginning this government seems to have proceeded on the theory that Waller was guilty, and to have been hunting for a pretext to abandon his case."[82] Proclaiming that the French had not proved a single charge against the illustrious Kansan, John Mitchell of the *Richmond Planet* (black) lashed Cleveland and Olney. "Backbone is lacking in the conduct of this administration," he wrote in late February, "and the color of the citizen had been a most potent factor in determining the result."[83] H. C. Smith of the *Cleveland Gazette* (black), always one of Waller's staunchest supporters, also refused to abandon the ex-consul: "The result of the Waller case is not wholly a surprise, but it is a disgrace to the government and country. . . . It is a parody on American citizenship."[84]

Such expressions of support for Waller and denunciations of the administration were exceptions to the rule. The *New York Times,* formerly one of Waller's most vociferous defenders, declared the day after his release: "With the departure of ex-consul Waller from the French prison, another experiment with the Negro in a diplomatic position comes to a close in a blaze of something unlike glory. . . . The State Department has managed to get the man out of jail but the fact remains that he was put there for good reason, and it is humiliating to reflect that this country . . . was forced to appeal not to international law or the laws of France but to the generosity and courtesy of the French government."[85] The *Providence Journal* (white) expressed a desire to "forget the whole unsavory affair" as soon as possible but saw in the incident a lesson for the American people. In the future the public should be more careful with whom it clothed the national interest.[86] The *Louisville Courier-Journal* (white) also believed the Waller matter to have instructional value. "The whole affair should teach a lesson to partisan politicians and newspapers," editorialized the *Journal* on February 22. "It is also a wholesome warning against the practice of bestowing office on a man because of the color of his skin."[87]

Black papers as well as white proved willing to accept the Cleveland report as the final word and, as a result, blasted Waller. The *Afro-American Sentinel* of Omaha wrote the day after the ex-consul's release: "Mr. Waller seems to have forgotten that he was the accredited representative of this country . . . and was on that account duty bound to maintain a neutral attitude. . . . The conduct which he has clearly proven to have engaged in not only laid him personally liable . . . but involved his government in serious trouble."[88] Most negative reaction within the black press, however, stemmed from the widespread fear that the Waller affair could be used by Negrophobes to further discredit the Afro-American and exclude him from the mainstream of American life. "The celebrated Waller case is ended, without honor to himself and in a manner that will enable our enemies to use it against the interests of the race," mourned George Knox of the *Indianapolis Freeman.*[89] "Alas for our sympathies, alas for patriotism, alas, also, for our race pride," declared the *Wichita National Reflector.* "Waller seems to have been another good man gone wrong."[90]

Ever the optimist and opportunist, John Waller had labored doggedly to make the most of his arrest and imprisonment. The biracial

175

and bipartisan brouhaha created in the United States by his incarceration might be utilized, he believed, to prod the Cleveland administration into intervening in the Franco-Hova dispute, protecting his concession, and forcing France to pay him a large indemnity. Waller and his supporters did not underestimate the degree of public outrage in the affair nor the willingness of the Cleveland administration to stand up both for America's interests in east Africa in general and Waller's rights in particular. What they did not anticipate was that the Quai d'Orsay, utilizing public demands in the United States for Waller's release, would be able to force the Cleveland administration to choose between freedom for the Kansan and preservation of America's economic and political interests in Madagascar. In the end Cleveland and Olney chose to repudiate the 1881 United States–Malagasy Treaty, recognize French hegemony in the island, and abandon Waller in his crusade for indemnity. In order to deflect charges that it had failed to protect the rights and to support the legitimate demands of an American citizen abroad, the Cleveland administration hit upon a plan whereby it would accept the ex-consul's release as a matter of grace and then portray him to the American people as a thief and scoundrel. Only in this way could Washington secure Waller's freedom and at the same time partially camouflage the fact that it had agreed to the abrogation of the 1881 treaty and in the process relinquished an American citizen's just claim to indemnity. Thus, it may be said that Waller's dreams of overseas empire were wrecked less on the rocks of American racism than on the reefs of European colonialism.

CHAPTER TEN

A Call to Arms and the Last Frontier

John Waller's lifelong quest for personal and racial advancement dramatically broadened his intellectual horizons and produced a world view that was ever more complex and universal. As a slave Waller existed in a milieu that was minuscule, limited as it was to the Sherwood plantation and its immediate environs. The peculiar institution, moreover, was as confining mentally as it was physically. Even within the context of his relatively privileged family, the overriding goals of life were, first, survival and, second, a minimal amount of personal freedom. Emancipation placed the young freedman in a position to experience the world beyond the Sherwood estate and New Madrid County, Missouri, a world he had only dreamed about previously. Dominating Waller's existence during the years immediately following the Civil War was a search, first, for knowledge and, subsequently, for a vocation that would allow him maximum growth—economically, professionally, and intellectually. As a former slave and contraband and as an Afro-American, Waller had lived in environments over which he had had little control; consequently, the drive in him to manage his own destiny and manipulate the societal factors that might affect it was particularly strong. Sometime in late adolescence or early manhood Waller realized that because he was a Negro personal achievement could not be separated from racial advancement. Responding to that perception, he began a lifelong search for a frontier where blacks could enjoy the blessings of democracy and capitalism, and yet be free of the blight of racism. He turned first to a domestic "out-back"—Kansas—and then to an overseas frontier—Madagascar. In each environment Waller's plans for personal and racial fulfillment went awry, his political plans in Kansas subverted by domestic racism and his concessionary scheme in Madagascar by colonialism. In his continuing effort to find the key that would unlock the door to equality and acceptance, Waller upon his return to the United States in 1896 dabbled in journalism, politics, education, military service, and, inevitably, empire building. These efforts, just as his pre-1896 exploits, ended in failure. As a result, by 1900 John Waller had developed a world view that was truly global and that recognized both the relationship between racism and colonialism, and the pervasiveness of the struggle between white and nonwhites for natural resources and living space.

Waller left Nimes, where he had served the bulk of his ten-month term, on the evening of February 21, 1896. The would-be entrepreneur had lost eighty pounds during his incarceration. He complained, in addition, of impaired vision. Nonetheless, Waller was in high spirits when he arrived in Paris on the twenty-second. He immediately called on Eustis, who gave him a chilly reception, but the ambassador, as he had been ordered, provided Waller with enough money for the return trip to the United States. Journeying to London, he conferred briefly with Underwood Harvey and other British investors who had evidenced an interest in Wallerland. After a six-week sojourn in England, Waller departed Southampton on April 1, arriving in New York eleven days later.[1]

For the ex-consul "the Waller case" was far from over. He still believed that he could use the wave of public outrage created by his imprisonment to extract a sizable indemnity from the French. Accordingly, no sooner had he stepped off the U.S.S. *New York* than he began blasting the Cleveland administration, particularly Wetter and Olney, in hopes of generating support for a claim to indemnification. In an address to the Twenty-ninth District Republican Club on April 13, he accused Wetter of betraying him to the French. He repeatedly denied that there was a shred of truth in the charges leveled at him by France and the Cleveland administration. The assembly responded by passing unanimously a resolution affirming Waller's innocence and requesting Congress to extract compensation from France. Following a brief outpouring of sympathy, however, the American public rapidly wearied of the affair. Abandoning his campaign for reparations, Waller decided to pursue another tack. After innumerable letters to the State Department, the French legation, and his acquaintances in Great Britain, the black Kansan succeeded in persuading France early in 1897 to purchase Wallerland for $10,000. How much of this money he actually received is unclear, for it was not transmitted through the State Department but paid to one of Waller's friends in England, presumably Underwood Harvey.[2]

Waller hoped not only to convert his experiences into cash but to turn a political profit from them as well. The now-famous former diplomat decided to repair to the scene of his past political triumphs. His return to Kansas was delayed by a whirlwind speaking tour which took him to Baltimore, Philadelphia, Washington, St. Louis, and Chicago. When John returned to America, Susan and the children were living in Baltimore where Warner McGuinn had secured lodgings for them. The lecture tour was necessary to raise money to finance the family's trip home and to buy a house once they reached their destination. Lectures completed and money in hand, Waller gathered the clan and set out for Topeka, arriving there on May 2, 1896. Following a flurry of receptions and "socials," the family moved to Kansas City and bought a small but comfortable house at 836 State Street.[3]

The America to which John Waller returned in 1896 had changed dramatically since his departure five years earlier. The nation was still struggling to extricate itself from the chronic depression that followed the panic of 1893; unemployment remained high in several areas, and a significant number of Americans lacked the necessities of life. Agrarian discontent had mushroomed into a full-fledged revolt; Populists and free-silver Democrats plotted the demise of the "plutocrats" who were allegedly exploiting and oppressing the common man. Further contributing to social unrest were a series of bloody clashes between labor and management—the Homestead and Pullman strikes were among the more notorious—confrontations which served to convince middle-class Americans that unions were tools of alien radicals bent on destroying the nation, and the laboring class that America was controlled by an unholy coterie of businessmen, politicians, and lawyers determined to exclude the common man from economic and political decision-making.

Nowhere were social and political cleavages deeper than in Kansas. Declining prices and increasing farm mortgage foreclosures continued to keep farmers up in arms, while bankers, businessmen, and professional people, fearful that the state's burgeoning reputation as the seedbed of agrarian radicalism would drive eastern capital away, mobilized to squash "Sockless" Jerry Simpson, Mary "Yellin'" Lease, and their Populist followers. In 1892 the Democrats and Populists fused at the state level. The Republicans responded with an attempt to steal the Populists' thunder, adopting a platform calling for public control of railroads and telegraphs, a redemption period for debtors, the Australian ballot, and woman suffrage. Convinced, moreover, that Benjamin Foster's nomination by the Populists in 1890 had had much to do with their success, the Republicans selected Blanche K. Bruce, principal of the South Leavenworth School and editor of the *Leavenworth Herald*, as their nominee for state auditor. The tide of agrarian discontent was running too high, however, and neither a radical platform nor a black face on the ticket prevented the fusionists from sweeping the state. Two years later, however, the Democrats and Populists were unable to reconcile their differences. As a result, the Republicans, headed by Leavenworth banker and real-estate promotor E. N. Morrill, returned to office.[4]

Morrill's election hardly signaled a return to Republican dominance. To the acute dismay of Cy Leland and other party leaders, the Leavenworth businessman managed in the space of two years to antagonize virtually every voting constituency in the state. In 1895 Morrill publicly pronounced prohibition a failure and called for modification. Fanatical drys decided then and there to bolt the party. The administration subsequently alienated western drought sufferers by refusing to call upon the legislature to appropriate moneys for direct relief, even though there was a surplus in the state treasury. Black leaders had been promised during the '94 convention that if they would agree to an all-white slate of candidates, and if the Republicans won, several of the best appointive positions in the state would go to Negroes. When Morrill limited his black appointees to B. K. Bruce, a number of black Republicans promised to retaliate at the polls. Further dimming the party's prospects for 1896 was the free-silver issue over which the Republicans were badly split and the Democrats and Populists solidly united. Finally, the Populists and Democrats decided to return to the strategy that brought success in 1890 and 1892—fusion.[5]

Indeed, one of the few things the Republican party had going for it in 1896 was the Waller affair. Kansas Democrats complained to Washington throughout 1895 that Congressmen R. W. Blue and Charles Curtis and Senator Lucien Baker were making bales of political hay out of the inability of the Cleveland administration to secure Waller's release and an indemnity from France. The whole affair, wrote one irate Democrat, "will enable the jingoistic Republican politicians, who are without number since the last election, in these parts, to further denounce the 'weak' foreign policy of this administration."[6] Criticism continued after the ex-consul's release. Addressing the Republican state convention (called to elect delegates to the national convention) in Wichita in March, the permanent chairman promised that if a Republican administration was voted into office Americans around the world would once again enjoy the full protection of their rights. "Then, no American will be tried by a court martial and the record of such a trial [will not be] refused a single day from immediate inspection, when properly demanded."[7]

This, then, was the political environment that John Waller entered upon his return to Kansas in 1896. The ex-consul was pressed into action by beleaguered Republicans almost as soon as he stepped off the train. He embodied an issue that could be used to attract white as well as black votes. In dozens of speeches delivered during the summer and fall he put his misadventures to use for himself and the Republican party. "Mr. Waller is an impressive speaker," reported the *American Citizen*, following a political rally at the Tenth Street Baptist Church, "and when he told about how the French spat upon him and tried to kill him with abuse, all because he was an American Negro and a Protestant, the audience groaned in sympathy. . . . When he denounced the present administration for having allowed an American citizen to be trampled on by a foreign nation, the audience hissed. . . . The names of Attorney General Olney and Mr. Eustis . . . were hissed again and again and when Mr. Waller said that James G. Blaine, the Negroes' friend, would have sent the whole American navy to rescue him, the audience applauded."[8] Waller's speech must have been impressive indeed, for the day he delivered it, George A. Dudley, the owner of the *Citizen*, hired him as editor-in-chief.

Although he continued to extol the virtues of sound money, a high tariff, and the home market, Waller's specialty during the 1896 campaign was, not surprisingly, foreign policy. In the editorial columns of the *Citizen* and on the speaker's stump he blasted Cleveland for abandoning the nonwhite peoples of the world to the evils of colonialism, and he promised an Anglo-American rapprochement if the Republicans regained control of the White House. "Our candidate will have a foreign policy that will look to and defend the honor of our flag and protect the rights and property of American citizens abroad," he wrote to William McKinley. "He will not flaunt the red flag of war in the face of Great Britain over Venezuela and at the same time allow France, Turkey, and Spain to ruthlessly imprison, pilfer, and rob American citizens."[9] In August Waller began a campaign swing that took him to Des Moines, St. Louis, and Chicago. In Iowa he recalled past victories and urged the state to help return the party of Lincoln and Blaine to power. In Chicago he joined Ferdinand Barnett and other prominent black Republicans in demanding the rejection of an administration that had made America a synonym for craven cowardice among the nations of the world.[10]

Waller's decision to immerse himself in the campaign of 1896 stemmed from a number of considerations. Politics, of course, was his business, and he had never known any home other than the Republican party. Despite the Compromise of 1877 and the lily-white tactics of Arthur and Harrison, the G.O.P. was still the party of Lincoln, Seward, and Stevens. The Populists were an unknown quantity, while the Democrats could hardly be trusted as long as they continued to accord ex-Confederates places of honor and power within the party. And, moreover, Waller continued to be angry with the Cleveland administration for not actively defending the Malagasies. Finally, there was as always the personal motive. Waller hoped that the publicity he had gained while in prison in France and while on the stump in Kansas would lead to his being named, if the Republicans won, recorder of deeds, the highest paying and most powerful federal office traditionally given to a black man. The recorder not only controlled dozens of jobs directly but advised the president on all black appointments made during his administration. C. H. J. Taylor filled the post during Cleveland's second term. It was not unreasonable to expect, Waller believed, that one good Kansas man could follow another.[11]

Many hopes were disappointed in the year 1896, not the least of which were those of Kansas Republicans and John Waller. Despite the fact that there were no less than six slates of candidates running for office in Kansas in 1896, and although once again most Negroes, grumbling all the way, voted Republican, the fusionists won a clear-cut victory. John W. Leedy, a political opportunist who had at one time or another been a member of all three major parties, was elected governor, while the Demo-Pops claimed majorities in both chambers of the legislature. Although William McKinley won the presidential contest, Waller's bid to succeed Taylor was not to be realized. He received a good deal of support from black Republicans for the position but none from white. Waller's dreams of filling the post made famous by Frederick Douglass, Blanche K. Bruce, and others vanished when in April, 1897, McKinley settled on Henry P. Cheatham of North Carolina.[12]

With the recordership decided, John and Susan Waller were free to turn their attention to more mundane matters such as earning a living and finding a niche in Kansas City society. For a black family with social standing and a steady income, life in Kansas City at the turn of the century was not unpleasant. Kansas City, Kansas, which had been consolidated in 1886, had a total population as of 1896 of 40,676, which included 5,055 blacks. Although there were enclaves in the northern and extreme western portions of the city, most Negroes lived in the heart of the community within a seven block band that paralleled the river. Kansas City's packing houses, stockyards, grain elevators, and flour mills provided employment for hundreds of Negroes. Others earned their live-lihood serving whites indirectly as waiters, porters, and barbers, or directly as domestics. As was the case in Topeka, Leavenworth, and Law-rence, the black community in Kansas City was stratified by education, church affiliation, degree of adherence to conventional morality, and, to a certain extent, place of residence. There was near the stockyards and close to the river a section called Smokey Row, a line of shanties inter-rupted here and there by a black bawdy house or saloon. Some of the stockyard, mill, and packing house workers were forced to live in Smokey Row, but those blacks with social pretensions, a group which would cer-tainly include the Wallers, avoided contact with the inhabitants of this area except at election time. The respectable element—including B. S. Smith and his family, the Dudleys, the Corvine Pattersons, and the Wallers—lived in tree-lined if dilapidated neighborhoods farther away from the river. The Waller's house at 836 State was located in one of these areas. Also like the other cities of eastern Kansas, Kansas City had its coterie of professional and business people. The handful of lawyers, doctors, and merchants comprised the city's Negro middle class. They attended one of a number of A.M.E. churches, debated current events and literary topics in Kansas City's three black literary societies, and took the lead in politics and civic affairs. Between the elite and the inhabi-tants of Smokey Row, both physically and socially, stood a mass of semi-educated black laborers who struggled to duplicate conventional behavior patterns and life-styles of the middle class. They belonged for the most part not to the A.M.E. church but to one of the city's Baptist churches. Lack of education, white racism, and grinding poverty closed so many doors to this group that their existence consisted primarily of a struggle for survival.[13]

Kansas City politics was noted for its cynicism and corruption. Vote purchasing, ballot box stuffing, and false counts characterized not only general elections for city, county, and state office but primary elections as well. In 1898 Populist Police Chief W. T. Quarles was accused of collecting $1,200 per month from the city's gamblers and "jointists," and splitting the boodle with Leedy. When Waller moved to Kansas City, the Republican county organization was badly split between two rival factions, one headed by former mayor C. W. Trickett, and the other by George A. Martin, editor of the *Kansas City Gazette*. While rank-and-file blacks in Kansas City traditionally voted Republican, the city's Negro politicians had a well-deserved reputation for rebellion. In 1891 Eagle-son, Turner Bell, and William D. Matthews had put up an all-black slate of candidates for municipal office. In 1896, in an effort to secure more recognition from the party leadership, a group of disgruntled black Republicans challenged the Democrats and regular Republicans with the Abraham Lincoln Republican ticket. C. H. J. Taylor used Kansas City as his base of operations during his intermittent residence in the state. Moves toward independence were not totally counterproductive, as evidenced by the fact that in 1896 blacks were employed on the police force and in the fire department, and one was on the city council. The city attorney was a Negro, and there was one black justice of the peace.[14] Waller was somewhat taken aback by the cynicism of Wyandotte county politics and frustrated with the fragmentation within the Republican party. Regarding city or county office as somewhat beneath him, Waller attempted to function as a conciliator and unifier. For the most part his efforts went unheeded.

As usual Waller supported himself and his family through a variety of activities. Evidently, a major source of his income during this period came from public lecturing. Among his advertised topics were "An American Consul and Citizen Abroad," "Experiences and Treatment in French Prisons," and "Madagascar, Her People, Customs, and Habits." Fees were scaled from $50 or $75 for lectures in opera houses or public halls to $25 for speeches sponsored by churches. The ex-consul obviously earned something as editor of the *Citizen* but certainly not enough to feed and house the family. Early in 1897 he opened a law office at 117 West Sixth Street in partnership with W. H. Payne, former principal of Lincoln Institute in Jefferson City, Missouri. Susan supplemented the family income by taking in boarders and lecturing to ladies clubs on the charms of Madagascar. Waller planned to publish a book recounting his experiences under the title, *Madagascar, Customs and Religion of the People, Eleven Months in a French Prison.* Whether or not it was ever written is unclear. Money came in bits and pieces, but such was the family's prosperity that John, Jr., was able to attend Emporia Normal school, and Minnie the Chicago Conservatory of Music, simultaneously.[15]

Waller's stay in a French prison had not diminished his ability to keep himself in the public eye. Despite the damning report delivered by the Cleveland administration to Congress just prior to his release from prison, many midwestern and western blacks viewed Waller as the most notable Negro the region had yet produced. On the first anniversary of his release from prison a monster celebration was held in his honor in Kansas City. Prominent blacks from Missouri, Iowa, Kansas, and Oklahoma Territory came and witnessed an extensive program featuring voice and instrumental presentations, a history of Waller's life and adventures, and a "cotillion." Telegrams were read from groups in Chicago and other cities where black leaders were holding commemorative celebrations concurrently.[16]

In the midst of his abortive bid for the recordership Waller became head of an association of well-to-do Kansas blacks, including old acquaintances Albert Thomas and James H. Guy, which had as its object the establishment of an Afro-American Industrial College in Cowley County in southeast Kansas. Waller had always been an exponent of racial solidarity and self-help; it was natural for him to become caught up in the mania for industrial education that seized leaders of both races during the last quarter of the nineteenth century. The purpose of the association, according to its charter, was "to facilitate, aid, foster, and encourage the general school, literary, mechanical, industrial, agricultural, physical, mental, and art education of the Afro-American."[17] Although the group filed articles of incorporation, raised money during 1897, and obtained an option on a $6,500 ranch near Winfield, the scheme came to naught, primarily because of the Spanish-American War and Waller's election to the rank of captain in the Twenty-Third Kansas Volunteers.[18]

Waller had been an ardent supporter of the Cuban revolution ever since his return to the United States. In July he proclaimed in the *American Citizen*: "The Cuban insurgents deserve the most hearty sympathy and encouragement of all who believe in liberty untrammeled . . . and we hope there will be no abatement of the war on their part until the Spanish shall have conceded the Independence of Cuba."[19] The United States government, he concluded, should recognize Cuban belligerency at once. In December, 1896, Waller headed a huge pro-Cuban rally at Chicago's Bethel Methodist Episcopal Church. "There are about six hundred thousand colored people in Cuba," he told the meeting, "and all of them are determined upon the independence of the island, and we are glad the colored people of Chicago, as elsewhere, are heart and soul for Cuban independence."[20] That Waller should express sympathy for the Cubans is hardly surprising. The black Kansan's overseas adventures, as well as his domestic experiences, had given him a broad sympathy for exploited, oppressed peoples of all regions. He continued to be deeply troubled, for example, by the plight of the Malagasies, even after it was clear that he would never be able to return and claim his concession. "The situation of Madagascar is such that the civilized, Christian world ought to intervene and put down the attempt of France to pillage and rob that people of their country," he wrote. "It is fully as unjust and revolutionary as it would be were she to undertake to invade the United States and set up a dominion over them."[21] Waller, like many of his brethren, hoped that the United States would act in the Caribbean basin, if not in East Africa, as a counterweight to European colonialism. He reasoned that American intervention into the Spanish-Cuban conflict would redound to the benefit of blacks everywhere. It would make the white majority in the United States more aware of its oppression of the Afro-American, serve as a warning to other colonial powers, and possibly lead to the establishment of a vigorous black republic that would command the respect of nations everywhere. A benefit of American intervention not immediately apparent to Waller was the opportunity for him to win a commission in the United States Army and ultimately a chance to revive his dream of commercial empire.

Congress voted to intervene in the Spanish-Cuban War in April, 1898, and immediately black Kansans began clamoring for the right to serve in the armed forces. This demand marked the culmination of a prolonged struggle by blacks to end exclusion from the state's militia. The right of Afro-Americans to bear arms has been one of the more controversial issues in American history. Viewing military service as an undeniable badge of citizenship, white supremacists struggled from the American Revolution through World War I to exclude blacks from the armed forces in general and combat units in particular. Simultaneously, civil rights activists, just as certain of the intimate relationship between military service and full membership in society, placed the right to bear arms at the top of their list of priorities.[22] This was no less true in Kansas than other areas. Although Kansas' founding fathers, determined to keep Negroes out of uniform, provided in Article VIII of the Wyandotte Constitution that "the militia shall be composed of all able bodied white male citizens," they could do nothing to bar blacks from federal service.[23] Consequently, upon the outbreak of the Civil War, blacks organized the First Regiment, Kansas Colored Volunteers, which was mustered into federal service in January, 1863, the fourth Negro regiment to enter the Union Army. Both this outfit and the Second Kansas Colored Regiment saw considerable action against Confederate units in Arkansas and in Indian Territory. Eventually, the Kansas regiments were merged with the Eleventh and Fifty-fourth United States Colored Troops, two all-black brigades. Following the close of the war, many of these G.A.R. veterans returned to Kansas. As the years passed, their ranks were swelled by Negro troopers who retired from units stationed in the West to fight Indians. Thus, the black community in Kansas that developed during the 1860s and 1870s could look with pride on a distinguished record of military service; that tradition made the militia clause in the Wyandotte Constitution particularly onerous and had much to do with the effort that began in the 1870s to abolish it.[24]

Blacks first tested the discriminatory provision during the Great Railroad Strike in 1878. No sooner had that walkout paralyzed the Atchison, Topeka, and Santa Fe than the managers of the road began to import strikebreakers. When the strikers mobilized to prevent scabs from operating the roads, the governor called for able-bodied men to join the militia and help quell any violence that might develop. Although Adjutant General Peter S. Noble later denied that there was any discrimination, it is clear that blacks who volunteered were turned away.[25]

The Negro community responded to exclusion first by organizing "independent" militia units; that is, companies specifically authorized and partially supported by the state. By 1880 there were in Kansas three all-black militia companies: the Lawrence Guards, commanded by John M. Mitchell; the St. John Guards of Topeka (later supplanted by the Morton Guards), captained by John M. Brown; and the Garfield Rifles of Leavenworth, with Captain George W. Jackson in command. In 1887 the black citizens of North Topeka formed the Logan Rifles and elected John Johnson company commander. By 1890 Kansas City Negroes had formed the Kansas City Colored Company, with Captain N. W. Overton in charge. Apparently, the Lawrence and Leavenworth units were the best organized and most prosperous. Each had its own armory, uniforms, and a hundred state-supplied rifles.[26]

Simultaneously, black activists with Waller in the lead opened an aggressive campaign to have the word "white" eliminated from Article VIII of the constitution.[27] Waller displayed a life-long interest in things military. Too young to fight in the Civil War, he joined the Lawrence Guards upon moving to Douglas County in 1879. He rose rapidly through the ranks and in 1881 was elected one of the unit's two lieutenants.[28] Waller's speeches were heavily laced with history and specific references to the prominent part played by Negro troops in past national conflicts. The ex-slave was drawn to the military because he perceived it to be a facet of republican citizenship and thus important to the Negroes' struggle for civil equality, not because he was particularly interested in tactics, strategy, or soldiering *per se*. From the stump and the editorial columns of the *Western Recorder* he denounced the discriminatory militia clause as a slap in the face to all black Kansans. "In the name of the devotion of the people of Kansas to equality, equity, and fair play," he wrote in the *Recorder*, "we demand that the word white be stricken from the Constitution of this State, not because we want to fight, but because of the justice of it."[29] Waller used his influence with John Martin and persuaded the governor to officially request the legislature in 1886 to end discrimination in the state militia. When a number of powerful white

Republicans, such as Joe Hudson of the *Capital*, joined the campaign, the Kansas legislature in 1887 passed and in November, 1888, the people of Kansas endorsed a constitutional amendment eliminating the word from section eight.[30]

Resistance to enlistment of blacks was still very strong, however, and succeeding administrations employed two tactics designed to maintain the racial purity of the state's citizen army. When the Garfield Rifles, Lawrence Guards, and other black units applied for incorporation into one of the state's four national guard regiments or asked to form a regiment of their own, they were told that the number of units in the guard was set by law and no black unit could be admitted until one of the white companies dropped out. As criticism of this position mounted among blacks, the adjutant general embarked in 1892 on another tack. He ordered his regimental commanders to "inspect" the black units to determine if they were fit for state service. In each case they were found wanting in equipment, leadership, or training.[31] This, then, was the situation upon the outbreak of the Spanish-American War.

In Kansas political conditions operated to the advantage of those blacks seeking military recognition. Governor Leedy, it will be remembered, had won election in 1896 on a fusion (Populist-Democrat) ticket, but by 1898 his political coalition was on the verge of disintegration. Democrats insisted that they had brought 100,000 votes to the alliance but had received just a handful of state and county appointments. In addition a number of Kansas Democrats objected to the party's penchant for free silver, while others were repelled by the Populists' call for woman suffrage. Moreover, the Leedy administration had alienated Kansas voters in general by failing to deliver on several campaign promises. The legislature rejected a measure calling for a secret ballot, which had often been listed as one of the party's prime objectives. Despite the fact that the fusion platform in 1896 had called for a repeal of the metropolitan police act which gave the governor the power to appoint police boards for each city in Kansas, both the legislature and Governor Leedy refused to localize the boards. If state control were abolished, Leedy declaimed, the cities would elect Republican police boards, which would effectively eliminate political opposition from every city, county, and state election.[32] State authority, apparently, was evil only when someone else controlled the machinery.

According to one estimation, Leedy had received 2,000 out of the 16,000 black votes cast in 1896. Encouraged by this figure, the governor was convinced that he could win a majority in 1898. To this end the Populists subsidized the *Colored Citizen*, a black Populist sheet founded in 1897 in Topeka by Albert Eagleson and Marshall Holloway. In addition the party nominated four blacks for county office in 1898, the Republicans none. James Beck, a black Populist from Wamego, was named assistant inspector of mines. By 1898 two colored organizations— the Independent Political League, claiming a membership of 1,643, and the Colored Free Silver League, which estimated its following at 3,000 —were working actively for Leedy's reelection.[33] Despite the frantic efforts of black independents, however, there was no reason to believe that a larger percentage of blacks would desert the Republican party than had done so in 1886 or even 1896. What was needed was a dramatic, highly symbolic act that would offset the "bloody shirt" rhetoric emanating from the party of Lincoln. The opportunity for such a gesture presented itself in the summer of 1898 when Kansas Negroes mounted a campaign to have the administration accept an all-black regiment with black officers as part of the state's quota of troops for the Spanish-American War.

As early as March, 1898, petitions began pouring in from prominent blacks asking Leedy not to discriminate against the Negro population in calling for volunteers if war came with Spain. Sympathy for the downtrodden, simple patriotism, and the hope of winning full citizenship were among the motives of those insisting that the Afro-American be allowed to serve.[34] Among those agitating for a black regiment was a group of individuals who, frustrated by the Afro-American's inability to turn Oklahoma into a Negro homeland, and anticipating that the United States would acquire an island empire as a result of the war, perceived that blacks might be allowed to fulfill their political and economic destiny in the nation's new overseas possessions. "I believe it to be a good idea for the colored people to all join in case of war with Spain," wrote William Buck of Paxico. "There is [sic] three islands that will be confiscated if the war goes on," he predicted. Blacks ought to be allowed to form their own "companies" and should be allowed to "take charge" of at least the Philippines and Puerto Rico. Clearly, it was the black man's destiny to rule himself, for "the bible tells us that the Ethiopian shall stretch forth their hands and become a great nation."[35] Eagleson and Holloway of the *Colored Citizen* concurred. Free from "degrading vices" and untrammeled by "color prejudice," the Afro-American would be able to establish farms and workshops, found educational institutions, and "work out our own solution without fear and trembling."[36]

Apparently, the state agreed initially to include an all-black company in the three regiments allocated to Kansas by the War Department, and recruiters enlisted blacks from Wyandotte, Shawnee, Leavenworth, and

189

Douglas counties. The state's Negro leaders, however, quickly voiced their dissatisfaction with this arrangement. In the first place, they argued, any black units mustered into service should be commanded by black officers. Indeed, many conditioned their offers of enlistment upon this. Negro spokesmen also complained that those of their brethren who had been recruited were being abused by their white compatriots at Camp Leedy, the temporary military facility established at the Topeka fairgrounds to house the state's volunteers. It seems that white soldiers whiled the time away by "blanketing" black troopers and their friends and relatives who came to visit. Blanketing consisted of seizing a victim and tossing him or her high into the air with a blanket. Much more offensive to Negroes were the "vile, wanton, and unprovoked insults" heaped upon black women who entered the campgrounds.[37] Such incidents produced at least one minor race riot.

The deteriorating political situation, racial tensions at Camp Leedy, and the obvious dissatisfaction of black leaders prompted Leedy to respond to the president's second call for volunteers, in June, by authorizing the formation of an all-black regiment—the Twenty-Third Kansas Volunteers—with a full complement of black officers. Leedy's decision to raise a Negro regiment provoked little comment, but announcement that it would be commanded by Negroes aroused the ire of a number of white Kansans. Some believed Negroes incapable of command and feared that the Twenty-Third would disgrace the state. Most of those who complained of Leedy's decision, however, merely resented the fact that blacks would be filling officer slots that might otherwise go to whites. There were in Kansas a number of G.A.R. members who had commanded Negro troops during the Civil War and who hoped to use their experience to obtain high rank in the Twenty-Third. Nonetheless, Leedy, who believed there was more to be gained politically by naming black officers to command the Twenty-Third, stuck to his decision.[38]

With a few notable exceptions the officers appointed to the Twenty-Third were Populists, or at least political independents. Leedy, fearful of political repercussions if Kansas' black regiment failed to perform well, first offered command of the regiment to Charles Young, the only black graduate of West Point, but Young declined, having accepted a similar post with an all-black Ohio unit. He then proffered the colonelcy to James Beck, the Wamego farmer who had held appointive posts under both Lewelling and Leedy.[39] Beck accepted. One of the exceptions to the governor's political rule of thumb was Waller. The ex-consul was among the first to pressure Leedy to appoint a Negro regiment with black officers. "Certainly, inasmuch as you have assured me in a former

Captain Waller (3rd from left, 2nd row from top) and other commissioned officers, Twenty-Third Regiment

letter that *all* the citizens of Kansas would be fairly treated in selecting volunteers in defense of the honor of the government and free Cuba," he wrote to the governor in April, "you will allow us one out of the three regiments to be raised."[40] At the same time, Waller began making his peace with the Populists. For example, although W. A. Harris was a former officer in the Confederate Army, Waller applauded the senator as a true friend of the black man. Blacks who had received patronage jobs at the hands of the fusionists came in for repeated praise as "representative men of the race."[41] The Populists, in turn, still respecting Waller's political clout, included him in the command structure of the Twenty-Third. Waller first asked to be named regimental commander but indicated that he would be willing to accept a battalion, if this were not possible.[42] In the end Leedy authorized him to raise a company of volunteers in Wyandotte, thus in effect appointing him to the rank of captain. On June 24, 1898, a notice appeared in the *American Citizen* calling upon "all persons who have signed with Mr. John L. Waller to enter one of the two colored battalions of volunteers and as many others who wish to enlist in Mr. Waller's Company" to meet at the *Daily*

191

American Citizen office on the following Friday evening. "Close up the ranks."[43]

More than a hundred Kansas City blacks, all of whom had been previously contacted by Waller, dutifully assembled outside the *Citizen's* press room, elected the ex-consul company commander, and agreed to meet at the Waller residence on Monday, July 3. Company C, as Waller's outfit was subsequently designated, was not able to leave until July 4; in order to prevent last-minute changes of heart, which would leave the company under strength, Susan, Helen, Jennie, and Minnie cooked three meals for the troops and bedded them down in the yard. Anticipating such an emergency, Waller had previously collected funds to pay for the provisions from Armour and other Kansas City merchants. On July 4 Waller and his 117 recruits entrained for Topeka where they were mustered in, issued equipment, and given a bivouac location. Two additional companies were subsequently recruited in Wyandotte, and in the final analysis that county furnished more troops for the Twenty-Third than any other, a fact of which Waller was exceedingly proud.[44]

There was some doubt at first among the officers of the Twenty-Third as to whether the regiment would even be ordered out of the country. The Twentieth, Twenty-First, and Twenty-Second Kansas Volunteers had not fared well in the matter of assignments. As of July, the first two were stationed at San Francisco and Chickamauga, respectively, and the Twenty-Second was located in Washington. Waller feared that the War Department would assign Kansas' black regiment to garrison some isolated post in the West.[45] In mid-August, however, Washington notified Colonel Beck that his command was to go to Cuba as part of the army of occupation.

The monotony of life at Camp Leedy during the six weeks prior to the unit's departure was broken by frequent visits from wives, girl friends, and delegations of appreciative black dignitaries. On July 27, for example, a contingent of Kansas City ladies headed by Susan Waller journeyed to Topeka and presented Company C with a large hand-made American flag. The women were appropriately attired in white dresses with red, white, and blue belts, and white sailor hats with red, white, and blue bands. On the day of departure, Monday, August 25, the Twenty-Third rose at 3:00 A.M., broke camp, paraded past a review stand full of dignitaries headed by Governor Leedy, and then marched to the train station. The scene there was one of jubilant confusion. Wives and friends filled the platform and spilled over into the space between the tracks. Women rushed about with baskets of lunch, glasses of lemonade, and sacks of smoking tobacco. Small boys competed to fill the soldiers'

Twenty-Third Regimental Band, 1898

canteens.[46] Finally, the train pulled out and the Twenty-Third was on its way to Cuba where, some hoped, black Kansans might eventually share in the fruits of a new American empire.

The Twenty-Third's journey to the Ever Faithful Isle carried it through the midwest, Pennsylvania, and finally to New York where it departed for Santiago aboard the *Vigilante*. The seas were very rough during the trip from New York to Cuba. Waller, probably because of his previous voyages, was one of the few who did not become seasick. Arriving late in the day on August 31, the eight companies of black troops were transported the next morning by train to their camp at San Luis, situated in the mountains some twenty-six miles inland from Santiago. Camped nearby were the Twenty-Fourth and Twenty-Fifth Infantry, and the Ninth Louisiana Immunes. Black occupation troops in Cuba were not assigned specific duties and were even spared the hard manual labor that so often had been reserved for black soldiers in past American conflicts. Many of the natives around Santiago were deprived of even the bare necessities of life, and the American command provided partial relief from their suffering by employing them as laborers. Relations between the Cubans and the black soldiers around San Luis were generally good, although the Ninth Immunes became involved in a drunken scrape with the local police which took the lives of two soldiers and two policemen. Members of the Twenty-Third seemed especially compatible with the natives; at least three married Cubans during the unit's six-month stay in the island. The black troopers encountered some discrimination at the hands of whites, both Cuban and American, but most found the racial climate tolerable.[47]

The lush vegetation, fertile soil, and abundant labor supply in Cuba turned Waller's mind once again to thoughts of commercial empire. In the fall of 1898 he wrote a series of letters to friends in Kansas City and Topeka extolling the virtues of the area. The fields were in need of cultivating; the mineral resources, of mining; and the native population, somewhat inferior to the Malagasies, of civilizing and uplifting. "A year's touch of American hand and civilization . . . will make Santiago one of the greatest places for money-making in Cuba because it sits in the midst of a rich agricultural and thickly populated country," he predicted. "We found the condition of the natives greatly changed for the better by the help of the Americans."[48] He was particularly struck by the swarm of naked orphans who begged in and about the camps. Laying the blame for their condition squarely on the Spanish, he praised the McKinley administration for making possible their salvation. Clearly, Waller began developing plans for locating permanently in Cuba while still on military duty there, for in January, 1899, he had Susan and the three girls come to San Luis and discuss the possibility of duplicating Wallerland.[49]

The Twenty-Third Kansas left Cuba in early March, 1899, arriving in Leavenworth some ten days later. When the all-black regiment was subsequently mustered out on April 10, each enlisted man received from $100 to $150 and each officer from $500 to $1,500. The Twenty-Third had seen no action, but unlike the Ninth Immunes it had earned a reputation for discipline and orderly conduct.[50]

Waller accompanied Company C back to Leavenworth and was duly mustered out. The ex-consul's return was temporary, however, for almost as soon as he stepped off the train in Leavenworth he announced the formation of the Afro-American Cuban Emigration Society, whose goal was the establishment of an agricultural colony that would provide a refuge for the frustrated black entrepreneurs of America.[51] "I think there is a good opportunity for enterprising people in Cuba," he told the *Kansas City Gazette*, "but one should not go there without a well-filled wallet. . . . We can get an option on about 100 acres of good land near Santiago, and we will cultivate tobacco exclusively."[52] In truth, Benjamin Harrison's former representative to Madagascar had never really abandoned his dream of overseas empire.

By the time he was released from prison in early 1896, Waller had rejected the idea of African emigration as impractical—not because the American Negro could not survive and thrive but because that continent already had been divided up by the Great Powers. "It is perhaps needless for me," he wrote a business acquaintance in 1896, "to draw your attention to the fact that all Europe is today making a raid on Africa with the view of finally and fully acquiring by conquest or otherwise all the most productive and tillable territory in Africa, not for the purpose of settling colored people, but to make havens for the poor white people of their respective countries, and to broaden and extend their empires and to enhance their political ascendency and perpetuation."[53] Waller's pessimism in regard to Africa did not mean that he had rejected the concept of emigration. When it became apparent that the United States had gone to war in 1898 for empire as well as idealism, he began to dream of developing black commercial operations in the territories about to come under the control of the United States. Cuba, Puerto Rico, and the Philippines appeared to offer all the advantages of Madagascar without some of its drawbacks. Waller, much impressed with the way the Twenty-Third had been treated in San Luis, surmised that the natives would greet Afro-American immigrants with open arms. At the same time, those who emigrated would not have to give up the blessings of American democracy and free enterprise. Finally, and perhaps most importantly, the Spanish-American War had rid Cuba of European colonialism forever. "There is before this people now an 'open door' as a result of the Spanish-American War," he wrote in June, 1899, "which makes it possible for the colored people of the states to emigrate in large numbers to the islands and still be under the protection of the Stars and Stripes."[54] In trying to sell his scheme to Afro-Americans and white Negrophiles, Waller resurrected a rationale that he had invoked in advocating emigration to first Oklahoma and then Africa. A partial immigration to Cuba would provide a final solution to the "Negro problem" in the United States. "There can easily be spared from the South 3,000,000 colored people, 2,000,000 of whom should emigrate to Cuba and the remainder be divided between the other two islands," he proclaimed in a circular which appeared in the *Washington Post* in 1899. Such an outpouring would create shortages of labor in the South so acute that businessmen and farmers would be forced to grant the Negro his rights and pay top wages. If the South continued to pursue its racist course, the remainder of its black population would leave, with the result that "the

Negro problem would be solved as was the Israelitish problem and Protestant problem."[55] Finally, just as Waller had hoped would be the case in Africa, Afro-Americans could utilize their racial affinity, adaptability to tropical climes, and knowledge of American technology and institutions to perform a civilizing and uplifting role: "The intermingling of our race with that of the Cuban will infuse new blood, new life and will awaken new enterprise in the people of this country that will make them one of the strongest, most energetic, and fearless people in the world."[56]

Waller departed Kansas City for San Luis in April, 1899. During the ensuing six months he flooded newspapers in the United States with circulars advertising his scheme. At one point he even considered petitioning Congress for $20,000,000 to finance Afro-American emigration to Cuba. Whether due to hostility on the part of United States occupation authorities, native resentment stemming from fear of job competition from Negro emigrants, or Afro-American apathy, Waller's grandiose plans came to nothing. Judging from Waller's subsequent complaints about the military command in Cuba and his denunciation of American imperialism in general, one suspects that the military government of General Leonard Wood played a large role in preventing the establishment of a Cuban Wallerland. While waiting for a response to his letters and circulars, Waller sank the family's savings in real estate around Santiago. It was, as one observer put it, "a poor investment." As a result, the opening weeks of 1900 saw the ex-consul to Madagascar working as superintendent of a street gang for Barber Asphalt Paving Company.[57] He, Susan, and the girls returned to the United States in September, 1900, this time to stay.

Waller's last years are even more obscure than his first. He and Susan remained in Kansas City only long enough to sell their house Late in 1900 he moved the family to Yonkers, New York. In essence Waller retired from public life after his return from Cuba. He edited the Yonkers *Progressive American* for a time, and during the last year of his life worked for the New York Customs House. One Sunday afternoon in October, 1907, Waller called on a friend who lived several miles outside Yonkers. Compelled to walk home in a cold rain, he contracted pneumonia and died within a week. He was fifty-six.[58]

The Cuban fiasco marked the final disillusionment of John Lewis Waller. As a young man full of dreams and expectations, he had left Iowa in search of a stage upon which he could play out his life free from the paralyzing effect of racial prejudice, an environment where he could realize his full potential. He turned first to a domestic frontier—Kansas.

There he plunged into politics and developed a philosophy of racial uplift—civil rights militancy and black capitalism—that he believed would simultaneously advance his interests and those of his race. That philosophy, while improving his political standing with his black brethren, did not significantly improve the position of the Negro community within the larger society. The Republican party's refusal in 1890 to nominate Waller—a man who had been previously designated by Kansas blacks as their political spokesman—for state auditor seemed to underscore the futility of his program for individual and collective advancement. The disappointment and frustration that followed his defeat did not force Waller into apathy or rebellion. Instead, he sought his idealized frontier abroad in Madagascar. Waller's attempt to gain control over an economically underdeveloped area and convert it into a Negro colony that would benefit himself and blacks everywhere ended even more disastrously than his bid for political power in Kansas. The culprit in 1895 was not domestic racism but European colonialism in the guise of French imperialism.

By 1897 Waller had begun to perceive the world as a giant battleground on which the white and nonwhite peoples of the world struggled for food, markets, and raw materials. Superior wealth and technology enabled whites to win victory after victory. In a letter to J. H. Lendenberger, president of the American National Bank of Louisville, Waller expounded on his views: "India (a black country) in the east is now firmly in the hands of England, as well as a great portion of South Africa, and the Army of Her Britannic Majesty is now operating in Egypt with a view to extending her colonial dominion not only in that country but in all Africa." France, he continued, had overrun "black" Algeria with "an army of Freebooters" and cemented her hold on east Africa. Germany was in black Samoa, "and although Italy lost all but 14 percent of her best troops in the attempt to take charge of a black country, yet she is 'up and at them' again." The European powers, Waller concluded, were "hellbent" on robbing the black peoples of the world of their liberty "at the point of the bayonet and by the aid of the Gatling guns in the name of humanity and Christian religion."[59] Conspicuously absent from this pantheon of colonial powers was the United States. As of 1897 Waller did not think of America as an "imperial" power. Washington's refusal to come to the aid of the Hovas was due to the apathy and weakness of the Cleveland administration, not American acquiescence in European colonialism. He did not see that racism and colonialism are just two sides of the same coin nor that United States expansion would bring in its wake colonial exploitation. As a result, when the United

197

States acquired overseas possessions at the end of its "splendid little war" with Spain, Waller convinced himself that there now existed an environment, a "frontier," that would be free of both racism and colonialism. Cuba boasted a multiracial environment and abundant, undeveloped natural resources—a veritable paradise for Afro-Americans bent on acting out the Horatio Alger myth. This time, moreover, no avaricious foreign power could intervene to rob him and other black entrepreneurs of their concessions. But in 1898–1900 Waller's plans fell victim not to racism or colonialism but to a combination of both. Generations of oppression and exploitation had rendered black Americans either unwilling or unable to taste the fruits of America's new empire. In addition, Waller quickly learned that the United States had not gone to war with Spain and acquired overseas possessions to satisfy frustrated black entrepreneurs. The United States protectorate that Congress subsequently established over Cuba by passing the Platt Amendment to the Army Appropriations Act of 1901 was designed in part to ensure that the island remained a safe and profitable area for investment by whites. Waller was finally forced to admit that the United States, no less than France or Italy, was guilty of exploiting nonwhites not only at home but abroad, and that in supporting American expansion he had in essence been supporting the exportation of American racism. John Waller's lifelong dream of founding a frontier where the black man could realize the promise of American life was dead at last.

Something remains to be said of Waller's role as race leader. According to Nell Irvin Painter, two leadership types predominated in the late nineteenth-century South. At one pole were those labeled by black and white newspapers as "representative colored men," a term meaning the best the race had to offer. Such individuals were not mass leaders but, rather, assimilated Negroes who had become adept at manipulating whites. For the most part, representative colored men imposed themselves and their ideas on the inarticulate rural masses. Because these individuals had a "Western" education and were acquainted with whites, black farmers and laborers made use of them when a clearly racial issue surfaced but refused to defer to their judgment in matters that cut across race lines. Painter argues that representative colored men, in criticizing black folk for deviating from conventional, Victorian norms of behavior, played into the hands of white demagogues. Instead of unequivocally demanding the enforcement of state and federal laws that would protect the person and property of rural blacks, they asked unskilled Negroes to change their life-styles. Through thrift, industry, sobriety, and conformity to prevailing mores, the black masses would gradually earn the respect of whites; and as a result institutionalized racism would diminish. Representative colored men discussed legal and political questions on a cultural level, allowing white supremacists to shift the blame for discrimination and exclusion from themselves to their victims.[60]

At the opposite pole in Painter's leadership continuum were the "executors." Contrary to myth, when rural blacks needed to take public, community action, they invariably reached commonsense conclusions hammered out in public meetings. Once participants had expressed and discussed their options, they would make a decision as a whole and designate a speaker or organizer to execute policy in their behalf. The executor was not empowered to decide policies without prior consent of the people. Because the executor's mandate was circumscribed, he necessarily had to remain in close contact with his constituency.[61]

Historians such as Allan Spear, David Katzman, and David Gerber have discovered the existence of two distinct leadership groups among blacks in northern urban areas. There was in Chicago, Cleveland, Detroit, and New York at the turn of the century an educated and acculturated black elite made up of men and women who enjoyed close relations with their white counterparts. Most were light-skinned, native northerners, and descendants of freedmen and abolitionists. Well-educated and relatively well-off, these individuals were uncompromising integrationists and civil rights agitators. Their ultimate goal was unquestioned: the integration of Negroes into the mainstream of American life. The means of attack were traditional: legal assaults on institutionalized segregation, political pressure to secure civil rights legislation, and frequent protest meetings. Attempts to form separate black institutions were looked down upon as self-segregation.

Between 1890 and 1910 a new group of community leaders, composed of businessmen, professional people with business interests, and a new breed of professional politician, emerged to challenge the old guard. Members of this new leadership were dependent upon the Negro community for support. Most were self-made men with no more than a rudimentary formal education—even the professional men among them had substandard training. They tended to be darker-skinned, and many were the sons and daughters of southern immigrants. The leaders of the new element often associated with the lower socioeconomic stratum of both black and white society. As individuals who had their primary economic and social ties in the black belt, they contributed to the development of a separate institutional life in their respective ghettos. They established Negro businesses, built a Negro political machine, and participated in the organization of Negro social agencies. In short, members of the new leadership were proponents of racial self-help and solidarity.[62]

Was Waller a "representative colored man" or an "executor" type? Did he exemplify the traits and attitudes of the traditional black leadership in the North or those of the rising black middle class? Of immeasurable significance for Waller's later career were his childhood and adolescent experiences. His parents' positive attitude toward themselves and their racial identity, together with the educational opportunities and biracial milieu he experienced in Iowa, generated the self-esteem and to some extent the inner control that led him to aspire to a leadership role, but no one in Waller's life defined that role. The most important factor in shaping Waller's concept of racial advancement and his role in that projected advance was his Kansas experience. The state in which he spent most of his adult life was neither southern nor northern, but western. Many of the state's black residents were born in the South, while a fewer but significant number migrated from the North. Still another group was native to Kansas. The black population was neither predominantly urban nor rural; Negroes were fairly evenly distributed between the state's towns and its farms. A substantial number of blacks were illiterate and inarticulate; even more, however, were literate, and, even if not articulate, were assertive toward their environment. Black Kansans were a unique blend of idealism and practicality. Like Benjamin Singleton, they imagined Kansas to be a New Canaan where blacks would be able to work out their destiny free from the scourge of racial prejudice. At the same time, they recognized the existence of institutional racism in the state and fought through the courts and legislature to destroy it. What they demanded from the white power structure was equal protection under the law, the right to vote, and the opportunity to become property owners. Limited success in the battle for civil equality, coupled with a relatively high degree of physical freedom and economic opportunity, encouraged many to believe that their dream of a multiracial society dedicated to equality of opportunity could become reality.

John Waller possessed all of these traits, and his racial philosophy embodied his contemporaries' expectations. In one sense he was a representative colored man. Adept at dealing with whites, steeped in "Western" education, he was a tireless advocate of Victorian standards and conventional moral behavior. Yet he never intimated that even the most "degraded" of his black brethren did not deserve full civil and political rights. Waller did not confuse the cultural with the legal and political spheres. He was committed to "uplift," to educating and refining his fellow blacks; but he quickly realized that, because of white society's undifferentiated view of the black community, the rights of one Negro could not be sacrificed without endangering the rights of all. As his activities in behalf of the Edward Washingtons in Lawrence, the Drake brothers in Leavenworth, and the Hovas in Madagascar indicate, Waller was no accommodationist. But neither could he be called an executor type. He was not thrust forward spontaneously by the black community to fulfill a specific commission; he plotted and planned every phase of his career. His constituency was not typically southern—that is, it did not consist of rural, unlettered farm laborers who, through bulldozing and political assassination, had been eliminated from the electoral process. Because they could vote, and because they were concentrated in and around the state's six largest towns, black Kansans exercised limited political power. For this reason traditional political practices and forms had some meaning for the black community. Waller attended conventions, organized meetings, delivered speeches, debated, and ran for office in much the same manner as white politicians in the Gilded Age. At innumerable barbeques, banquets, and parades he attacked white Democrats and even Republicans who he thought had abandoned the black race. His views on inter- and intraracial matters were subjected to scathing attack by other black speakers and newspaper editors. Carefully gauging the temper of his constituency, Waller devised a comprehensive plan for racial advancement—civil rights militancy, political activism, and black capitalism—that accurately mirrored the attitudes and expectations of black Kansas. Both the black opportunists who came to Kansas from Iowa, Illinois, and New York and the downtrodden Negroes who fled the South after 1875 were committed to the goals which Waller's stratagem was designed to accomplish. Equal protection under the law, the franchise, and property ownership would be the primary fruits of the New Canaan. The protection and relative economic opportunity that they subsequently encountered in Kansas heightened the expectations of both the opportunists and the exodusters.[63] In effect Waller was arguing that the means to power were the very ends that had drawn so many blacks to Kansas. In his philosophy, object became subject, ends became means. His blueprint for racial advancement consisted of the expectations and goals of his fellow blacks.

Characteristically, black politicians in late nineteenth-century America had to appeal to two, often mutually antagonistic, constituencies—one black and one white. Waller refused to place white over black. In a state where Negroes could vote and did not always vote the color line (for example, in W. D. Kelley's race for the auditorship), to have placed the interests of party above race would have been political suicide. When segregationist and discriminatory policies called for criticism of the Republican party, Waller rarely hesitated, calling upon racist elements to return to the ways of their Radical forefathers. Thus did he criticize James G. Blaine for emphasizing the tariff at the expense of a free ballot and a fair count, and Chester Arthur for pursuing a lily-white southern policy. At the state and local level he blasted the G.O.P. for its betrayal of G. I. Currin and its racist attacks on W. D. Kelley. Moreover, Waller's advocacy of Republican tenets was more than mere lip service. As his exploits in Madagascar and Cuba indicate, he was willing to act on the assumption that blacks could compete successfully within the capitalist system.

At first glance Waller would seem to be a typical member of the new urban middle class. He was a dark-skinned politician dependent primarily upon a black constituency. Conversely, he grew up in a biracial milieu and he participated in a service trade (barbering) that served both blacks and whites. In addition he fully accepted white society's cultural standards. Thus, predictably, there was in Waller's racial philosophy a clear ambivalence on the issue of integration versus separation. At one level he was an integrationist. Self-help and self-reliance were admirable, but self-segregation was counterproductive of the race's long-term goals. Waller belonged to a number of all-black organizations, but his speeches and editorials gave the impression that America's ultimate goal should be the establishment of an egalitarian, multiracial society. Thus, in the late 1880s, on the eve of his bid for the auditorship, Waller joined with Fairfax and Price in urging the legislature to pass a civil rights bill that would eliminate public school segregation wherever blacks objected to it, and he agreed to represent in court a Negro who had been denied service at a theater and another who had been barred from a lunch counter. While he accepted white Kansas' definition of conventional behavior and even flirted with the idea of the moral depravity of the poor, Waller could not accept the doctrine of parallel development. The concept still required segregation in certain spheres, and forced physical separation of the races implied the innate inferiority of one group and the native superiority of the other.

At another level Waller believed in the autonomy of the race, the ability of blacks to control their own destiny. Only massive, direct relief and free land grants could have significantly improved the Negroes' economic and political status in Kansas. Although a belief that the federal government would provide such aid was at the heart of the Kansas Fever idea, few Kansans other than Daniel Votaw publicly advocated substantial, long-term federal and state aid to blacks; it was contrary to the

American creed of self-reliance, individualism, and *laissez faire*, a creed accepted not only by the white leadership of the Republican party but its black element as well. At heart Waller was an idealist. He and other members of his generation were to serve as a bridge across which blacks would march on their journey from slavery to freedom. His version of the "talented tenth" and the way to racial uplift was for blacks to find a mechanism that would give them economic and political power, and to lead exemplary lives. Because he accepted the American creed and because he believed his generation could play the role destiny had assigned it, Waller would never concede that blacks could not overcome on their own those two most pressing problems—poverty and prejudice.

Notes

INTRODUCTION

1. August Meier, *Negro Thought in America, 1880–1915* (Ann Arbor, 1963), 22, 26.
2. Letter from W. B. Townsend, *Western Recorder*, May 2, 1884.
3. For a typical rationale for disfranchisement, see John C. Wickliffe, "Negro Suffrage a Failure: Shall We Abolish It," *The Forum* 14 (September, 1892–February, 1893).
4. Meier, *Negro Thought*, 19.
5. See, for example, George M. Frederickson, *The Black Image in the White Mind* (New York, 1971), xi–xii, 228.
6. Martin E. Dann, *The Black Press, 1827–1890: The Quest for National Identity* (New York, 1971), 11–12. Ironically, Social Darwinism was a philosophy much used by anti-Negro thinkers in the late nineteenth century. Its function was to justify a policy of repression and neglect coming in the wake of the alleged failure of blacks during Reconstruction. Frederickson, *Black Image*, 254–255.
7. *American Citizen*, January 6, 1899.
8. E. Franklin Frazier argues that from its inception the education of the Negro was shaped by bourgeois ideals. The northern missionaries who established schools after the Civil War taught the Yankee virtues of thrift and industry. When the triumphant industrial capitalism of the North assumed support of Negro education in the South, bourgeois ideals were given greater support. E. Franklin Frazier, *Black Bourgeoise* (Glencoe, Ill., 1957), 60.
9. "New Empire" is a term popularized by Walter LaFeber. He uses it as a synonym for American overseas economic development during the last quarter of the nineteenth century. Walter LaFeber, *The New Empire* (Ithaca, 1963), 1–60.

CHAPTER 1

1. "John L. Waller," *Topeka Capital-Commonwealth*, March 7, 1889; and "John L. Waller," *New York Age*, May 9, 1891.
2. Resolution of Missouri House of Representatives to Secretary of State, May 1, 1895, Miscellaneous Letters,

RG 59, Department of State, National Archives (hereafter DOS); Eighth Census of the United States, 1860, Slave Schedule, New Madrid County, Missouri, Center for Research Libraries (hereafter CRL); "John L. Waller," *Topeka Capital-Commonwealth*, March 7, 1889; and "John L. Waller," *New York Age*, May 9, 1891.

3. Eighth Census of the United States, 1860, Free Schedule, New Madrid County, Missouri, CRL. See also *New Madrid Southeast Missourian*, February 28, 1896.

4. Seventh Census of the United States, 1850, Free Schedule, New Madrid County, Missouri, CRL; and Eighth Census of the United States, Slave Schedule, New Madrid County, Missouri, CRL.

5. Citizens of Buchanan County, Missouri, to Governor of Missouri, April 30, 1895, Miscellaneous Letters, RG 59, DOS; "The Next State Auditor," *Indianapolis Freeman*, May 10, 1890; and "John L. Waller," *Topeka Capital-Commonwealth*, March 7, 1889.

6. Citizens of Buchanan County, Missouri, to Governor of Missouri, April 30, 1895, Miscellaneous Letters, RG 59, DOS.

7. For discussions of the slave community and especially the role of the household servant, see Eugene Genovese, *Roll, Jordon, Roll* (New York, 1976), 1–158, 325–397, and John Blasingame, *The Slave Community: Plantation Life in the Antebellum South* (New York, 1972), 77–103, 154–200.

8. Citizens of Buchanan County, Missouri, to Governor of Missouri, April 30, 1895, Miscellaneous Letters, RG 59, DOS; and *Cedar Rapids Evening Gazette*, March 26, 1895.

9. *Topeka Capital*, September 3, 1890; *American Citizen*, September 4, 1896; and J. L. Waller to Laura Martin, *Cedar Rapids Evening Gazette*, July 9, 1895.

10. "The Next State Auditor," *Indianapolis Freeman*, May 10, 1890; and

"Hon. John L. Waller," *Indianapolis Freeman*, December 17, 1892.

11. "The Next State Auditor," *Indianapolis Freeman*, May 10, 1890.

12. "John L. Waller," *Topeka Capital-Commonwealth*, March 7, 1889; and "John L. Waller," *New York Age*, May 9, 1891. See also *New York Times*, March 24, 1895.

13. *Cedar Rapids Evening Gazette*, March 27, 1895; "John L. Waller," *Topeka Capital-Commonwealth*, March 7, 1889; "John L. Waller," *New York Age*, May 9, 1891; and John D. Glass to Thomas Updegraff, March 28, 1895, Miscellaneous Letters, RG 59, DOS.

14. "John L. Waller," *Topeka Capital-Commonwealth*, March 7, 1889.

15. I. Garland Penn, *The Afro-American Press and Its Editors* (New York, 1969), 188–192; and "The Next State Auditor," *Indianapolis Freeman*, May 10, 1890.

16. *American Citizen*, July 27, 1888; "Day at Mt. Vernon," *Cedar Rapids Evening Gazette*, May 11, 1895; "Hon. John L. Waller," *Indianapolis Freeman*, December 17, 1892; and Penn, *Afro-American Press*, 188–192.

17. "Was a Rapids Man," *Cedar Rapids Evening Gazette*, March 25, 1895. Waller may have had relatives or friends living in Cedar Rapids. During the massive movement of contrabands into Iowa following the Emancipation Proclamation, the largest number came from Missouri. The United States Census shows that in 1870 the majority of Negroes living in Iowa were born in Missouri. Leola Nelson Bergman, *The Negro in Iowa* (Iowa City, 1969), 32.

18. "Was a Rapids Man," *Cedar Rapids Evening Gazette*, March 25, 1895.

19. *Western Recorder*, May 31, 1883; Penn, *Afro-American Press*, 188–192; and "Hon. John L. Waller," *Indianapolis Freeman*, December 17, 1892. Colonel Charles A. Clark ran for governor of Iowa on the Democratic ticket in the 1890s. *Cedar Rapids Evening Gazette*, March 20, 1895.

20. Charles A. Clark to W. Q. Gresham, April 15, 1895, Miscellaneous Letters, RG 59, DOS.
21. *Topeka Capital*, September 3, 1890.
22. G. R. Struble to Charles A. Clark, April 4, 1895, Miscellaneous Letters, RG 59, DOS.
23. For a brief description of some of Waller's personal characteristics, see "John L. Waller," *Cedar Rapids Evening Gazette*, July 31, 1895. See also the poignant description of Waller's return to his home in Iowa in 1896 in *American Citizen*, September 4, 1896.
24. Roy Garvin, "Benjamin or 'Pap' Singleton and His Followers," *Journal of Negro History* 33 (January, 1948): 18–19

CHAPTER 2

1. Leland Smith, "Early Negroes in Kansas," master's thesis (Wichita State University, 1932), 27.
2. See *Leavenworth Times*, January 1, 1879; and *Topeka Capital*, February 23, 1886.
3. Jennie M. Kemp to E. N. Morrill, September 23, 1895, Governor Morrill Letters Received, Women's Rights, Kansas State Historical Society (hereafter K.H.S.).
4. Smith, "Early Negroes," 27; "Leavenworth Miner's Strike", *Topeka Capital*, February 17, 1888; *Western Recorder*, June 21, 1883; A. T. Andreas, *History of the State of Kansas*, vol. 1 (Chicago, 1883): 432; *Leavenworth Advocate*, March 14, 1891; and *American Citizen*, December 28, 1888.
5. *Topeka Colored Citizen*, August 9, 1878; and I. Garland Penn, *The Afro-American Press and Its Editors* (New York, 1969), 188–192.
6. "Letter from John Waller," *Topeka Colored Citizen*, August 30, 1878.
7. See, for example, Court Records, Court Calendars, and Trial Dockets, 1878, nos. 7466, 10123, and 2484, Leavenworth County District Court.
8. *Topeka Colored Citizen*, August 9, 1878.

9. *Topeka Colored Citizen*, November 9, 1878.
10. *Leavenworth Advocate*, August 17, 1889; and *Topeka Colored Citizen*, November 9, 1878.
11. William H. Chafe, "The Negroes and Populism: A Kansas Case Study," *Journal of Southern History* 34 (August, 1968): 411. See also *Western Recorder*, April 12, 1884.
12. Shawnee County Clippings, vol. 2 (1888): 83, K.H.S.
13. See, for example, *Western Recorder*, February 1 and April 12, 1884; *American Citizen*, February 23 and March 1, 1888; and *Leavenworth Advocate*, August 16, 1890.
14. *Western Recorder*, June 21, 1883.
15. John Waller to Benjamin Harrison, August 14, 1888, Papers of Benjamin Harrison, Library of Congress.
16. *Western Recorder*, June 21, 1883.
17. Chafe, "Negro and Populism," 404; John Waller to Harrison Kelley, February 28 and May 4, 1889, Papers of Harrison Kelley, K.H.S.; *Western Recorder*, March 7 and July 25, 1884; and *American Citizen*, July 6 and August 7, 1888.
18. Department of the Interior, Census Office, *Statistics of the Population of the U.S. at the Eleventh Census: 1890*, vol. 1 (Washington, 1895): xcii, xciv, ci, 916.
19. "John L. Waller," *Cedar Rapids Evening Gazette*, July 31, 1895.
20. "Closing Remarks of the Address Delivered by John L. Waller at Blue Rapids," *Western Recorder*, August 10, 1883.
21. Kenneth Wiggins Porter, "William Bolden Townsend," manuscript filed in Kansas Historical Society Library; Historic Sites Survey, Kansas State Historical Society, *Black Historic Sites: A Beginning Point* (Topeka, 1977), 24–25; *Leavenworth Advocate*, June 13, 1891; and *Topeka Plaindealer*, January 12, 1923.
22. Rashey B. Moton, "Negro Press of Kansas," master's thesis (University of Kansas, 1938), 56; *Topeka Commercial*, March 5, 1879; and Robert A. Swann, "The Ethnic Heritage of

Topeka, Kansas: Immigrant Beginnings" (n.p., Institute of Comparative Ethnic Studies, 1974), 49.

23. *Topeka Colored Citizen*, November 9, 1878. See also *Topeka Colored Citizen*, September 20, and October 4, 1878. Eagleson and Henderson boomed Waller for city marshal, city attorney, and several other local offices in 1879, but he chose not to run. *Topeka Colored Citizen*, March 8 and March 15, 1879.

24. *Topeka Colored Citizen*, September 20 and October 4, 1878; "John L. Waller," *Topeka Capital-Commonwealth*, March 7, 1889; and *Topeka Colored Citizen*, October 26, 1878.

CHAPTER 3

1. For an in-depth analysis of Adams' and Singleton's careers, see Nell Irvin Painter, *Exodusters: Black Migration to Kansas after Reconstruction* (New York, 1977), 71–95, 108–117. See also Historic Sites Survey, Kansas State Historical Society, *Black Historic Sites: A Beginning Point* (Topeka, 1977), 11.

2. "Succeeding Hugely," *Topeka Colored Citizen*, January 11, 1879. See also Robert G. Athearn, *In Search of Canaan: Black Migration to Kansas 1879–1880* (Lawrence, 1978), 76.

3. Marie Deacon, "Kansas As The Promised Land: The View of the Black Press, 1890–1900," master's thesis (University of Arkansas, 1973), 5–6.

4. *New Orleans Louisianan*, February 15, 1879.

5. John P. St. John to R. H. Lanier, *Topeka Commonwealth*, June 14, 1879, in Negroes-Clippings, vol. 3–4, K.H.S.

6. Billy D. Higgins, "Negro Thought and the Exodus of 1879," *Phylon* 22 (Spring, 1971): 43–44.

7. H. H. Hill to John P. St. John, November 28, 1879, Governor St. John Letters Received, Negro Exodus, K.H.S.; and "The Next State Audi-

tor," *Indianapolis Freeman*, May 10, 1890.

8. A. Neely to John P. St. John, September 17, 1879, Governor St. John Letters Received, Negro Exodus, K.H.S.

9. *Black Historic Sites*, 16.

10. Deacon, "Promised Land," 1.

11. Painter, *Exodusters*, 177–178.

12. *Black Historic Sites*, 15. For a detailed description of St. Louis' reaction to black refugees from the South in 1829, see Athearn, *In Search of Canaan*, 12–36. See also *Leavenworth Times*, March 12, 1879.

13. Nellie McGuinn, *The Story of Kansas City, Kansas* (Kansas City Public Schools, 1961); Roy Garvin, "Benjamin or 'Pap' Singleton and His Followers," *Journal of Negro History* 33 (January, 1948): 14; and Robert A. Swann, Jr., "The Ethnic Heritage of Topeka, Kansas: Immigrant Beginnings" (n.p., Institute of Comparative Ethnic Studies, 1974), 65–68.

14. Lee Ella Blake, "The Great Exodus of 1879 and 1880 to Kansas," master's thesis (Kansas State University, 1942), 56.

15. Nell Blythe Waldron, "Colonization in Kansas from 1861–1890," doctoral dissertation (Northwestern University, 1925); and Blake, "Exodus of 1879 and 1880," 53.

16. William Frank Zornow, *Kansas: A History of the Jayhawk State* (Norman, 1957), 186. Nell Painter points out that the sustained migration of some 9,500 blacks from Tennessee and Kentucky during the 1870s far exceeded the much-publicized migration of 1879, which netted no more than about 4,000 people from Louisiana and Mississippi. Painter, *Exodusters*, 146–147.

17. *Topeka Colored Citizen*, September 6, 1878.

18. *Herald of Kansas*, March 26, 1880.

19. "The Convention of Colored Men," *Herald of Kansas*, April 16, 1880.

20. *Western Recorder*, April 5, 1883.

21. "Letter from John L. Waller," *Topeka Colored Citizen*, August 30, 1878.

22. "Let Us Have a State Convention," *Topeka Colored Citizen*, February 1, 1879.
23. John Waller to J. P. St. John, April 22, 1879, Governor St. John Letters Received, Negro Exodus, K.H.S.
24. "The Cause of the Exodus," *Topeka Commonwealth*, May 13, 1879.
25. W. M. Fortescue to J. P. St. John, May 2, 1879, and John Waller to J. P. St. John, April 22, 1879, Governor St. John Letters Received, Negro Exodus, K.H.S.; and *Leavenworth Times*, March 13, 1879.
26. *Topeka Commonwealth*, May 13, 1879.
27. *Emporia Ledger*, quoted in *Herald of Kansas*, April 9, 1879.
28. *Topeka Commonwealth*, April 22, 1879, in Negroes-Clippings, vol. 1–2, K.H.S.
29. *Topeka Commonwealth*, April 23, 1879, in Negroes-Clippings, vol. 1–2; and *Black Historic Sites*, 13.
30. *Salina Herald*, July 26, 1879, in Negroes-Clippings, vol. 3–4, K.H.S.; J. P. St. John to Editor of *Wa-Keeny World*, June 8, 1880, Governor St. John Letter Press Books, vol. 30: 308–320; and Elizabeth Comstock to J. P. St. John, November 20, 1880, Governor St. John Letters Received, Negro Exodus, K.H.S.
31. S. A. Hackworth to J. P. St. John, May 19 and June 20, 1879, and November 20, 1880, Governor St. John Letters Received, Negro Exodus, K.H.S.; and Lawrence D. Rice, *The Negro in Texas, 1874–1900* (Baton Rouge, 1971), 207.
32. *Topeka Commonwealth*, June 28, 1879, in Negroes-Clippings, vol. 3–4, K.H.S.
33. Laura S. Haviland to Unknown Correspondent, 1879, in Negroes-Clippings, vol. 1–2, K.H.S.
34. J. P. St. John to H. C. Weeden, September 2, 1879, Governor St. John Letters Received, Negro Exodus, K.H.S.
35. *Topeka Commonwealth*, June 28, 1879, in Negroes-Clippings, vol. 3–4, K.H.S. There was apparently another reason for the inability of the K.F.R.A. to follow through with its colonization plan. On February 7, 1880, the ambitious and evidently unscrupulous John Brown was named general superintendent of the organization. This officer was to receive into the Topeka facility all destitute black refugees, provide for their physical wants while there, and arrange for their removal as rapidly as possible to colonies and other places where employment was available. Apparently, Brown preferred to use the moneys at his disposal to provide direct material aid to those under his care for as long as possible, rather than to purchase western lands or to aid those who had already removed. There was little effort at organized colonization by the K.F.R.A. after February, 1880, and western colonists would complain bitterly of being neglected by the association. Under Brown's supervision the association appeared to be more interested in making "political capital," E. P. McCabe of Nicodemus complained to St. John, than in furthering the long-term well-being of the colonists. *Herald of Kansas*, April 30, 1880, and E. P. McCabe to John P. St. John, Governor St. John Letters Received, Negro Exodus, K.H.S. Some would later charge that Brown profited financially as well as politically from his position as K.F.R.A. superintendent. *Leavenworth Herald*, August 4, 1894.
36. Henry King, "A Year of the Exodus in Kansas," *Topeka Commonwealth*, May 23, 1880, in Negroes-Clippings, vol. 3–4, K.H.S.
37. W. O. Lynch to J. P. St. John, March 31, 1880, Governor St. John Letters Received, Negro Exodus, K.H.S.
38. For the origins of the Quaker community in Kansas, see A. T. Andreas, *History of the State of Kansas*, vol. 1 (Chicago, 1883): 327. Also J. A. Ball to J. P. St. John, August 26, 1879, and Daniel Votaw to J. P. St. John, August 14, 1882, Governor St. John Letters Received, Negro Exodus, K.H.S.

39. Wilmer Walton to John P. St. John, March 26, 1880, Governor St. John Letters Received, Negro Exodus, K.H.S.
40. Wilmer Walton to John P. St. John, March 26, 1880, Governor St. John Letters Received, Negro Exodus, K.H.S. More than one freedman complained to St. John that Walton was doling out supplies in such a way that "some get all and some get none." Glass Floyd to J. P. St. John, March 22, 1880, Governor St. John Letters Received, Negro Exodus, K.H.S.
41. Johnathan E. Pickering to J. P. St. John, January 31, 1881, and W. S. Newton to J. P. St. John, March 11, 1881, Governor St. John Letters Received, Negro Exodus, K.H.S.; *Topeka Weekly Times*, April 22, 1881, in Negroes-Clippings, vol. 5–6, K.H.S.; and Minutes of Board of Directors of Kansas Freedman's Relief Association (April 1, 1881), 77–78, K.H.S.
42. Several prominent Quakers, including Comstock and Haviland, were named to the Board of Trustees; the board in turn named Johnathan E. Pickering, a Quaker and an "old time abolitionist," as president; S. W. Winn, "an educated and competent refugee from Mississippi," secretary; and L. M. Pickering, son of the president and for three years head of the Sac and Fox Indian agency, superintendent. Votaw and other blacks later accused Pickering of selling donated goods to destitute exodusters and other missionary groups. Daniel Votaw to J. P. St. John, May 5, 1882, Governor St. John Letters Received, K.H.S.
43. *Topeka Commonwealth*, May 14, 1881, in Negroes-Clippings, vol. 5–6, K.H.S.; and Laura Haviland to J. P. St. John, April 11, 1881, Governor St. John Letters Received, Negro Exodus, K.H.S.
44. Daniel Votaw to J. P. St. John, November 25, 1880, and June 27 and September 12, 1881, Governor St. John Letters Received, K.H.S. ,See also *Topeka Capital*, June 15, 1881, in Negroes-Clippings, vol. 5–6, K.H.S.
45. Elizabeth Comstock to J. P. St. John, June 4, 1881, Governor St. John Letters Received, Negro Exodus, K.H.S. See also S. W. Winn to J. P. St. John, June 2 and June 7, 1881, and Daniel Votaw to J. P. St. John, June 27, 1881, Governor St. John Letters Received, Negro Exodus, K.H.S.
46. Daniel Votaw to J. P. St. John, April 19, 1882, Governor St. John Letters Received, Negro Exodus, K.H.S.; and *Black Historic Sites*, 21. The Quakers were not the only religious organization that interested itself in the welfare of the exodusters. In the spring of 1880 the Presbyterian Synod sent a missionary, Reverend John M. Snodgrass, to the Dunlap Colony. He established a free school for adults, which operated for seven months out of the year, and persuaded local whites, at first very hostile to establishment of a Negro colony, to admit children of the exodusters to the public schools. Under his auspices a racially mixed association was established to relieve the county of having to care for the needy, to assist blacks with land purchases, to acquire land to be sold to the refugees in small lots at no interest, and to establish a literary and business academy. Andrew Atchison to John P. St. John, August 22, 1881, Governor St. John Letters Received, Negro Exodus, K.H.S.
47. A. N. Moyer to John P. St. John, April 17, 1879, Governor St. John Letters Received, Negro Exodus, K.H.S.
48. Anonymous to John P. St. John, March 4, 1880, Governor St. John Letters Received, Negro Exodus, K.H.S.
49. N. W. Duffield to George W. Glick, June 18, 1883, Governor Glick Letters Received, box 1, K.H.S.; and *Leavenworth Advocate*, July 13, 1889. See also George M. Frederickson, *The Black Image in the White Mind* (New York, 1971), 254–255.

50. *Kansas Democrat,* quoted in *American Citizen,* September 27, 1889.
51. See, for example, *Atchison Globe,* July 21, 1882.
52. Nell Painter quotes from the diary of Sir George Campbell, M.P., who while on a visit to Kansas City, Missouri and Kansas, in 1878, found blacks very well treated: "On the Kansas side they form quite a large proportion of the population. They are certainly subject to no indignity or ill-usage. They ride quite free in the trains and railways along side the whites . . . and there seems to be no prejudice whatever against personal contact with them. . . . Here the negroes seem to have quite taken to work at trades." Quoted in Painter, *Exodusters,* 238. See also *Lawrence Journal,* quoted in *Topeka Capital,* April 25, 1879, in Negroes-Clippings, vol. 1–2, K.H.S.; and Kenneth Wiggins Porter, *The Negro on the American Frontier* (New York, 1971), 360–368.
53. *Topeka Capital,* July 2, 1886.
54. See, for example, "The Indian Land Question," *Topeka Capital,* January 7, 1886.
55. See, for example, M. M. Campbell to George W. Glick, August 13, 1883, Governor Glick Letters Received, box 1, K.H.S.; "Letter from L. C. Chase," *Topeka Capital,* March 2, 1890; and Harrison Kelley to John A. Martin, January 24, 1885, Governor Martin Letters Received, box 1, K.H.S.
56. "Kansas," *Topeka Colored Citizen,* November 15, 1879.
57. *Topeka Capital,* January 10, 1890.
58. See, for example, article written by Captain Henry King, white postmaster of Topeka, which appeared in *Scribner's Monthly.* "Kansas," *Topeka Colored Citizen,* November 15, 1879. See also "Progress of the Colored Race," *Wichita Eagle,* July 25, 1888, in Negroes-Clippings, vol. 5–6, K.H.S.; *Topeka Capital,* April 24, 1879 in Negroes-Clippings, vol. 1–2, K.H.S.; "Letter from Hon. Sidney Hook, Speaker of Kansas House of Representatives," *Topeka Colored Citizen,* April 19, 1879; *Topeka Capital,* April 13, 1879, in Negroes-Clippings, vol. 1–2, K.H.S.; and *Topeka Commonwealth,* April 3, 1880.
59. "The Afro-American," *Kansas City Star,* quoted in *Topeka Colored Citizen,* November 4, 1897.
60. Frederickson, *Black Image,* 178–182.
61. "The rich men do not know or care anything for a poor colored man in Wakeeny and if I ask someone that will help me I may starve for what they care," wrote a black exoduster to St. John in 1880. William Louis Brown to J. P. St. John, January 25, 1880, Governor St. John Letters Received, Negro Exodus, K.H.S. See also "A Rebus Solved," *Topeka Capital,* April 28, 1889; and *Topeka Capital,* July 2, 1886.
62. *Western Recorder,* April 5, 1883.

CHAPTER 4

1. W. E. B. Du Bois, *The Souls of Black Folk* (New York, 1961), vii–ix.
2. Robert L. Crain and Carol Sacks Weisman, *Discrimination, Personality, and Achievement* (New York, 1972), 179.
3. "The City of Lawrence," *Lawrence Journal,* January 22, 1880.
4. Department of the Interior, Census Office, *Statistics of the Population of the U.S. at the Tenth Census,* vol. 1 (Washington, 1883): xxxviii; A. T. Andreas, *History of the State of Kansas* (Chicago, 1883), 327; *American Citizen,* January 25, 1888; *Leavenworth Advocate,* April 5, 1890; and *Western Recorder,* June 14, 1883.
5. See, for example, "Speech Delivered by Mrs. J. L. Waller," *American Citizen,* November 6, 1896. See also *American Citizen,* March 23, 1888; *Leavenworth Advocate,* March 8, 1890; and *Western Recorder,* April 5 and July 13, 1883, and September 5, 1884.
6. *Topeka Capital,* September 21, 1890.
7. *Leavenworth Herald,* February 1, 1896.
8. *Western Recorder,* March 22, 1883.

9. J. P. St. John to John L. Waller, September 3, 1881, Governor St. John Letter Press Books, vol. 39, 86–87; *Western Recorder*, April 12, 1883; and *Leavenworth Times*, March 29, 1895.

10. Waller began writing a "social column" for the *Colored Citizen* almost as soon as he arrived in Kansas. *Topeka Colored Citizen*, September 6, 1879. See also Lawrence D. Rice, *The Negro in Texas, 1874–1900* (Baton Rouge, 1971), 171; "Churches and Booms," *Topeka Capital*, March 20, 1887; *Leavenworth Advocate*, February 22, 1890; *Kansas City Gazette*, May 7, 1896; "Washing the Feet," *Topeka Capital*, May 4, 1886; and John L. Waller to John P. St. John, November 19, 1880, Governor St. John Letters Received, Negro Exodus, K.H.S.

11. See, for example, "Larph," *Southern Argus*, September 3, 1891; Interview between Edwin Uhl and E. G. Woodford, October 22, 1895, Waller Case Papers, *Papers Relating to the Foreign Relations of the United States* (hereinafter referred to as *PRFRUS*), 371; "Influence," *American Citizen*, January 1, 1897; and John L. Waller to Laura Martin, August 7, 1895, *Cedar Rapids Evening Gazette*, September 11, 1895.

12. For posture of Negro Congregationalists, see B. F. Foster, "The Coming of a Colored Evangelist," *Topeka Capital*, June 4, 1886.

13. "Communion Services," *Western Recorder*, July 13, 1883. Susan and John Waller apparently had two additional children, girls, Celia and Effie, who died in infancy. *American Citizen*, September 4, 1896.

14. "Dividing Line," *Ft. Scott Colored Citizen*, June 14, 1878.

15. See, for example, *Topeka Colored Citizen*, July 1, 1897; *Historic Times*, October 7 and November 7, 1891; Allan H. Spear, *Black Chicago: The Making of a Ghetto, 1890–1920* (Chicago, 1967), 51–90; *Southern Argus*, July 16, 1891, and August 13, 1894; *American Citizen*, May 25, 1888, and

October 12, 1894; *Leavenworth Herald*, April 21 and December 22, 1894; *Leavenworth Advocate*, November 30, 1889, and March 15, 1890; *Kansas City Gazette*, November 18, 1897; and *Western Recorder*, December 21, 1883.

16. See, for example, *Topeka Colored Citizen*, March 15, 1879. Here Waller, after hearing of an eleven-year-old orphan girl being severely beaten by her brothers and sisters, writes a letter to the editor urging blacks to build a home for black orphans. He repeatedly reminds the more well-to-do members of the black community that they have a responsibility toward their less fortunate brethren.

17. *Lawrence Journal*, January 8 and 14, 1880; Mary E. Griffith to John P. St. John, April 20, 1880, Governor St. John Letters Received, Negro Exodus, K.H.S.; *Lawrence Journal*, January 14, 1880; *Topeka Tribune*, September 18, 1880; *Herald of Kansas*, April 30, 1880; and *Western Recorder*, April 5 and June 7, 1883.

18. "Letter from John L. Waller," *Herald of Kansas*, February 6, 1880; and "School for Colored Adults," *Lawrence Journal*, January 24, 1880.

19. *Topeka Commonwealth*, February 20, 1880; and *Lawrence Journal*, March 5, 1880.

20. "The State Convention," *Topeka Colored Citizen*, August 30, 1878.

21. "Letter from J. C. Embry," *Topeka Colored Citizen*, September 13, 1878.

22. *Topeka Colored Citizen*, January 18, 1879.

23. *Topeka Colored Citizen*, September 27 and October 11, 1879; *Lawrence Journal*, January 6, 1881; and Joel Williamson, *After Slavery: The Negro in South Carolina during Reconstruction, 1861–1877* (New York, 1975), 343.

24. "Colored Convention," *Lawrence Journal*, March 17, 1880.

25. *Topeka Tribune*, August 5, 1880.

26. See "Mr. Waller Has a Word to Say," *Lawrence Journal*, March 24, 1880; *Herald of Kansas*, March 26, 1880; and *Topeka Tribune*, August 12, 1890.

27. *Topeka Tribune*, August 26, 1880.

28. *Topeka Tribune*, September 2 and 9, 1880; and "John L. Waller," *New York Age*, May 9, 1891.

29. *American Citizen*, July 17, 1891; and *Herald of Kansas*, April 2, 1890.

30. "The Colored Republicans Decline," *Lawrence Journal*, September 4, 1880.

31. John L. Waller to John P. St. John, September 3, 1880, Governor St. John Letters Received, Negro Exodus, K.H.S.

32. *Topeka Tribune*, July 15, 1880, and September 23, 1890.

33. *Leavenworth Times*, quoted in *Topeka Tribune*, July 29, 1880; and W. D. Matthews to John P. St. John, November 11, 1880, Governor St. John Letters Received, box 1, K.H.S.

34. "The Convention of Colored Men," *Topeka Colored Patriot*, June 1, 1882; and J. H. McGill to John P. St. John, March 5, 1881, Governor St. John Letters Received, Negro Exodus, K.H.S.

35. W. B. Stone to J. P. St. John, August 11, 1882, and Wilmer Walton to J. P. St. John, November 6, 1882, Governor St. John Letters Received, Negro Exodus, K.H.S. See also *Atchison Globe*, July 8, 1882; Daniel Votaw to J. P. St. John, Governor St. John Letters Received, Negro Exodus, K.H.S.

36. Kenneth Wiggins Porter, "Edward P. McCabe," manuscript filed in Kansas Historical Society Library. See also Jere W. Roberson, "Edward P. McCabe and the Langston Experiment," *Chronicles of Oklahoma* 51 (Fall, 1973); and E. P. McCabe to John P. St. John, November 4, 1879, Governor St. John Letters Received, box 5, K.H.S.

37. *Topeka Commonwealth*, August 11, 1882, in Negroes-Clippings, vol. 5–6, K.H.S.

38. William Frank Zornow, *Kansas: A History of the Jayhawk State* (Norman, 1957). See also William J. Simmons, *Men of Mark* (Chicago, 1970), 761–762; *Leavenworth Advocate*, September 21, 1889; and *Western Recorder*, July 18, 1884; *New York Age*,

September 2, 1891; and *Leavenworth Advocate*, July 5, 1890.

39. Memorandum to Paul Wilson, Files re *Brown* vs. *Topeka, Kansas, Board of Education* (1954), 1–4, K.H.S.

40. *Leavenworth Advocate*, May 4, 1889.

41. "Ought to be Moved," *Leavenworth Advocate*, June 29, 1889.

42. *Kansas City Gazette*, January 14, 1897; Andreas, *History of Kansas*, 1: 545, 2: 226; *Leavenworth Advocate*, April 5, 1890, and May 11, 1889; and *Parsons Weekly Blade*, October 22, 1892.

43. Andreas, *History of Kansas*, 2: 1073, 1453; *Western Recorder*, August 29, 1884; *Topeka Colored Citizen*, November 8, 1879; and *Leavenworth Herald*, September 29, 1884. In a few communities a white backlash following the exodus of 1879–1882 led to segregation where integration had formerly existed. In Olathe, for example, whites and blacks attended the same school in the 1870s, but with the influx of several hundred Negroes during the 1879–1881 period the school board decided that it would be better if the black community had its own school with its own teachers. "Race Troubles," *Leavenworth Advocate*, May 3, 1890. See also *Leavenworth Advocate*, December 21, 1889.

44. Andreas, *History of Kansas*, 2: 1225.

45. *Leavenworth Herald*, September 28, 1895, and June 5, 1897; *Afro-American Advocate*, November 25, 1892, and May 26, 1893; *American Citizen*, February 23 and June 15, 1888; *Colored Patriot*, May 18, 1882; *Topeka Capital*, May 3, 1895; *Leavenworth Herald*, September 28, 1895; "Debarred," *Topeka Colored Citizen*, September 27, 1879, and October 12, 1898; and *Times-Observer*, September 26, 1891.

46. "Distinction with a Vengence," *American Citizen*, January 25, 1888, and March 15, 1889; "Prejudiced Teachers," *Historic Times*, October 24, 1891; *American Citizen*, January 25, 1888; and *Topeka Colored Citi-*

zen, June 21, 1879. The attitude of white teachers toward their black students is exemplified by an interview T. Dwight Thacher of the *Lawrence Journal* conducted with two elementary school teachers in 1880. Asked about differences in learning abilities between the two races, she said "in writing, drawing, or anything which they could imitate, colored children were in advance of the whites. . . . In mathematics, reading, or any branch which requires invention on the part of the pupil, the colored children are behind the whites. . . ." The ladies did admit, however, that black pupils who had attended school as long and as regularly as whites matched them in overall performance. *Lawrence Journal*, April 2, 1880.

47. Petition from Colored Citizens of Independence, Kansas, to J. P. St. John, September 27, 1880, Governor St. John Letters Received, Negro Exodus, K.H.S.; "More School Buildings Necessary," *Topeka Capital*, January 17, 1885; and *Topeka Tribune*, October 23, 1880.

48. *American Citizen*, March 5, 1889. In the fall of 1888 the black citizenry of Fort Scott brought suit against the city school board for refusing to admit black children on account of their color. Blacks in Fort Scott resented not only segregation but the grossly inferior facilities their children had to suffer. The *American Citizen*, a black Topeka newspaper, solicited funds to finance the litigation. The issue at stake, editorialized the *Citizen*, was whether or not blacks were to remain "half slaves." On March 5, 1889, the Kansas Supreme Court ruled that the board had erred in not admitting the children when they applied. The point was now moot, however, for as of January 1, 1889, Fort Scott had become a city of the first class and hence could legally maintain a separate school system. "The Color Line Fight," *Topeka Capital*, December 18, 1887; *Topeka Capital*, March 15,

1888; and *American Citizen*, March 5, 1889.

49. *Leavenworth Advocate*, November 19, 1889. In 1889 the black citizens of Tonganoxie, a suburb of Leavenworth and a city of the third class, asked District Court Judge Robert Crozier for a writ of mandamus compelling the school board to admit black children. They had been debarred even though there were two vacant school rooms in the schoolhouse for whites. Crozier, citing *Board of Education* v. *Tinnon* and the 1874 Civil Rights Act, found for the plaintiffs. "Tonganoxie School Trouble," *American Citizen*, November 15, 1889; and *Leavenworth Advocate*, November 19, 1889, and January 4, 1890. In 1890 the parents of Luella Johnson, aged nine, sued for a writ of mandamus to force the Olathe School Board to admit her to a previously all-white primary school. In the summer of 1889 Olathe built two new ward schools. Although Luella lived but 600 yards from one of them, the board forced her to go to the all-black school over two miles from her home. District Judge John T. Burris found for the Johnsons and ordered their daughter admitted. *Leavenworth Advocate*, November 19, 1889, and January 4, 1890.

50. *Topeka Colored Citizen*, April 18, 1903.

51. *Topeka Tribune*, August 26, 1880.

52. *Western Recorder*, March 7, 1884; and "John L. Waller," *New York Age*, May 9, 1891.

53. *American Citizen*, January 25, 1888; and "William Abram Price," *American Citizen*, March 1, 1889.

54. *American Citizen*, January 25, 1888, and February 8 and March 8, 1889; and *Leavenworth Advocate*, February 14, 1891.

55. J. L. Waller to John P. St. John, June 14, 1880, Governor St. John Letters Received, box 4, K.H.S.

56. *Western Recorder*, May 24, 1883.

57. I. Garland Penn, *The Afro-American Press and Its Editors* (New York, 1969), 188–192; *Topeka Tribune*, July

8, 1880; and *Western Recorder,* June 14, 1883.

58. *Western Recorder,* March 17, 1883.

59. *Leavenworth Herald,* August 28, 1897.

60. See, for example, *Western Recorder,* May 9, 1889. See also "Death of E. P. Washington," *Western Recorder,* March 17, 1883; and *Western Recorder,* March 22, March 29, and May 10, 1883.

61. E. G. Woodford to James B. Eustis, August 21, 1895, no. 362, Dispatches of the United States Minister to France (hereinafter referred to as DUSMF), RG 59, DOS.

CHAPTER 5

1. *Western Recorder,* December 21, 1883.

2. *St. Louis Advance,* August 3, 1883.

3. "Proceedings of the State Convention of Colored Men," *Western Recorder,* September 7, 1883.

4. Ibid.

5. "Proceedings of the National Convention of Colored Men," *Western Recorder,* September 28, 1883.

6. Ibid.

7. "Colored People of Washington, D.C., and the Administration," *Western Recorder,* April 26, 1883. See also "Where Shall It Be Held?" *Western Recorder,* May 10, 1883.

8. *Lawrence Journal,* April 18, 1884; "The Chicago Convention," *Western Recorder,* April 12, 1884; and "Commissioner to the World's Fair," *Western Recorder,* August 29, 1884. See also *Western Recorder,* September 5 and November 7, 1884.

9. See, for example, *American Citizen,* July 6 and August 7, 1888.

10. "Negro Immigration," *The New West Monthly* 1 (April, 1879): 131.

11. *Topeka Capital,* June 19, 1886. See also "The Color Line in Kansas City," *Topeka Capital,* November 21, 1886; "The Sectional Issue Again," *Topeka Capital,* November 20, 1888; and *Hiawatha World,* October 25, 1883.

12. *Leavenworth Advocate,* November 8,

1890. See also *Afro-American Advocate,* May 20, 1892; *Historic Times,* September 26, 1891; *American Citizen,* November 22, 1889; and *Kansas State Ledger,* September 30, 1892.

13. *Topeka Colored Citizen,* September 20, 1878.

14. *Leavenworth Herald,* January 12, 1895; and *Afro-American Advocate,* August 12, 1892.

15. Leland Smith, "Early Negroes in Kansas," master's thesis (Wichita State University, 1932), 27; Nellie McGuinn, *The Story of Kansas City, Kansas* (Kansas City Public Schools, 1961), 76; Robert A. Swann, Jr., "The Ethnic Heritage of Topeka, Kansas: Immigrant Beginnings" (n.p., Institute of Comparative Ethnic Studies, 1974), 65; Department of the Interior, Census Office, *Statistics of the Population of the U.S. at the Tenth Census,* vol. 1 (Washington, 1883): xxvi–xxxvii; and Department of the Interior, Census Office, *Statistics of the Population of the U.S. at the Eleventh Census,* vol. 1 (Washington, 1895): xciii, xcvi, and ci.

16. "To people living outside Kansas this may seem strange, but it is nevertheless true," reported the editor of the *American Citizen* in 1889. "There are homes and lots and additions in and near this city where no Negro can rent or buy at any price, let him be ever so talented, cultured, or refined, and there are others where if he rents or buys his life and property are in danger." *American Citizen,* February 15, 1889. John R. Davis, a black minister of Topeka who had been warned by a note on his door to leave the white suburb of Oakland if he valued his health, complained that many of Topeka's finest white citizens—teachers, lawyers, and doctors—moved into the worst white slums rather than live by a Negro. Those whites who dared stand up for the black man's right to live where he wanted were denounced and boycotted. "Damnable Race Prejudice," *American Citizen,* February 18, 1889.

215

17. *Topeka Capital*, September 25, 1889. See also *Topeka Colored Citizen*, September 20, 1887; and *American Citizen*, February 5, 1892.
18. *Topeka Colored Citizen*, May 31, 1879; *Leavenworth Herald*, October 13, 1894, and January 12, 1895; S. S. Peterson to L. U. Humphrey, August 16, 1890, Governor Humphrey Letters Received, box 5, K.H.S.; *American Citizen*, February 5, 1892; and B. D. Eastman to L. U. Humphrey, November 26, 1890, Governor Humphrey Letters Received, box 2, K.H.S.
19. See, for example, *Topeka Colored Citizen*, June 16, 1898. See also John P. St. John to J. H. Sallee, March 27, 1879, Governor St. John Letter Press Books, vol. 14, K.H.S.; "A Black Brute," *Topeka Capital*, February 1, 1887; *Atchison Blade*, September 17, 1892; *Topeka Capital*, September 10, 1889; and Genevieve Yost, "History of Lynchings in Kansas," *Kansas Historical Quatrerly* 2 (May, 1933): 192.
20. *Leavenworth Advocate*, May 18, 1889; and *Kansas Blackman*, May 18, 1894.
21. "The Penitentiary," *Leavenworth Times*, February 5, 1888; and "Prison Life," *Topeka Capital*, November 23, 1890. See also *Topeka Capital*, January 9, 1885; and *Leavenworth Herald*, January 11, 1896. As was true in other urban areas, the incidence of interpersonal violence among city-dwelling Negroes in Kansas was high. See *Kansas City Gazette*, June 2, 1898, and May 31, 1900; *Leavenworth Herald*, April 25, 1896; and *American Citizen*, November 30, 1894. See, in addition, *Herald of Kansas*, March 19, 1880; "A Black Fiend," *Topeka Capital*, January 10, 1885, and May 4, 1890; *Afro-American Citizen*, March 25, 1892; "Negroes Sue Judge Pfost," *Kansas City Gazette*, September 23, 1897; *Kansas City Gazette*, January 12, 1899; *American Citizen*, December 13, 1890, and January 11, 1895; *Leavenworth Advocate*, May 31, 1890; *Leavenworth Herald*, April 4, 1896, and May 1, 1896; *Kansas Blackman*, May 18, 1894; and "The Same Old

Thing," *Kansas Herald*, February 6, 1880.
22. "The Future of the Negro in America," *Topeka Capital*, January 3, 1886; "The Difference in Souls," *American Citizen*, August 3, 1888, and February 7, 1890; and "Colored People in Theaters," *Topeka Capital*, February 7, 1889.
23. A. T. Andreas, *History of the State of Kansas*, vol. 1 (Chicago, 1883): 295.
24. *General Statutes of Kansas* (Annotated) 1949 (Topeka, 1950), 61–64; and *Western Recorder*, May 31, 1883.
25. There were no antimiscegenation laws on the books in Kansas. Newspapers around the state contained numerous reports of mixed marriages, most of which were tolerated. Editorial and private comment indicate that the lack of violent reaction to these cases by white Kansans was because whites believed that these relationships stemmed from aberrations limited to the dregs of society rather than from a growing commitment to racial amalgamation. See *Leavenworth Times*, May 1, 1878; *American Citizen*, January 25, 1895; *Leavenworth Herald*, December 7, 1895; and *American Citizen*, June 21, 1895. There were, however, isolated incidents in which whites reacted violently to interracial marriage. In 1878 in Parsons a white man married a black woman; a group of whites subsequently paid the couple a pre-dawn visit, dragged the man from his house, and brutally beat him. *Leavenworth Times*, May 1, 1878.
26. *Leavenworth Advocate*, March 14, 1891; "United Order of Immaculates," *American Citizen*, December 28, 1888; *American Citizen*, December 24, 1897; "Kansas Colored Pythians," *Kansas City Gazette*, July 30, 1896; and *Topeka Tribune*, July 22, 1880. See, in addition, *Afro-American Advocate*, July 29, 1892; *American Citizen*, September 7, 1888, and April 19, 1897; *Afro-American Advocate*, April 7, 1893; "The Negro Hospital," *Kansas City Gazette*, No-

vember 17, 1898; *Topeka Journal,* June 16, 1896; *Kansas City Gazette,* January 26, March 9, and April 20, 1899; "Colored Stone Masons," *Topeka Capital,* March 1, 1877; "The Color Line in a Union," *Leavenworth Advocate,* March 21, 1891; and *Kansas Blackman,* June 1, 1894.

27. *Western Recorder,* September 7, 1883. See also *Topeka Colored Citizen,* October 21, 1898; and "Lynch Law and Its Effects," *Topeka Capital,* October 23, 1887.

28. *Western Recorder,* September 7, 1883. See also *Topeka Colored Citizen,* October 21, 1898.

29. *Western Recorder,* May 31, 1883; and John A. Martin to John L. Waller, November 30, 1885, Governor Martin Letter Press Books, vol. 5, K.H.S.

30. "The Next State Auditor," *Indianapolis Freeman,* May 10, 1890; and *Topeka Capital,* January 7, 1887.

31. *American Citizen,* August 17, 1888; "Colored People in Theaters," *Topeka Capital,* February 7, 1889; and *Kansas State Ledger,* September 2 and 30, and October 7, 1892. In 1894 W. B. Townsend authored a comprehensive civil rights measure eliminating the contradictions that had led to invalidation of the 1874 statute. Townsend persuaded a group of Negrophiles in the legislature to introduce the measure, but it remained permanently bottled up in the judiciary committee. *Leavenworth Advocate,* February 23, 1895, and March 6, 1897.

32. *Afro-American Citizen,* March 25, 1892; and *American Citizen,* June 4, 1897.

33. *Topeka Tribune,* August 5, 1880.

34. "Colored Men Should Form Syndicates," *American Citizen,* March 16, 1888.

35. *American Citizen,* February 3 and July 13, 1888. Black leaders such as Waller, Bruce, and Townsend also recognized that unemployment was a major cause of crime among Negroes. By providing jobs for young men and women, black capitalists could reduce crime and improve the race's collec-

tive image. "The Issue," *Leavenworth Herald,* June 24, 1894.

36. *American Citizen,* February 3 and July 13, 1888.

37. *American Citizen,* April 10, 1888.

38. *American Citizen,* June 22, 1888.

39. John A. Garraty, *The New Commonwealth* (New York, 1968), 165.

40. John L. Waller to J. A. Martin, April 12, 1886, Governor Martin Letters Received, General Correspondence, K.H.S.

41. John A. Martin to John L. Waller, April 15, 1886, Governor Martin Letter Press Books, vol. 6, K.H.S.; and John L. Waller to J. A. Martin, April 21, 1886, Governor Martin Letters Received, General Correspondence, K.H.S.

42. *American Citizen,* April 10, 1888.

43. *American Citizen,* March 19, 1897.

44. "Our Business Men," *American Citizen,* July 20, 1888; *American Citizen,* December 13, 1889, and June 6, 1897; *Leavenworth Advocate,* March 29, 1890; *Black Historic Sites,* 31–32; and *Afro-American Advocate,* August 11, 1893.

45. "The Anglo-African," *Ft. Scott Colored Citizen,* June 14, 1878.

46. *Lawrence Journal,* April 18, 1884; John Waller to Harrison Kelley, February 28, 1889, Kelley Papers, K.H.S.; and *Western Recorder,* July 4, 1884.

47. See, for example, *Atchison Globe,* July 17, 1882.

48. "Armour Pkg. Co.," *American Citizen,* February 21, 1896. See also *Kansas State Ledger,* May 13, 1896.

49. *Leavenworth Herald,* January 25, 1896. See, in addition, Thomas H. Mitchell to L. U. Humphrey, February 11, 1892, Governor Humphrey Letters Received, General Correspondence, K.H.S. Relations between black and white miners were often strained. Frequently, blacks would refuse to strike or would agree to go to work for a lower wage. In the early 1890s hundreds of black strikebreakers were imported from Alabama to work the mines near Weir City. Despite threats from local whites to lynch, shoot, or tar and

feather Negroes, the Alabama blacks stayed. By 1894, however, most of the strikebreakers had either become union members or had decided to back the union in its confrontations with management. *Kansas Blackman*, June 1, 1894; *Southern Argus*, June 25, 1891; and *Benevolent Banner*, May 28, 1887. The convention of black men that met in Hutchinson in 1887 reported that black farmers in southwest Kansas owned 167,000 acres of land.

50. "Pictures in Pauperdom," *Topeka Capital*, February 9, 1887.

51. *American Citizen*, January 15, 1897.

52. While Negroes suffered discrimination and sometimes exclusion at the hands of management, the chief obstacle to their effort to find a secure means of livelihood was the hostility of white labor. In 1880, for example, one C. H. Peck, who was in the process of constructing a new packing house at Atchison, hired a number of laborers at $1.25 per day rather than at the usual $1.50. Among the new employees were three blacks. White workers blamed the Negroes for the cut in wages, an angry mob formed, and the three blacks fled. Unappeased, the crowd of laborers proceeded to the Seip and Company brickyard and forced more than a dozen black employees to flee for their lives. In 1878 six white laborers threw down their shovels and walked off a construction site when they were forced to work alongside a Negro. The black was retained. In 1894 in Leavenworth the management of the electric streetcar system promoted James Brown, a black, from shop foreman to motorman. A majority of the white employees voted to strike but changed their minds when management expressed indifference and publicized the fact that the waiting list for positions with the municipal transit system numbered more than 200. The hostility manifested by white workers toward their black counterparts created a marked distrust of unions, even the Knights of Labor, among black Kansans. "It is a well-known fact," editor George A. Dudley wrote in the *American Citizen*, July 13, 1894, "that the opposition to and oppression of the Negro in this country do not come from the wealthy and intelligent classes but from the laboring and less intelligent masses." If blacks joined with their natural enemies in trying to bring down the "money powers," they would find themselves totally isolated. See also *Topeka Colored Citizen*, April 14, 1898; *Leavenworth Herald*, June 2 and July 21, 1894; and "A Sample of Democracy," *Topeka Tribune*, July 29, 1880.

53. In 1894 the *American Citizen* praised the Barnes Coffee, Tea, and Spice Company of Kansas City for making one Fred Turner head of its shipping department. In 1879 the *Colored Citizen* of Topeka lauded a local banker, John D. Knox, for taking on a Negro as a teller in his bank. In addition black periodicals indicated that the W. L. Thomas Furniture Co. of Kansas City occasionally employed Negroes as clerks. "The Color Line Obliterated," *American Citizen*, October 16, 1894; and *Topeka Colored Citizen*, October 18, 1897.

CHAPTER 6

1. William H. Chafe, "The Negro and Populism: A Kansas Case Study," *Journal of Southern History* 34 (August, 1968): 416–417.

2. John L. Waller to John A. Martin, August 16, 1886, Governor Martin Letters Received, box 8, K.H.S., and *Topeka Capital*, October 15, 1886.

3. William Frank Zornow, *Kansas: A History of the Jayhawk State* (Norman, 1951), 194–196. See also John L. Waller to John A. Martin, April 27, 1885, Governor Martin Letters Received, box 8; and John A. Martin to John L. Waller, August 12, 1886, Governor Martin Letter Press Books, vol. 7, K.H.S.

4. See *Leavenworth Times*, February 18, 1886.

5. "The Penitentiary," *Leavenworth Times*, February 5, 1888; and "Prison Life," *Topeka Capital*, 1895.

6. John L. Waller to John A. Martin, November 21, 1885, and August 10, 1886, Governor Martin Letters Received, box 8, K.H.S.; L. W. Pulies to John L. Waller, August 9, 1886, Governor Martin Letters Received, box 3, K.H.S.; and John A. Martin to John L. Waller, August 12, 1886, Governor Martin Letter Press Books, vol. 7, K.H.S.

7. See John H. Smith to John A. Martin, April 27, 1885, and John L. Waller to John A. Martin, May 14, 1885, and August 16, 1886, Governor Martin Letters Received, box 8; John A. Martin to John H. Smith, April 29, 1885, Governor Martin Letter Press Books, vol. 1, K.H.S.; *Leavenworth Times*, August 11, 1878; and *Topeka Capital*, October 15, 1886.

8. "Colored Mass Meeting," *Topeka Capital*, February 10, 1886.

9. *Troy Chief* quoted in *Topeka Capital*, March 27, 1886; *Hiawatha World*, April 13, 1886; "Endorsing Auditor E. P. McCabe," *Topeka Capital*, February 19, 1886; and *Leavenworth Times*, March 21, 1886.

10. John L. Waller to P. I. Bonebrake, March 3, 1886, Governor Martin Letters Received, box 8, K.H.S.

11. "Brown vs. Smith," *Topeka Capital*, January 23, 1887; "The Colored Man in State Politics," *Topeka Capital*, June 20, 1886; and "A Libel Suit," *Topeka Capital*, September 8, 1886.

12. "State Convention," *Topeka Capital*, July 6, 1886; "At Fever Heat," *Topeka Capital*, July 7, 1886; "No Third Term," *Topeka Capital*, July 9, 1886; and John H. Smith to John A. Martin, September 1, 1886, Governor Martin Letters Received, box 8, K.H.S.

13. *Topeka Democrat*, quoted in *Leavenworth Times*, July 14, 1886.

14. G. W. Glick to John L. Waller, November 26, 1884, Governor Glick

Letter Press Books, vol. 54, K.H.S.; and *Topeka Capital*, August 5, 1886.

15. *Topeka Democrat*, quoted in *Topeka Capital*, August 8, 1886.

16. *Topeka Capital*, August 7, 1886.

17. "The Democratic Ticket," *Leavenworth Times*, quoted in *Topeka Capital*, August 7, 1886.

18. "Short-Sighted Colored Men," *Topeka Capital*, October 4, 1885. See also "Colored Men in Politics," *Topeka Capital*, November 1, 1885; and *Leavenworth Times*, March 6, 1886.

19. "Short-Sighted Colored Men," *Topeka Capital*, October 4, 1885.

20. John A. Martin to P. I. Bonebrake, August 16, 1886, Governor Martin Letters Received, box 29, K.H.S.

21. John Waller to John A. Martin, September 11, 1886, Governor Martin Letters Received, box 29, K.H.S.

22. John L. Waller to John A. Martin, September 11 and 14, 1886; John L. Waller to Captain John H. Smith, no date, Governor Martin Letters Received, box 8, K.H.S.; John H. Smith to John A. Martin, September 1, 1886, Governor Martin Letters Received, box 8, K.H.S.; John A. Martin to John L. Waller, September 14, 1886, Governor Martin Letter Press Books, vol. 29, K.H.S.; *American Citizen*, February 23, 1888; and *Topeka Capital*, October 1, 1886.

23. "The Political Arena," *Topeka Capital*, October 13, 1886.

24. "Mr. Waller's Version," *Atchison Champion*, quoted in *Topeka Capital*, September 3, 1886.

25. *Topeka Capital*, November 21, 1886.

26. Adrian Reynolds to John A. Martin, November 5, 1886, Governor Martin Letters Received, box 4, K.H.S.

27. *American Citizen*, February 23, 1888.

28. *American Citizen*, February 23 and March 28, 1888, and March 15, 1889.

29. "A New State Paper," *Topeka Capital*, February 16, 1888.

30. *American Citizen*, February 23, 1888.

31. See *Topeka Capital*, January 6, 1886, and August 3, 1888.

32. *Topeka Colored Citizen*, November 29, 1879; "Our Businessmen," *Amer-*

ican Citizen, July 13, 1888; "The Anniversary," *American Citizen,* March 1, 1889; "Emancipation Day," *Topeka Capital,* August 2, 1890; and *Leavenworth Advocate,* January 4, 1890.

33. *Benevolent Banner,* September 3 and October 3, 1887.
34. *American Citizen,* June 29, 1888; "Letter from John L. Waller," *Topeka Capital,* August 3, 1888; and "Democratic Sympathy for the Colored Man," *Topeka Capital,* May 12, 1888.
35. *American Citizen,* July 6, 1888.
36. "John L. Waller," *Topeka Capital-Commonwealth,* March 7, 1889; "The Next State Auditor," *Indianapolis Freeman,* May 10, 1890; "A Lynching Prevented," *Topeka Capital,* October 1, 1887; *American Citizen,* March 30, August 3 and 17, 1888; and *Topeka Capital,* April 3 and August 17, 1888.
37. *American Citizen,* April 13, 1888.
38. "Political Speeches by Well-Known Republicans Last Night," *Topeka Capital,* April 17, 1888.
39. *Topeka Capital,* July 5, 1888.
40. *Topeka Capital,* July 26 and 27, 1888.
41. "To Colored Men," *Topeka Capital,* November 6, 1888; *American Citizen,* June 15 and July 6, 1888; and *Topeka Capital,* August 26, September 1 and 29, 1888.
42. Humphrey had endeared himself to blacks when in 1887, as a state senator, he introduced in the upper chamber a resolution to strike the word "white" from the Kansas constitution. "John L. Waller," *Topeka Capital-Commonwealth,* March 7, 1889. See also Zornow, *Kansas,* 197.
43. *Topeka Capital,* November 11, 1888.
44. "Topeka's Jubilee," *Topeka Capital-Commonwealth,* November 15, 1888.
45. Zornow, *Kansas,* 194–196.
46. See, for example, "Letter from M. W. Twine," *American Citizen,* May 11, 1888; *Washington Bee,* March 19, 1887; and *Cleveland Gazette,* April 9, 1887.
47. *American Citizen,* December 28, 1888; and *Topeka Capital-Commonwealth,* April 19, 1889.

48. "An Address to the Colored Voters of Kansas," *American Citizen,* October 9, 1896.
49. *American Citizen,* May 11, 1888.
50. *American Citizen,* August 16, 1889.
51. August Meier, *Negro Thought in America, 1880–1915* (Ann Arbor, 1963), 32; *American Citizen,* January 22, 1892; *Nebraska Morning World Herald,* August 14, 1891; *Leavenworth Advocate,* September 22, 1888; and *Afro-American Advocate,* February–December, 1891.
52. C. H. J. Taylor, "Every Colored Voter Should Read This Letter," Republican Party-Clippings, K.H.S.
53. "Colored Kickers," *Topeka Capital,* June 1, 1888. As of 1891, Bell was depicted as the leading black Democrat of Leavenworth by the *Advocate. Leavenworth Advocate,* March 20, 1891. See also "Taylor's Convention," *American Citizen,* June 18, 1888.
54. *American Citizen,* April 2, 1897. For a brief history of the *Citizen,* see *American Citizen,* May 4, 1888.
55. *Benevolent Banner,* May 28, 1887.
56. *American Citizen,* May 4, 1888.
57. Peter H. Argersinger, "Road to a Republican Waterloo: The Farmers' Alliance and the Election of 1890 in Kansas," *Kansas Historical Quarterly* 33 (Winter, 1967): 443–444.
58. *Leavenworth Advocate,* August 16, 1890. The Kansas Farmers' Alliance was surprisingly a member of the Southern rather than the Northern Alliance. The constitution of the Southern Alliance barred Negroes from membership. When the two groups attempted to fuse in 1890 at St. Louis, the southern organizations did agree to state option. "An Anomaly in Politics," *Topeka Capital,* July 27, 1890; and "The National Alliance," *Topeka Capital,* September 13, 1890.
59. According to historian Jack Abramowitz, "the potentialities awaiting the Populist movement should it seek to win the Negro vote and integrate the Negro into the party itself, were first discernible in Kansas where there was less a tradition of anti-Negro sentiment to hinder this develop-

ment." Jack Abramowitz, "The Negro in the Populist Movement," in Sheldon Hackney, ed., *Populism: The Critical Issues* (Boston, 1971), 40–41.

60. Chafe, "Negro and Populism," 410.
61. *Western Recorder*, June 6, 1884.
62. *Leavenworth Advocate*, April 20, May 4, and June 15, 1889; "Ex-Auditor E. P. McCabe Pleased with It," *American Citizen*, May 25, 1888. See also *American Citizen*, December 7, 1888, and February 15 and 22, 1889.
63. *Leavenworth Advocate*, May 11, 1889.
64. *Leavenworth Advocate*, July 6 and September 7, 1889; John Waller to Harrison Kelley, February 28, 1889, Kelley Papers, K.H.S.; and *American Citizen*, February 8, 1889.
65. *American Citizen*, July 26, 1889.
66. See *Topeka Capital*, September 12, 1888; L. U. Humphrey to J. L. Waller, February 18, 1890, Governor Humphrey Letter Press Books, vol. 86, K.H.S.; and *American Citizen*, September 27, 1889.
67. See *Topeka Capital*, June 9, 1890; and *American Citizen*, April 18 and June 6, 1890. See also Allen Buckner to L. U. Humphrey, May 1 and December 3, 1889, Governor Humphrey Letters Received, box 1, K.H.S.; "Trouble at a Blind Asylum," *Leavenworth Advocate*, February 22, 1890; and *Leavenworth Advocate*, March 1, 1889.
68. *Leavenworth Advocate*, July 26, 1890.
69. Ibid.
70. "Must the Negro Go?—Answer by a Negro," *Topeka Capital-Commonwealth*, April 21, 1889; "A Combination," *Topeka Capital*, January 2, 1890; "Col. John M. Brown's Candidacy," *Topeka Capital*, October 27 and November 7, 1889; and *American Citizen*, November 15, 1889.
71. See, for example, *Lawrence Record*, quoted in *Leavenworth Advocate*, August 23, 1890; and *Topeka Capital*, August 12, 1890
72. *Leavenworth Advocate*, July 26, 1890.
73. See, for example, E. P. McCabe to

A. N. Harper, *American Citizen*, December 14, 1888.
74. *Leavenworth Advocate*, August 16, 1890.
75. Ibid.
76. A portion of the South Carolina Farmers' Alliance platform passed in 1890 read: "We recognize the imperative necessity of Anglo-Saxon unity in our state and pledge ourselves to abide by the arbitraments of the democratic party, relying upon the sense of justice and enlightened self interest of a majority of our white fellow citizens to secure all needed reforms." *Topeka Capital*, August 1, 1890.
77. *Topeka Capital*, August 6, September 3 and 5, 1890; Zornow, *Kansas*, 198; *Abilene Reflector*, May 3, 1890; *Salina Republican*, quoted in *Topeka Capital*, August 16, 1890; "What It Means," *American Citizen*, September 12, 1890; *Leavenworth Advocate*, September 6, 1890; and "Kansas Republicans," *Topeka Capital*, September 3, 1890.
78. See, for example, "The Colored Man's Threats," *Topeka Capital*, May 7, 1889. See also *Leavenworth Advocate*, July 26, 1890.
79. See, for example, *Kansas City Gazette*, July 19, 1900.
80. *Topeka Capital*, August 12, 1890.
81. *American Citizen*, April 10, 1888.
82. *American Citizen*, August 7, 1888.

CHAPTER 7

1. See, for example, Earl E. Thorpe, *The Mind of the Negro: An Intellectual History of Afro-Americans* (Westport, Conn., 1961), 32; and August Meier, *Negro Thought in America 1880–1915* (Ann Arbor, 1963), 66.
2. The most authoritative work on black America's interest in African colonization at the turn of the century is Edwin S. Redkey, *Black Exodus: Black Nationalist and Back to Africa Movements, 1890–1910* (New Haven, 1969).

3. Meier says of the black community in the 1890s: "The passing of the Knights of Labor, the failure of southern agrarians to wipe out the color line, and a parallel decline of radical leanings among the few outstanding men who had subscribed to them, combined to give Negro thought an even more conservative cast than it otherwise would have had at this time. Both the decline in political fortunes and the failure to achieve unity with the white working classes forced Negroes to turn their greatest efforts toward achieving wealth and middle-class respectability by their own efforts." Meier, *Negro Thought*, 47.

4. For varying interpretations of this phenomenon, see Julius Pratt, *The Expansionists of 1898* (Baltimore, 1936); Walter LaFeber, *The New Empire* (Ithaca, 1963); Albert Weinberg, *Manifest Destiny* (Baltimore, 1935); and Milton Plesur, *America's Outward Thrust: Approaches to Foreign Affairs, 1865–1890* (DeKalb, 1971).

5. *New York Globe*, April 5, 1884; and Willard B. Gatewood, Jr., *Black Americans and the White Man's Burden* (Urbana, 1974), 300. By 1890 there were in America a sizable number of Negro entrepreneurs, operating mostly in the fields of banking and insurance, with sufficient capital to invest in overseas enterprises. Thorpe, *Mind of the Negro*, 420.

6. Gatewood, *Black Americans*, 306, 315.

7. "A New Field," *Coffeyville American*, May 28, 1898.

8. *Cleveland Gazette*, May 4, 1895.

9. "Manifest Destiny," *Topeka Plaindealer*, August 15, 1900.

10. Thomas J. McCormick, *China Market: America's Quest for Informal Empire, 1893–1901* (New York, 1967), 17; Meier, *Negro Thought*, 57; and LaFeber, *New Empire*, 64. See also "Negro Colonization Scheme," *Chattanooga American*, January 28, 1899.

11. In addition, a number of blacks, including Booker T. Washington, believed that the Afro-American had a civilizing and uplifting role to play in Africa. Louis R. Harlan, "Booker T. Washington and the White Man's Burden," *American Historical Review* 71 (January, 1966): 441–467.

12. Stewart, for example, after spending two years in Liberia and then returning to the United States in 1885, denied that he was a colonizationist but argued vigorously in behalf of black participation in informal empire. Convinced that Negroes would always remain within the American nation, though as a distinct people, he advised simply a voluntary movement of self-supporting people. Meier, *Negro Thought*, 66.

13. Robert G. Weisbord, *Ebony Kinship: Africa, Africans, and the Afro-American* (Westport, Conn., 1973), 29; and Gatewood, *Black Americans*, 300.

14. Edward W. Blyden, "The African Problem and the Method of Its Solution," in Howard Brotz, ed., *Negro Social and Political Thought, 1850–1920: Representative Texts* (New York, 1966), 126–170. See also Gatewood, *Black Americans*, 305; Louis R. Harlan, *Booker T. Washington: The Making of a Black Leader, 1856–1895* (New York, 1972), 75–76; and Harlan, "White Man's Burden," 441–447.

15. "Cuba and Hawaii," *Parsons Weekly Blade*, September 21, 1895.

16. "A New Field," *Coffeyville American*, May 28, 1898.

17. See, for example, an article by Kelly Miller entitled "The Effect of Imperialism on the Negro Race," quoted in George P. Marks, *The Black Press Views American Imperialism, 1898–1900* (New York, 1971), xi.

18. See, for example, "Resolutions by the Colored People," *Topeka Capital*, April 14, 1886. See also *Topeka Capital*, October 12, 1886, in Negroes-Clippings, vol. 5–6, K.H.S.; Charles Charles to John A. Martin, December 1, 1887, Governor Martin Letters Received, box 4, K.H.S.; "The Liberian Movement," *Topeka Capital*, January 30, 1887; and "The Exodus Movement—The Scheme to Colonize

Colored People in Brazil and the Argentine Republic," *Topeka Capital*, February 3, 1888.

19. "The Oklahoma Situation," *Topeka Capital*, March 15, 1885; "Oklahoma Boomers," *Topeka Capital-Commonwealth*, April 13, 1889; *American Citizen*, July 26, 1889; "Negro Colonies," *Topeka Capital*, July 7, 1889; "Topeka's Contingent," *Topeka Capital-Commonwealth*, April 21, 1889; "A Flourishing Colony," *Topeka Capital*, August 6, 1889; and *Afro-American Citizen*, April 1, 1892.

20. *Topeka Capital*, October 16, 1889.

21. "McCabe's Boom," *Topeka Capital*, February 5, 1890; "Driven Away," *Topeka Capital*, March 5, 1890; "Charges against the Oklahoma Townsite Officials," *Topeka Capital*, March 15, 1890; and "Takes Defeat Gracefully," *Topeka Capital*, May 9, 1890.

22. *Topeka Commonwealth*, May 13, 1879.

23. *American Citizen*, March 11, 1888. Actually, Waller had visualized Oklahoma as a western haven for blacks as early as 1883. See "Oklahoma," *Western Recorder*, April 5, 1883.

24. *Topeka Capital*, March 6, 1890.

25. "Mr. Waller Rejoins," *Topeka Capital*, March 11, 1890. See also *Western Recorder*, May 31, 1883.

26. "To the Colored Citizens of Kansas," *Topeka Capital*, September 28, 1890. See also October 18 and 23, and August 15, 1890.

27. *Leavenworth Advocate*, October 11, 1890.

28. Peter H. Argersinger, "Road to a Republican Waterloo: The Farmers' Alliance and the Election of 1890 in Kansas," *Kansas Historical Quarterly* 33 (Winter, 1967): 443; and *Topeka Capital*, November 5, 1890.

29. B. W. Perkins to Benjamin Harrison, October 18, 1890, Waller Appointment File, RG 59, DOS.

30. Preston B. Plumb to James G. Blaine, June 18, 1890, Waller Appointment File, RG 59, DOS.

31. J. H. Robertson to Grover Cleveland,

October 17, 1890, Waller Appointment File, RG 59, DOS.

32. *Leavenworth Advocate*, October 25, 1890; and *Afro-American Advocate*, September 29, 1892.

33. "C. H. J. Taylor—The Leader," *American Citizen*, June 22, 1888.

34. *Leavenworth Advocate*, February 21 and March 7, 1891; and *Leavenworth Times*, February 28, 1891.

35. *American Citizen*, June 19, 1891.

36. Ibid.

37. I. Garland Penn, *The Afro-American Press and Its Editors* (New York, 1969), 182.

38. Frederick Taylor, "Madagascar," *The North American Review* 158 (October, 1896): 479–487; "The French in Madagascar," *Harper's Weekly* 39 (July 6, 1895): 640; Stephen H. Roberts, *History of French Colonial Policy, 1870–1925*, vol. 2 (London, 1925): 377; and Prime Minister Ratsimanana to John Waller, February 29, 1895, Waller Case Papers, *PRFRUS*, 358.

39. Roberts, *French Colonial Policy*, 379; Alf Andrew Heggoy, *The African Policies of Gabriel Hanotaux, 1894–1898* (Athens, 1972), 73, 77–78; *New York Daily Tribune*, October 9, 1895; and Henri Brunschwig, *French Colonialism, 1871–1914* (London, 1966), 87.

40. *Revue Bleu* (Paris), November 8, 1894, quoted in *Literary Guide* 10: 25.

41. Heggoy, *Hanotaux*, 77–78.

42. *New York Times*, January 28, 1894.

43. Ibid.

44. Heggoy, *Hanotaux*, 77–78; Herbert I. Priestly, *France Overseas: A Study of Modern Imperialism* (New York, 1938), 311, 306; and "Madagascar," *London Times*, January 10, 1895.

45. Ronald Robinson and John Gallagher, *Africa and the Victorians* (New York, 1968), 127, 302; and "Declarations exchanges entre le Gouvernement de la République Française et la Gouvernement de sa Majesté Britannique au sujet des territoires d'Afrique," August 5, 1890, no. 4,

Documents Diplomatique: Affaires de Madagascar, 1885–1895 (Paris, Imprimerie Nationale, 1895).

46. John Campbell to William Wharton, September 24, 1890, no. 89, Dispatches of the United States Consul at Tamatave (hereinafter referred to as DUSCT), RG 59, DOS.

47. *Madagascar News*, August 12, 1893; "Madagascar," *The Parliamentary Debates* (June 12, 1894), vol. 25, Twenty-fifth Parliament, Third Session, 921; and Roberts, *French Colonial Policy*, 381–384.

48. "Excerpts from Prime Minister's Speech," September 24, 1890, no. 89, DUSCT, RG 59, DOS.

49. *The Madagascar Mail*, January 12, 1892.

50. A desire to involve the United States in the Franco-Malagasy dispute was not limited to the Hovas and the English colony in Madagascar. In March, 1894, Sir Charles Dilke in the House of Commons proposed joint action by Great Britain and the United States to prevent a French takeover. "Madagascar," *The Parliamentary Debates* (March 15, 1894), vol. 25, Twenty-fifth Parliament, Third Session, 315.

51. Taylor, "Madagascar," 483.

52. "Ranavalona and Waller," *Cedar Rapids Evening Gazette*, August 20, 1895.

53. *American Citizen*, September 18, 1891; and Prime Minister Rainilaiarivony to John Waller, April 12, 1893, no. 17, DUSCT, RG 59, DOS.

54. *New York Age*, February 18, 1892.

55. *American Citizen*, September 18, 1891; and Prime Minister Rainilaiarivony to John Waller, April 12, 1893, no. 17, DUSCT, RG 59, DOS; Queen Ranavalona to Grover Cleveland, June 6, 1893, no. 65, DUSCT, RG 59, DOS; *Madagascar News*, August 21, 1893, Petition to Edward Wetter, January, 1896, Waller Case Papers, *PRFRUS*, 396; and Robert Cornish to John Waller, October 31, 1891, no. 11, DUSCT, RG 59, DOS.

56. Heggoy, *Hanotaux*, 81.

57. Prime Minister to Secretary of State, August 27, 1887, no. 13, DUSCT, RG 59, DOS.

58. John Waller to William Wharton, August 10, 1891, no. 1, DUSCT, RG 59, DOS; and A. Ribot to M. Bompard, September 30, 1891, no. 14, *Documents Diplomatique*.

59. The United States concluded treaties of peace, friendship, and commerce with the Hova monarchy on February 14, 1867, and May 13, 1881. Richard Olney to James B. Eustis, March 30, 1896, No. 635, DUSMF, RG 59, DOS.

60. *Manchester Guardian*, August 28, 1895.

61. William R. Day, acting secretary of state under John Sherman, and later secretary in his own right, advised Congress that "the output of United States manufactures . . . has reached the point of large excess above the demands of home consumption." Day urged a vigorous commercial expansion into the southern half of the Western Hemisphere and "the vast underdeveloped regions of Asia and Africa." McCormick, *China Market*, 38.

62. Milton Plesur, *American's Outward Thrust: Approaches to Foreign Affairs, 1865–1890* (DeKalb, Ill., 1971), 147–148. Even extreme racists within the white community could in good conscience support Waller because they saw in him a stimulus to black emigration. In an article penned in 1890, Alabama Senator John T. Morgan declared that it was the duty of the United States to return the descendants of the slaves to the land from which they had been brought. Africa should be opened up so Negroes could return and promote commerce among their own people. Plesur, *Outward Thrust*, 149.

63. *Lagos Weekly Record*, August 22, 1891.

64. Campbell, *China Market*, 64; and Alvey Adee to Richard Olney, February 7, 1896, vol. 44, Papers of Richard Olney, Library of Congress.

65. Henry A. Sanford, "American Inter-

ests in Africa," *The Forum*, 9 (March–August, 1890): 428–429.

66. "France and Madagascar," *The Literary Digest* 9 (May–November, 1894): 713; Edward Wetter to E. H. Strobel, March 27, 1894, no. 22, DUSCT, RG 59, DOS; John Waller to Alvey Adee, November 26, 1892, no. 34, DUSCT, RG 59, DOS; Edward Wetter to Edwin Uhl, July 23, 1895, no. 105, DUSCT, RG 59, DOS; and "The Madagascar Difficulty between France and England," *Commercial and Financial Chronicle*, September 29, 1894. See also "France and Madagascar," *New York Times*, June 17, 1896.

67. John Campbell to William Wharton, September 24, 1890, no. 89, DUSCT, RG 59, DOS.

68. C. Vann Woodward, *The Strange Career of Jim Crow* (New York, 1966), 54. See also Redkey, *Black Exodus*, 58–60.

69. Richard E. Welch, Jr., "The Federal Elections Bill of 1890: Postscript and Prelude," *The Journal of American History* 52 (December, 1965): 512.

70. Joseph Bradfield to Benjamin Harrison, July 22, 1889, Papers of Benjamin Harrison, Library of Congress.

71. *Leavenworth Advocate*, June 22, 1889.

72. George Sinkler, "Benjamin Harrison and the Matter of Race," *Indiana Magazine of History* 65 (September, 1969): 195–196.

73. See, for example, *Executive Documents of the House of Representatives*, Fifty-second Congress, Second Session, vol. 1 (Washington, 1893): 165–168, 229, 231, 234; and *American Citizen*, July 3, 1896.

74. LaFeber, *New Empire*, 127–130.

75. The two most recently published works on Liberian history are Richard West, *Back to Africa: A History of Sierra Leone and Liberia* (New York, 1971), and Charles Morrow Wilson, *Liberia: Black Africa in Microcosm* (New York, 1971).

76. In his first annual message to Congress in 1886, President Cleveland proclaimed that it "was the moral right and duty of the United States to assist in the maintenance of Liberia's integrity." Elizabeth Brett White, *American Opinion of France* (New York, 1927), 214–215.

77. See, for example, *Executive Documents of the House of Representatives*, Fifty-second Congress, Second Session, vol. 1 (Washington, 1893): 165–168, 229, 231, 234.

78. John Waller to William Wharton, October 26, 1891, no. 11, DUSCT, RG 59, DOS. At one point Waller urged the State Department to empower him to go to Tananarive and mediate between the Hovas and the French. Protection of American interests, he argued, demanded it. Alvey Adee ruled out such a move, intimating to Josiah Quincy that in his opinion "the eventual supremacy of the French in Madagascar was inevitable." By 1894, however, Adee was one of the most vociferous advocates within the State Department of American resistance to a French takeover. John Waller to William Wharton, April 25, 1893, no. 53, and Alvey Adee to Josiah Quincy, June 2, 1893, Interdepartmental Memo, DUSCT, RG 59, DOS.

79. Edward Wetter to Edwin Uhl, November 27, 1894, no. 64, DUSCT, RG 59, DOS.

80. *Madagascar News*, April 12, 1895; and William Rockhill to W. E. Faison, March 27, 1894, no. 64, DUSCT, RG 59, DOS.

81. *Madagascar News*, April 12, 1895.

82. John Waller to James R. Ruff, *Afro-American Advocate*, June 24, 1892. During his two years as consul in Madagascar, Waller and his stepson sent over 500 letters to blacks and influential whites extolling the economic opportunities and racial climate of east Africa. *Parsons Weekly Blade*, June 22, 1895.

83. *Le Madagascar*, March 29, 1894; and "Exonerates Eustis," *Cedar Rapids Evening Gazette*, October 18, 1895.

84. Actually, Waller had begun negotiating with the Hovas for a concession as early as the spring of 1893. John

Waller to Forrest White, March 17, 1893, Miscellaneous Letters, RG 59, DOS.

85. "Agreement between John Waller and the Malagasy Government," March 15, 1894, no. 34, DUSCT, RG 59, DOS.

86. See *Madagascar News*, August 8, 1890, and April 8, 1895; Queen Ranavalona to Grover Cleveland, June 6, 1893, no. 5, DUSCT, RG 59, DOS; John Duder to E. L. Poupard, March 19, 1894, Telegram, DUSCT, RG 59, DOS; and John Waller and Paul Bray to John Mercer Langston, December 4, 1894, Papers of John Mercer Langston, Microfilm in Amistad Research Center, Dillard University (originals at Fisk University, Nashville).

87. *Madagascar News*, March 17, 1894, and May 3, 1894.

88. M. Larrouy to M. Develle, July 22, 1893, no. 21; September 5, 1893, no. 23; and September 27, 1894, no. 24, *Documents Diplomatique*. See also *Madagascar*, April 14, 1893; and Le Myer de Vilers to Gabriel Hanotaux, November 2, 1894, no. 54, *Documents Diplomatique*.

89. M. Casmir-Perier to M. Larrouy, January 26, 1894, no. 31, *Documents Diplomatique*.

90. Heggoy, *Hanotaux*, 78–79; and E. G. Woodford to James B. Eustis, August 21, 1895, no. 362, DUSMF, RG 59, DOS.

91. Robert McLane to T. F. Bayard, February 3, 1886, Waller Case Papers, *PRFRUS*; and *Madagascar News*, August 8, 1890.

92. The French had obtained an 1891 memorandum from an American merchant in Madagascar to the Hova prime minister outlining "the whole policy of granting concessions on a very large scale to Americans." That some Frenchmen feared attempts at massive economic penetration of Madagascar by the U.S. is not surprising. Interview between Edwin Uhl and Ethelbert Woodford, October 22, 1895, Waller Case Papers, *PRFRUS*, 377.

93. *Progres de l'Imerina*, October 13, 1894, in *Literary Guide* 9: 13.

94. *Le Madagascar*, March 29, 1894, and April 15, 1894.

95. G. R. Struble to Charles A. Clark, April 4, 1894, Miscellaneous Letters, RG 59, DOS.

96. John Waller to John Mercer Langston, May 12, 1894, Langston Papers.

97. *American Citizen*, March 16, 1888, and July 26, 1889; *Topeka Plaindealer*, July 5, 1901; and *Leavenworth Advocate*, November 16, 1889, and April 5, 1890.

98. John Waller to John Mercer Langston, March 30, 1894, Langston Papers; *Madagascar News*, May 3, 1894; and Agreement between John L. Waller and the Malagasy Government, March 15, 1894, no. 34, DUSCT, RG 59, DOS.

99. John Waller to John Mercer Langston, March 30, 1894, Langston Papers.

100. John Waller to John Mercer Langston, July, 1894, Langston Papers.

101. *Cedar Rapids Evening Gazette*, June 7, 1895.

102. John Waller to John Mercer Langston, August 20, 1894, Langston Papers.

103. John Waller to John Mercer Langston, May 12, 1894, Langston Papers.

104. Warner T. McGuinn to John Mercer Langston, October 3, 1894, Langston Papers.

105. "John L. Waller Again," *Parsons Weekly Blade*, June 22, 1895.

106. Crammond Kennedy to Richard Olney, May, 1895, Miscellaneous Letters, RG 59, DOS; and Edwin Uhl to John Mercer Langston, October 10, 1894, Langston Papers.

107. "France and Madagascar," *Progres de l'Imerina*, October 13, 1894.

108. John Waller to Susan Waller, November 2, 1894, Waller Case Papers, *PRFRUS*.

109. Edward Wetter to E. H. Strobel, December 8, 1893, no. 5, DUSCT, RG 59, DOS; and Edward Wetter to E. H. Strobel, January 27, and February 7, 1894, no. 7, DUSCT, RG 59, DOS.

110. Aside from being racially and polit-

ically prejudiced against Waller, Wetter disliked Waller because he had attempted to help one Charles T. Lyons, the representative of a Boston commercial firm doing business in Madagascar. Lyons, who had arrived in Madagascar in September, 1894, had replaced a friend of Wetter's, and in retaliation the consul charged Lyons with tampering with official mail. Waller and Bray subsequently helped Lyons jump bail and escape. Upon his return to the United States, Lyons complained vigorously of his treatment at Wetter's hands. *New York Sun*, September 4, 1895.

111. Edwin Wetter to Edwin Uhl, October 26, 1894, no. 60, DUSCT, RG 59, DOS; and Richard Olney to Grover Cleveland, December, 1895, vol. 41, Olney Papers.

112. M. Le Myer de Vilers to Gabriel Hanotaux, November 2, 1894, no. 54, *Documents Diplomatique.*

113. M. Le Myer de Vilers to Gabriel Hanotaux, October 26, 1894, no. 52, and October 20, 1894, no. 49, *Documents Diplomatique*. See also Gabriel Hanotaux to M. Le Myer de Vilers, November 27, 1894, no. 57, and December 8, 1894, no. 58, *Documents Diplomatique*; and Heggoy, *Hanotaux*, 83.

114. "Waller's Acts in Madagascar," *New York Times*, February 23, 1895; Waller's Deposition, August 27, 1895, no. 362, DUSMF, RG 59, DOS; and Edward Wetter to Edwin Uhl, November 27, 1894, no. 64, DUSCT, RG 59, DOS. See also Edward Wetter to Edwin Uhl, November 7, 1894, no. 63, DUSCT, RG 59, DOS.

115. Edward Wetter to Edwin Uhl, April 20, 1895, no. 88, DUSCT, RG 59, DOS.

116. Record of First Permanent Court Martial Sitting at Tamatave, June 24, 1895, enclosure 4, no. 327, DUSMF, RG 59, DOS.

117. John Waller to Daniel W. Voorhees, June 14, 1895, Miscellaneous Letters, RG 59, DOS; and "John Waller's

Story," *Indianapolis Freeman*, April 11, 1896.

118. John Waller to Edward Wetter, March 18, 1895, Waller Case Papers, *PRFRUS*.

119. Edward Wetter to Edwin Uhl, March 11, 1895, no. 8, DUSCT, RG 59, DOS.

120. Edward Wetter to John Waller, March 20, 1895, Waller Case Papers, *PRFRUS*, 322–323.

121. Captain Kiesel to Edward Wetter, March 22, 1895, Waller Case Papers, *PRFRUS*, 324–325.

122. Statement of Paul H. Bray in re expulsion from Madagascar of Ex-Consul Waller, May 19, 1895, Waller Case Papers, *PRFRUS*. For other accounts of Waller's arrest and trial, and Wetter's role, see J. O. Ryder to Alvey Adee, May 2, 1895, Miscellaneous Letters, RG 59, DOS; and Waller's Deposition, August 27, 1895, no. 362, DUSMF, RG 59, DOS.

CHAPTER 8

1. Interview between Edwin Uhl and Ethelbert G. Woodford, October 22, 1895, Waller Case Papers, *PRFRUS*, 369–380.

2. There is no evidence that Booker T. Washington attempted to help Waller, but he was certainly aware of the Kansan's predicament. H. Walter Webb to Booker T. Washington, 1895, container 113, Papers of Booker T. Washington, Library of Congress.

3. C. H. J. Taylor to Grover Cleveland, March 10, 1894, Papers of Grover Cleveland, Library of Congress.

4. "Waller's Still on Top," *American Citizen*, March 15, 1895. In the midst of the controversy created by Waller's imprisonment, on June 15, 1895, editor Monroe Dorsey of the *Parsons Weekly Blade* wrote an open letter to Waller in which he proclaimed that the entire race was proud to view the imprisoned Kansan as "a typical American Negro."

5. *St. Louis American Eagle*, January 25, 1896, as quoted in the *Cleveland Gazette*.

6. *Salt Lake City Broad Ax,* February 8, 1896.
7. "The Waller Case," *Cleveland Gazette,* May 4, 1895.
8. *Parsons Weekly Blade,* May 11, 1895,
9. *St. Paul Broad Ax,* February 8, 1896; *Richmond Planet,* December 21, 1895; *Leavenworth Herald,* December 21, 1895; and *Omaha Enterprise,* December 14, 1895.
10. *Parsons Weekly Blade,* December 28, 1895.
11. *Cleveland Gazette,* August 31, 1895.
12. *Kansas City Journal,* August 11, 1895. The *Omaha Enterprise* of January 4, 1896, argued that Waller's incarceration posed a threat to the freedom and safety of every person in the United States. "Something more vital than the Monroe Doctrine is at stake," warned editor G. F. Franklin, "when an American citizen is lawlessly imprisoned and despoiled of his property by a foreign power with which the United States is at peace." In the ultimate attempt to shame the nation into defending its black representative abroad, the *Wichita National Reflector,* in its issue of February 8, 1896, made a provocative comparison: "There is no doubt of the fact that had John Waller been a subject of Great Britain he would have been released long ago."
13. *Cleveland Gazette,* May 4, 1895.
14. *Richmond Planet,* May 11, 1895.
15. T. McCants Stewart to Grover Cleveland, March 28, 1895, Miscellaneous Letters, RG 59, DOS.
16. *Parsons Weekly Blade,* March 29 and May 15, 1895.
17. "The Waller Case," *Indianapolis Freeman,* April 27, 1895.
18. *Washington Bee,* September 28, 1895.
19. *Cleveland World,* August 3, 1895.
20. August Meier, "The Negro and the Democratic Party, 1875–1915," *Phylon* 17 (Summer, 1956): 175. In his *The Democratic Party and the Negro* Lawrence Grossman argues that following the election of 1872 Democratic moderates seized control of the party and devised a clever long-range plan to regain power. During the two decades that followed, the Democratic leadership acquiesed in Reconstruction, accepting the Republican governments established in the South in 1867–68 and the Reconstruction Amendments, and at the same time called for local self-government in the South. Official acceptance of Reconstruction would renew Democratic respectability among northern voters, while a hands-off southern policy justified by states' rights theory might allow Dixie Democrats to recapture control of the South. This stratagem became known as the "new departure." Simultaneously, blacks and Democrats in the North began to explore the possibilities of political rapprochement above the Mason-Dixon line. On some occasions and in some places Negroes took the initiative by adopting an independent political stance in state and local elections. In other situations the Democrats made the first move with patronage or favorable state legislation. As governor and president, Grover Cleveland came to symbolize the positive northern Democratic attitude toward Negroes; he did not undermine the position of Negroes in the federal bureaucracy, and he rebuked outright violence against them in the South. Lawrence Grossman, *The Democratic Party and the Negro: Northern and National Policies, 1868–1892* (Urbana, 1976), 15, 57, 65–66, 115.
21. *Marquette (Wisconsin) Monitor,* April 27, 1888.
22. Meier, "Negro and Democratic Party," 177.
23. Donald E. Drake, "Militancy in Fortune's New York Age," *Journal of Negro History* 55 (October, 1970): 309.
24. In 1895 Astwood was pastor of the Bethel A.M.E. Church in Harrisburg, Pennsylvania. H. C. C. Astwood to Grover Cleveland, November 11, 1895, Cleveland Papers. See also H. C. C. Astwood to Henry Turber, November 13 and August 29, 1893, and George T. Downing to Grover

Cleveland, April 8, 1888, Cleveland Papers; *Washington Bee*, October 4, 1890, and September 19, 1891; *New York Age*, August 29, 1891; C. H. J. Taylor to Henry Thurber, July 13, 1894, Cleveland Papers; and Meier, "Negro and Democratic Party," 177–190.

25. H. C. C. Astwood to Henry Thurber, November 13, 1893, and April 15, 1895, Cleveland Papers.
26. C. H. J. Taylor to Grover Cleveland, March 10, 1894, and C. H. J. Taylor to Henry Thurber, October 15, 1895, Cleveland Papers.
27. "France and Madagascar," *Chicago Tribune*, June 2, 1895.
28. "The Capture of Antananarivo," *New York Times*, October 9, 1895.
29. Charles H. Booth to Grover Cleveland, April 30, 1895, Miscellaneous Letters, RG 59, DOS.
30. Rev. James M. Whiton, "The Crime Against Madagascar," *Outlook* 52 (September 28, 1895): 503–504.
31. See, for example, *Memphis Commercial Appeal*, August 22, 1895.
32. David Healy maintains that events of the 1890s, particularly the Venezuelan Affair, "forced the phenomenon of imperialism upon the attention of Americans, and led them to think more seriously about their foreign relations. One of the results of this development was "the growing advocacy of a sort of proscriptive imperialism, a conviction that the United States should seize desirable areas before a rival power got them." David Healy, *U.S. Expansionism: The Imperialist Urge in the 1890s* (Madison, 1970), 28.
33. W. C. Tetrick to Richard Olney, July 19, 1895, Miscellaneous Letters, RG 59, DOS. The issue at point, declared the *New York World*, February 22, 1896, was "the right of American citizens to live abroad without being subjected to execution and imprisonment."
34. "A Direct Affront," *Memphis Commercial Appeal*, August 24, 1895.
35. *New York Daily Tribune*, November 29, 1895.

36. See, for example, John D. Glass to Thomas Updegraff, March 28, 1895, Miscellaneous Letters, RG 59, DOS; "The Case of Waller," *New York Times*, December 4, 1895; "The Diplomatic Tangle," *Chicago Tribune*, March 25, 1895; and "The Persecution of Waller," *New York Daily Tribune*, August 25, 1895.
37. *Chicago Tribune*, March 5, 1895.
38. *New York Daily Tribune*, May 19, 1895.
39. Healy, *U.S. Expansionism*, 163. Ironically, Reid was a close friend and avid political supporter of Alexandre Ribot. Whitelaw Reid to Henry Vignaud, November 1, 1895, reel 68, Papers of Whitelaw Reid, Library of Congress.
40. "Indifferent to Waller's Fate," *New York Daily Tribune*, March 28, 1895. *The Journal of Commerce*, however, best summarized the views of those who saw the Waller affair primarily in economic terms. "We have no sympathy whatever with jingoism," declared the editors. "We recognize the subjection of our citizens and our ships to foreign jurisdiction when they are within the boundaries of foreign powers, but we certainly owe it to our citizens to protect them from violence and injustice." The United States must not waive this right simply because France was a great power. "France and the Waller Case," *Journal of Commerce* (New York), August 31, 1895.
41. *Cleveland Gazette*, October 12, 1895.
42. "Our Foreign Policy," *Leavenworth Herald*, May 4, 1895.
43. *Cleveland World*, August 3, 1895.
44. See, for example, Walter Gresham to Albert S. Willis, January 23, 1895, Letterbook, Papers of Walter Q. Gresham, Library of Congress; and Rubin F. Weston, *Racism in United States Imperialism* (Columbia, S.C., 1972), 12.
45. "Indifferent to Waller's Fate," *New York Daily Tribune*, March 28, 1895.
46. *Kansas City Journal*, February 22, 1896. Even members of the president's own party attacked his policy

toward Madagascar. *The New Orleans Times-Picayune*, already angry with the Cleveland administration over its refusal to back Cuban independence, declared Waller "unjustly condemned" and pronounced the federal government's failure to secure his release as "one of the most extraordinary exhibitions of lack of national pride that could be imagined." "The Case of Ex-Consul Waller," *New Orleans Times-Picayune*, August 23, 1895. Reflecting mounting fear within Democratic circles that inactivity in the Waller affair would cost the party dearly at the polls, the *Memphis Commercial Appeal* and the *Arkansas Gazette*, both of which were sound-money, antiannexationist, pro-Cleveland papers, alternately pleaded and demanded that the administration take a more aggressive stand in the matter. *Memphis Commercial Appeal*, September 11, 1895, and *Arkansas Gazette*, August 27, 1895.

CHAPTER 9

1. "John L. Waller's Story," *Indianapolis Freeman*, April 11, 1896.
2. A number of Waller's defenders charged that the career foreign-service officers within the State Department deliberately mishandled the case because they were extreme Negrophobes. The charge appears to be unfounded, at least insofar as it applied to Alvey Adee, who headed the departmental bureaucracy. See, for example, Alvey Adee to Richard Olney, July 27, 1895, container 30, Olney Papers.
3. "Another Colored Causa Belli," *Washington Post*, March 26, 1895. See also Charles Curtis to Walter Gresham, March 30, 1895; Thomas Updegraff to Walter Gresham, March 30, 1895; and Citizens of Buchanan County, Missouri, to Walter Gresham, April 30, 1895, all Miscellaneous Letters, RG 59, DOS.

4. Walter LaFeber, *The New Empire* (Ithaca, 1963), 197.
5. Ibid. Gresham was, however, "unalterably opposed to stealing territory, or of annexing people against their consent." Walter Gresham to John Overmeyer, July 25, 1894, vol. 43, Gresham Papers.
6. At the same time, American representatives in Madagascar were advising the State Department that the French protectorate was proving very harmful to United States–Malagasy trade. In collusion with the resident general, French firms had been avoiding Hova import duties through a system of false invoices. Edward Wetter to E. H. Stroble, January 26, 1894, no. 6, DUSCT, RG 59, DOS.
7. Walter Gresham to James B. Eustis, April 10, 1895, Waller Case Papers, *PRFRUS*, 260.
8. "The Court Martial of Waller," *New York Times*, March 24, 1895.
9. Edward Wetter to Edwin Uhl, April 20, 1895, no. 88, DUSCT, RG 59, DOS.
10. *Le Courier des Etats-Unis*, March 25 and April 13, 1895.
11. *Le Figaro*, August 28, 1895.
12. *Estafette*, August 31, 1895. See also James B. Eustis to Walter Gresham, April 5, 1895, vol. 43, Gresham Papers.
13. James Eustis to Walter Gresham, May 1 and April 25, 1895, no. 297, DUSMF, RG 59, DOS.
14. *Cleveland Gazette*, May 4, 1895; and Mora Claims, July 17, 1895, container 28, Olney Papers.
15. Langston and Kennedy's first task was to defend Waller against charges that he was no longer an American citizen. W. B. Townsend, still smarting at Waller's "defection" to C. H. J. Taylor, had started a rumor that the ex-consul had returned to the United States in 1894 and then gone abroad again without a passport. Certain white Negrophobes joined with Townsend in arguing that Waller had forfeited his citizenship by returning to Madagascar "illegally" and hence was not due protection

from the United States government. Langston and Kennedy had no trouble, however, in proving that the Kansan had not been in the United States since 1891. "Without a Passport," *Washington Post*, March 28, 1895.

16. Paul Bray to John Mercer Langston, September 11, 1894, Langston Papers; Edward Wetter to Edwin Uhl, April 20, 1895, no. 87, DUSCT, RG 59, DOS; James Eustis to Walter Gresham, May 3, 1895, Telegram, DUSMF, RG 59," DOS; "Ex-Consul Waller's Stepson," *New York Times*, May 19, 1895; and "P. M. Bray in Washington," *New York Times*, May 20, 1895.

17. Benjamin Harrison to James G. Blaine, December 31, 1891, container 17, Papers of James G. Blaine, Library of Congress; and Kenneth J. Hagan, *American Gunboat Diplomacy in the Old Navy* (Westport, Conn., 1973), 85–87.

18. Commander Thomas Perry to Secretary of the Navy, May 15, 1895, container 33, Olney Papers.

19. See *New York Times*, August 23, 1895; Edward Wetter to Edwin Uhl, June 11, 1895, no. 97, DUSCT, RG 59, DOS; and "An Incident at Tamatave," *New York Times*, August 25, 1895. The Navy Department, after consultation with State, subsequently approved Perry's refusal at Tamatave to salute the French flag. "The Madagascar Campaign," *Manchester Guardian*, August 26, 1895.

20. David Healy, *U.S. Expansionism: The Imperialist Urge in the 1890s* (Madison, 1970), 39; and LaFeber, *New Empire*, 256–258.

21. James Eustis to Gabriel Hanotaux, May 31, 1895, no. 316, DUSMF, RG 59, DOS.

22. James Eustis to Richard Olney, June 21, 1895, no. 323, DUSMF, RG 59, DOS; James Eustis to Gabriel Hanotaux, June 22, 1895, no. 327, enclosure 5, DUSMF, RG 59, DOS; and Edwin Uhl (Acting Secretary) to James Eustis, July 3, 1895, Waller Case Papers, *PRFRUS*, 269. The administration was even besieged by pleas in Waller's behalf from foreign politicians. In late August, J. E. Gordon, a member of the House of Commons who had met Waller aboard ship in 1891, wrote to Olney asking Washington to protect him from "the cruel treatment of the French court." J. E. Gordon to Richard Olney, August 23, 1895, Miscellaneous Letters, RG 59, DOS.

23. The French distrusted Woodford almost as much as they did Waller, seeing in him an agent of United States economic expansion. *Le Temps*, May 16, 1895. E. G. Woodford to Grover Cleveland, March 5, 1893, Cleveland Papers, E. G. Woodford to James Eustis, August 21, 1895, no. 362, DUSMF, RG 59, DOS; John Campbell to Edwin Uhl, June 18, 1895, container 27, Olney Papers; and Susan Waller to John Waller, June 20, 1895, no. 358, DUSMF, RG 59, DOS.

24. "The Waller Case Again," *Indianapolis Freeman*, July 13, 1895.

25. "Waller in Prison," *Cedar Rapids Evening Gazette*, July 9, 1895; "John L. Waller Writes," *Cedar Rapids Evening Gazette*, August 15, 1895; and John L. Waller to Laura Martin, August 7, 1895, *Cedar Rapids Evening Gazette*, September 11, 1895.

26. John L. Waller to Laura Martin, August 1895, *Cedar Rapids Evening Gazette*, September 11, 1895.

27. J. H. Gallinger to Richard Olney, July 1, 1895, Miscellaneous Letters, RG 59, DOS.

28. J. Sims to Jacob Gallinger, July 2, 1895; John Waller to Daniel Voorhees, June 14, 1895; and Daniel Voorhees to Richard Olney, July 15, 1895; Charles Curtis to Richard Olney, July 11, 1895, all Miscellaneous Letters, RG 59, DOS. See also "In Behalf of Ex-Consul Waller," *New York Daily Tribune*, July 20, 1895. Olney proved remarkably sensitive to public opinion in the Waller case, always demanding that his subordinates keep him posted as to any new development or fresh criticism. See, for example, E. J. Penick (Chief

Clerk of State Department) to Richard Olney, March 3, 1895, container 28, Olney Papers.

29. E. N. Morrill to the President, July 25, 1895, Governor Morrill Letter Press Books, vol. 116, K.H.S.

30. "Ex-Consul Waller's Case," *New York Times*, July 16, 1895.

31. Alvey Adee to James Eustis, July 5, 1895, Waller Case Papers, *PRFRUS*; Richard Olney to Alvey Adee, August 4, 1895, container 31, Olney Papers; Richard Olney to James B. Eustis, November 7, 1895, Telegram, DUSMF, RG 59, DOS; and Alvey Adee to Richard Olney, July 8, 1895, container 28, Olney Papers.

32. Alvey Adee to James Eustis, July 10, 1895, Waller Case Papers, *PRFRUS*.

33. Alvey Adee to Richard Olney, July 29, 1895, container 30, Olney Papers.

34. Alvey Adee to Richard Olney, July 31, 1895, container 30, Olney Papers.

35. Edward Wetter to Edwin Uhl, July 23, 1895, no. 103, DUSCT, RG 59, DOS. The "Siam adventure," of course, referred to France's colonial effort in Southeast Asia. See also Gabriel Hanotaux to James Eustis, August 5, 1895, no. 349, enclosure 4, DUSMF, RG 59, DOS.

36. "Ex-Consul Waller's Case," *New York Daily Tribune*, September 11, 1895. See also "Waller's Arrest by France," *New York Times*, April 23, 1895; and Crammond Kennedy to Richard Olney, August 2, 1895, Miscellaneous Letters, RG 59, DOS.

37. Although a member of the Bourbon aristocracy, Eustis was hardly enlightened in his views on race. In an 1888 article in *The Forum* he observed that blacks had made absolutely no progress since emancipation, and he called for an end to all federal aid to the Negro. James B. Eustis, "Race Antagonism in the South," *The Forum* 6 (September, 1888–February, 1889): 144–154.

38. Paul Bray to H. C. Smith, *Cleveland Gazette*, August 10, 1895.

39. *Cleveland Gazette*, July 13, 1895.

40. *Chicago Tribune*, August 28, 1895.

41. *Chicago Times-Herald*, August 21, 1895; and Richard Olney to Alvey Adee, August 16, 1895, and Alvey Adee to Richard Olney, August 17, 1895, container 32, Olney Papers.

42. Alvey Adee to James Eustis, August 23, 1895, Olney Papers.

43. Alvey Adee to Richard Olney, August 23, 1895, container 33, Olney Papers. During Cleveland's first administration, Eustis and Cleveland had warred over patronage in Louisiana. They "buried the hatchet" in 1886, and Eustis was one of Cleveland's most ardent supporters in 1892. Eustis' appointment as minister to France was regarded by many as a personal one by the president. "Mr. Eustis and the Administration," *Washington Post*, August 26, 1895. Eustis, who was extremely upset by the State Department's criticism of him, demanded to know of Adee if Cleveland had actually criticized him or if State had merely used the president's name. The next day a number of papers reported that, according to reliable sources, the White House had decided to recall Eustis. Alvey Adee to Richard Olney, September 6, 1895, container 34, Olney Papers. See also James Eustis to Richard Olney, September 6, 1895, no. 368, DUSMF, RG 59, DOS.

44. "The Waller Case," *Chicago Tribune*, August 24, 1895.

45. "Ex-Consul Waller's Case," *New York Times*, August 22, 1895; and "France Not So Firm," *Chicago Tribune*, August 23, 1895.

46. "The Waller Incident," *New Orleans Times-Picayune*, August 25, 1895.

47. *Omaha Enterprise*, August 24, 1895.

48. Crammond Kennedy to Alvey Adee, September 6, 1895, Miscellaneous Papers, RG 59, DOS.

49. "Ex-Consul Waller's Case," *New York Sun*, September 6, 1895.

50. James Eustis to Richard Olney (personal), August 30, 1895, container 33, Olney Papers.

51. Waller's Deposition, August 27, 1895, no. 362, enclosure, DUSMF, RG 59, DOS.

52. James Eustis to Alvey Adee, August

30, 1895, Confidential Communique, DUSMF, RG 59, DOS.

53. Treaty between France and Malagasy Government Signed October 1, 1895, January 16, 1896, no. 444, DUSMF, RG 59, DOS; and *Chicago Tribune*, October 9, 1895. See, in addition, Edward Wetter to Edwin Uhl, December 9, 1895, no. 120, DUSCT, RG 59, DOS; James Eustis to Richard Olney, October 5 and 17, 1895, Telegrams, and Gabriel Hanotaux to James Eustis, October 16, 1895, no. 391, DUSMF, RG 59, DOS.

54. James Eustis to Richard Olney, October 21, 1895, Telegram, DUSMF, RG 59, DOS.

55. Alvey Adee to W. E. Faison, September 13, 1895, Interdepartmental Memo, DUSCT, RG 59, DOS.

56. LaFeber, *New Empire*, 263.

57. "Injured by American Friends," *New York Times*, October 31, 1895. See also James Eustis to Richard Olney, and Richard Olney to James Eustis, November 6, 1895, Telegrams, DUSMF, RG 59, DOS.

58. James Eustis to Marcelin Berthelot, November 7, 1895, no. 401, DUSMF, RG 59, DOS.

59. Susan Waller to John Waller, July 11, 1895, no. 358, enclosure, DUSMF, RG 59, DOS; "Exonerates Eustis," *Cedar Rapids Evening Gazette*, October 18, 1895; Interview between Edwin Uhl and Ethelbert G. Woodford, October 22, 1895, Waller Case Papers, *PRFRUS*, 369–380; "Mrs. Waller Talks More Freely," *New York Times*, October 18, 1895; and "Exonerates Eustis," *Cedar Rapids Evening Gazette*, October 18, 1895.

60. "Ex-Consul Waller's Despair," *New York Daily Tribune*, October 30, 1895; and "France Offers Waller's Release," *New York Times*, November 10, 1895.

61. "Ex-Consul Waller's Troubles," *New York Daily Tribune*, November 16, 1895.

62. John Waller to James Eustis, November 22, 1895, no. 413, DUSMF, RG 59, DOS.

63. James Eustis to Richard Olney, November 15, 1895, no. 404, DUSMF, RG 59, DOS.

64. *New York Press*, quoted in *New York Age*, November 30, 1895; "The Freeman Waller Fund," *Indianapolis Freeman*, November 30, 1895; and *Omaha Enterprise*, November 30, 1895.

65. G. P. Fenlon to Richard Olney, December 3, 1895, container 38, Olney Papers.

66. "Letter from John G. Jones to Walter Q. Gresham, March 30, 1895, Miscellaneous Letters, RG 59, DOS; "Ex-Consul Waller Sent to Nimes," *New York Daily Tribune*, October 19, 1895; and C. H. J. Taylor to Henry Thurber, October 15, 1895, Cleveland Papers.

67. "Liberty or Blood," *Cedar Rapids Evening Gazette*, December 7, 1895.

68. "Case of John L. Waller," *Congressional Record*, December 6, 1895, Fifty-fourth Congress, First Session, vol. 28: 51; and "Imprisonment of John L. Waller," *Congressional Record*, December 9, 1895, Fifty-fourth Congress, First Session, vol. 28: 62.

69. Richard Olney to James Eustis, December 4, 1895, no. 414, enclosure 5, DUSMF, RG 59, DOS.

70. James Eustis to Richard Olney, December 7, 1895, Telegram, DUSMF, RG 59, DOS.

71. "It was quite apparent to me from the first," Woodford told Eustis, "that Waller had been outrageously treated . . . . In no way had he acted otherwise than in accordance with his rights as a man and his treaty rights as an American citizen." E. G. Woodford to James B. Eustis, August 21, 1895, no. 362, DUSMF, RG 59, DOS.

72. "Waller and the Message," *Indianapolis Freeman*, December 7, 1895.

73. Olney apparently got the idea for the bribery angle from an old dispatch of Wetter's. See Edward Wetter to Edwin Uhl, April 21, 1895, no. 89, DUSCT, RG 59, DOS.

74. Richard Olney to President, December, 1895, container 41, Olney Papers.

75. "Imprisonment of John Lewis Waller," *Congressional Record*, January 27, 1896, Fifty-fourth Congress, First Session, vol. 28: 973.
76. Richard Olney to James Eustis, January 7, 1896, no. 439, DUSMF, RG 59, DOS. See also Richard Olney to James Eustis, January 23, 1896, no. 454, and James Eustis to Richard Olney, January 24, 1896, Telegram, DUSMF, RG 59, DOS.
77. James Eustis to Richard Olney, February 6 and 21, 1896, Telegrams, DUSMF, RG 59, DOS.
78. Congress called for the relevant documents in the Waller case on December 9. The State Department immediately shipped its records to the White House, but they were held up there. The *New York Times* speculated that the administration wanted to be able to announce Waller's impending release before Congress proceeded with its investigation. "Waller May Be Soon Released," *New York Times*, February 1, 1896.
79. "Imprisonment of John L. Waller," *Congressional Record*, February 11, 1896, Fifty-fourth Congress, First Session, vol. 28: 1573; and President's Message to House of Representatives, February 11, 1896, Waller Case Papers, *PRFRUS*, 251–259.
80. LaFeber, *New Empire*, 267–270.
81. *Kansas City Journal*, February 29, 1896.
82. *Indianapolis Journal*, as quoted in *Omaha Enterprise*, February 29, 1896.
83. "Mr. Waller's Predicament," *Richmond Planet*, February 22, 1896.
84. *Cleveland Gazette*, February 18, 1896.
85. *New York Times*, February 22, 1896.
86. "The Release of Ex-Consul Waller," *Providence Journal*, February 22, 1896, quoted in *Literary Guide* 12: 48.
87. "The Release of Ex-Consul Waller," *Louisville Courier Journal*, February 22, 1896, quoted in *Literary Guide* 12: 48.
88. "Waller's Release," *Afro-American Sentinel* (Omaha), February 22, 1896.
89. *Indianapolis Freeman*, March 7, 1896.

90. *Wichita National Reflector*, February 15, 1896.

CHAPTER 10

1. "Waller to Lecture," *Kansas City Gazette*, April 23, 1896; James Eustis to Richard Olney, February 26, 1896, no. 464, DUSMF, RG 59, DOS; and "Ex-Consul Waller's Story," *New York Tribune*, April 12, 1896.
2. "Ex-Consul Waller Here," *New York Times*, April 12, 1896; "A Reception for Ex-Consul Waller," *New York Tribune*, April 14, 1896; *Topeka Capital*, October 19, 1907; and John L. Waller to William R. Day, July 15, 1897, and John L. Waller to John Sherman, March 31, 1898, Miscellaneous Letters, RG 59, DOS.
3. *Kansas City Gazette*, June 25, 1896; and "Waller's Talk," *American Citizen*, June 26, 1896.
4. William Frank Zornow, *Kansas: A History of the Jayhawk State* (Norman, 1951), 199–201; *American Citizen*, November 6, 1891; *Historic Times*, November 7, 1891. *Kansas State Ledger*, November 18, 1892; and *Leavenworth Advocate*, November 15, 1890.
5. See, for example, M. W. Weeks to E. N. Morrill, April 20, 1895, Governor Morrill Letters Received, General Correspondence, K.H.S.; and "Brewers to Pay for It," *Kansas City Gazette*, January 2, 1896. See also Harrison Kelley to E. N. Morrill, February 3, 1895, and Young Men's Colored Republican State League to E. N. Morrill, 1895, Governor Morrill Letters Received, General Correspondence, K.H.S.; *American Citizen*, August 7 and September 18, 1896; and *Kansas City Gazette*, March 26 and July 30, 1896.
6. G. P. Fenlon to Richard Olney, December 3, 1895, Papers of Richard Olney, box 38, Library of Congress.
7. *Kansas State Ledger*, March 13, 1896. See also *Leavenworth Herald*, August 3, 1895.

8. "Waller's Talk," *American Citizen*, June 26, 1896.
9. *American Citizen*, July 3, 1896.
10. "Waller in Iowa," *Kansas City Gazette*, August 27, 1896; and *American Citizen*, September 11, 1896.
11. "John Waller for Recordership," *Iowa State Bystander*, November 27, 1896; and "John L. Waller," *Kansas City Gazette*, May 6, 1897.
12. "Six Tickets in Kansas," *Kansas City Gazette*, September 17, 1896. The editor of the *American Citizen*, however, claimed that enough blacks voted Populist in the First and Third Congressional Districts to cost the Republicans the election. *American Citizen*, November 13, 1896. See also *Topeka Colored Citizen*, October 6, 1898; "Ex-Consul Waller's Ambition," *New York Times*, December 24, 1896; *Iowa State Bystander*, March 12, 1897; and *American Citizen*, May 7, 1897.
13. *Kansas City Gazette*, March 5, 1895; January 9, June 25, July 27, and September 10, 1896; May 6, 1897; and January 6 and June 2, 1898.
14. *Kansas City Gazette*, April 16 and October 8, 1896, and November 23, 1899. See also *Leavenworth Advocate*, March 28, 1891; and *American Citizen*, March 31, 1898.
15. John L. Waller to William R. Day, July 5, 1897, Miscellaneous Letters, RG 59, DOS; *American Citizen*, July 27 and August 7, 1896, and January 8, April 23, and June 18, 1897; and "To Publish a Book," *Kansas City Gazette*, December 9, 1897.
16. *Kansas City Gazette*, February 25, 1897.
17. *American Citizen*, October 23, 1896.
18. "Waller To Run a College," *Kansas City Gazette*, August 6, 1896.
19. *American Citizen*, July 3, 1896.
20. "Demand Cuba's Liberation," *Chicago Times-Herald*, December 25, 1896.
21. *American Citizen*, October 23, 1896.
22. See Dudley T. Cornish, *The Sable Arm: Negro Troops in the Union Army, 1861–1865* (New York, 1956); and Benjamin Quarles, *The Negro*

in the American Revolution (Chapel Hill, 1961).
23. *Topeka Capital*, January 20, 1886.
24. Dudley T. Cornish, "Kansas Negro Regiments in the Civil War," *History of Minority Groups in Kansas*, Commission on Civil Rights (Topeka, 1969). See also *Western Recorder*, May 3 and August 10, 1883.
25. *Ft. Scott Colored Citizen*, May 24 and June 14, 1878.
26. *Topeka Colored Citizen*, February 8 and December 13, 1879; *Lawrence Journal*, January 15, 1880; *Benevolent Banner*, May 1, 1887; and *Leavenworth Advocate*, December 14, 1883. See also George W. Jackson to L. U. Humphrey, August 20, 1890, Governor Humphrey Letters Received, box 10, K.H.S.
27. John L. Waller to J. W. Leedy, April 26 and June 22, 1898, Governor Leedy Letters Received, Military-Applications, K.H.S.
28. John L. Waller to J. W. Leedy, April 1, 1898, Governor Leedy Letters Received, Military Applications, K.H.S.
29. *Western Recorder*, May 31, 1883.
30. *Topeka Capital*, January 20, 1886; and *General Statutes of Kansas* (Annotated) 1949 (Topeka, 1950), vol. 64.
31. J. W. Roberts (Adjutant General) to L. U. Humphrey, February 4, 1892, and J. W. Roberts to L. U. Humphrey, May 13, 1892, Governor Humphrey Letters Received, box 1, K.H.S.
32. *Kansas City Gazette*, February 11, October 28, and March 18, 1897.
33. *Topeka Colored Citizen*, June 17, July 1, July 17, July 22, and October 12, 1898.
34. See E. D. Moore to John Leedy, March 1, 1898; George W. Jackson to J. W. Leedy, April 25, 1898; and Paul Jones to J. W. Leedy, April 25, 1898, all Governor Leedy Letters Received, Military-Applications, K.H.S.
35. William Beck to J. W. Leedy, April 24, 1898, Governor Leedy Letters Received, Military-Applications, K.H.S.
36. *Topeka Colored Citizen*, May 12, 1898.
37. *Topeka Colored Citizen*, April 28 and May 12, 1898. See also Dennis

A. Jones to John Leedy, April 30, 1898, and A. M. Wilson to J .W. Leedy, May 26, 1898, Governor Leedy Letters Received, Military-Applications, K.H.S.

38. Willard B. Gatewood, Jr., "Kansas Negroes and the Spanish-American War," *Kansas Historical Quarterly* 37 (Autumn, 1971): 305–306. See also H. H. Brown to J. W. Leedy, April 25, 1898, Governor Leedy Letters Received, K.H.S.; and *Topeka Colored Citizen,* June 23, 1898.

39. Gatewood, "Kansas Negroes," 305–306; *Topeka Colored Citizen,* June 23, 1898; Charles Young to Col. Lindsay, June 30, 1898, Governor Leedy Letters Received, Military-General, K.H.S.; and "The Negro Populists' Venture," *Topeka Plaindealer,* June 15, 1890.

40. John L. Waller to J. W. Leedy, April 26, 1898, Governor Leedy Letters Received, Military-General, K.H.S.

41. *American Citizen,* January 8 and 29, 1897.

42. John L. Waller to J. W. Leedy, April 26 and June 22, 1898, Governor Leedy Letters Received, Military-Applications, K.H.S.

43. *American Citizen,* June 24, 1898.

44. "The Colored Troops," *Kansas City Gazette,* July 7, 1898; and *Topeka Colored Citizen,* July 14, 1898.

45. *Kansas City Gazette,* July 21, 1898.

46. *Topeka Colored Citizen,* July 27 and August 25, 1898.

47. "Captain Waller Writes," *Kansas City Gazette,* September 22 and November 17, 1898. See also "They Bring Cuban Wives," *Kansas City Gazette,* March 16, 1899; and *Topeka Colored Citizen,* November 11, 1898.

48. "Captain Waller Writes," *Kansas City Gazette,* September 22, 1898.

49. "Conditions in Cuba," *Kansas City Gazette,* October 20, 1898; and *Topeka Plaindealer,* January 27, 1899.

50. *Kansas City Gazette,* April 6, 1899; and Edward Everett Henry to John Leedy, Governor Leedy Letters Received, Military-General, K.H.S.

51. *Topeka Plaindealer,* March 27, 1899.

52. "Captain Waller and Cuba," *Kansas City Gazette,* April 20, 1899.

53. John Waller to J. H. Lindenberger, *Chicago Times-Herald,* October 23, 1896.

54. "Refuge of the Negro," *Washington Post,* July 2, 1899.

55. Ibid.

56. Ibid.

57. Willard B. Gatewood, Jr., *Black Americans and the White Man's Burden* (Urbana, 1974), 235; and *Colored American,* February 24, 1900.

58. Waller did become involved in one more overseas investment scheme. In 1907 he and a group of New York blacks attempted to establish a syndicate of Afro-Americans to purchase and develop lands in the Gold Coast, West Africa. Alfred C. Cowan to W. H. Sweaton, August 31, 1907, *New York Age,* September 12, 1907; and John L. Waller to T. Thomas Fortune, September 19, 1907, *New York Age,* September 19, 1907. See also *Colored American,* February 6, 1904; *Official Register,* 1907, vol. 1 (Washington, 1907): 604; and "Death of John L. Waller," *New York Age,* October 24, 1907.

59. John Waller to J. H. Lindenberger, *Chicago Times-Herald,* October 23, 1896.

60. Nell Irvin Painter, *Exodusters: Black Migration to Kansas after Reconstruction* (New York, 1977), 15–16.

61. Ibid., 22–23.

62. Allan H. Spear, *Black Chicago: The Making of a Negro Ghetto, 1890–1920* (Chicago, 1967), 51–53; David A. Gerber, *Black Ohio and the Color Line, 1860–1915* (Urbana, 1976), 320–416; and David M. Katzman, *Before the Ghetto: Black Detroit in the Nineteenth Century* (Urbana, 1973), 151–169, 187–194, 209. Actually, these authors document and expand a concept developed by August Meier in his *Negro Thought in America, 1880–1915* (Ann Arbor, 1963).

63. By 1886, according to Painter, a small sample of exoduster heads of household in Wyandotte were earning an average of $262.75 annually,

while comparable white laborers were averaging $333.09 per year. Nearly all the exoduster wives worked, usually as washerwomen, and the combined incomes of husband and wife brought the yearly average to $363.28. About three-quarters of the families owned their own homes. Painter, *Exodusters*, 257.

Selected Bibliography

There are no Waller papers as such. The diplomatic records (RG 59) of the National Archives, the Waller case papers published in *Papers Relating to the Foreign Relations of the United States,* the governors' papers in the Kansas State Historical Society, *Documents Diplomatique,* the manuscript collection of the Library of Congress, and various newspapers have yielded approximately 500 pieces of correspondence that shed some light on John Lewis Waller's personal life. Of these, 150 were written by Waller himself. Most of the documents deal with Waller's political and diplomatic life and mention his family, personality, and economic condition only in passing. Consequently, there are vast gaps in the story of his life. At times he virtually disappears from the narrative. Yet, given the relative invisibility of blacks as individuals in the written record of American history, there is a relative wealth of material on Waller. Obviously, I felt there was enough to warrant a biography.

Identifying the forces and personalities that shaped the black experience in Kansas during the last quarter of the nineteenth century proved a much simpler task than uncovering information on Waller's personal life. The Kansas Historical Society at Topeka contains an abundance of information. Particularly valuable are the papers of the various governors who held office from 1878 through 1900. These papers, which comprise the bulk of the society's manuscript holdings, contain correspondence to and from the governors, and the records and correspondence of the various departments of state during that particular chief executive's tenure. The society's newspaper collection is immense. Between 1875 and 1900 Kansas blacks were publishers of nearly thirty newspapers; at least remnants of almost all have been preserved at Topeka. The files

239

pertaining to *Brown* vs. *Board of Education* contain much valuable information on the history of racial discrimination in Kansas.

For Waller's exploits in Madagascar, United States policy toward Madagascar, and the byzantine maneuverings in Washington and Paris relating to the Waller affair, see first the Waller case papers published in *Papers Relating to the Foreign Relations of the United States*. The case papers are the documents gathered together by the State Department at the request of Congress. Also helpful are the miscellaneous letters of the Department of State and the correspondence of the American diplomatic representatives at Tamatave and Paris. The Harrison, Washington, Cleveland, Blaine, Gresham, and Olney papers all contain correspondence concerning the Waller affair. The Olney papers are the most significant. John Mercer Langston was chief counsel to both Waller and Wallerland. His papers, available on microfilm at the Amistad Research Center of Dillard University (the originals are at Fisk University), are invaluable. *Documents Diplomatique: Affaires de Madagascar, 1885–1895* is a compilation of French diplomatic correspondence on Franco-Malagasy relations during the decade in which France drew Madagascar into its orbit. It contains a wealth of information on Waller, Wallerland, and the Waller affair.

UNPUBLISHED SOURCES

Chicago. Center for Research Libraries.
Eighth Census of the United States, 1860, Free Schedule and Slave Schedule, New Madrid County, Missouri.
Seventh Census of the United States, 1850, Free Schedule and Slave Schedule, New Madrid County, Missouri.
Leavenworth. Leavenworth County (Kansas) District Court. Court records, calendars, and trial dockets (1878).
New Orleans. Amistad Research Center, Dillard University. John Mercer Langston papers, microfilm (originals at Fisk University, Nashville).
Topeka. Kansas State Historical Society.
George W. Glick papers, general and subject correspondence sent and received.
L. U. Humphrey papers, general and subject correspondence sent and received.
Harrison Kelley papers.
John W. Leedy papers, general and subject correspondence sent and received.
John A. Martin papers, general and subject correspondence sent and received.

E. N. Morrill papers, general and subject correspondence sent and received.
John P. St. John papers, general and subject correspondence sent and received.
Files in case of *Brown* vs. *Topeka, Kansas, Board of Education* (1954).
Manuscript on file, Robert A. Swann, "The Ethnic Heritage of Topeka, Kansas: Immigrant Beginnings" (Institute of Comparative Ethnic Studies, 1974).
Manuscripts on file, Kenneth Wiggins Porter, "Edward P. McCabe" and "William Bolden Townsend."
Minutes of Board of Directors of Kansas Freedmen's Relief Association. Shawnee County Clippings, vol. 2 (1888).
Washington, D.C. Library of Congress.
James G. Blaine papers.
Grover Cleveland papers.
Walter Q. Gresham papers.
Benjamin Harrison papers.
Richard Olney papers.
Booker T. Washington papers.
Washington D.C. National Archives. Record Group 59, Department of State.
Dispatches of the U.S. Consul at Tamatave.

Dispatches of the U.S. Minister to France.
Miscellaneous letters.
Waller appointment file.

PUBLISHED DOCUMENTARY SOURCES

Congressional Record, Fifty-fourth Congress, First Session (Washington, 1896).

Department of the Interior, Census Office, *Statistics of the Population of the U.S. at the Eleventh Census: 1890* (Washington, 1895).

Department of the Interior, Census Office, *Statistics of the Population of the U.S. at the Tenth Census,* 1880 (Washington, 1883).

Documents Diplomatique: Affaires de Madagascar, 1885–1895 (Paris, 1895).

Executive Documents of the House of Representatives, Fifty-second Congress, Second Session, vol. 1 (Washington, 1893).

General Statutes of Kansas (Annotated) 1949 (Topeka, 1950).

Historic Sites Survey, Kansas State Historical Society, *Black Historic Sites: A Beginning Point* (Topeka, 1977).

Official Register, 1907, vol. 1 (Washington, 1907).

Parliamentary Debates, vol. 25, Twenty-fifth Parliament, Third Session (London, 1895).

Waller Case Papers, *Papers Relating to the Foreign Relations of the United States* (Washington, 1896).

NEWSPAPERS

Abilene (Kans.) *Reflector*
Afro-American Sentinel (Omaha, Nebr.)
Afro-American Advocate (Coffeyville, Kans.)
American Citizen (Topeka and Kansas City, Kans.)
Arkansas (Little Rock) *Gazette*
Atchison (Kans.) *Blade*
Atchison (Kans.) *Champion*
Atchison (Kans.) *Globe*
Benevolent Banner (Topeka, Kans.)
Cedar Rapids (Iowa) *Evening Gazette*

Chattanooga (Tenn.) *American*
Chicago Times-Herald
Chicago Tribune
Cleveland Gazette
Cleveland World
Coffeyville (Kans.) *American*
Commercial and Financial Chronicle (N.Y.)
Emporia (Kans.) *Ledger*
Estafette (Paris)
Ft. Scott (Kans.) *Colored Citizen*
Herald of Kansas (Topeka)
Hiawatha (Kans.) *World*
Historic Times (Lawrence, Kans.)
Indianapolis Freeman
Iowa State Bystander (Des Moines, Iowa)
Journal of Commerce (N.Y.)
Kansas Blackman (Topeka)
Kansas City (Kans.) *Gazette*
Kansas City (Mo.) *Journal*
Kansas City (Kans.) *Star*
Kansas Democrat
Kansas State Ledger (Topeka)
Lagos (West Africa) *Weekly Record*
Lawrence (Kans.) *Journal*
Leavenworth (Kans.) *Advocate*
Leavenworth (Kans.) *Herald*
Leavenworth (Kans.) *Times*
Le Courier des Etats-Unis (N.Y.)
Le Figaro (Paris)
Le Madagascar
Le Tempe (Paris)
Madagascar News
Manchester (England) *Guardian*
Marquette (Wis.) *Monitor*
Memphis (Tenn.) *Commercial Appeal*
Nebraska Morning World Herald (Omaha)
New Madrid Southeast Missourian
New Orleans Louisianan
New Orleans Times-Picayune
New York Age
New York Daily Tribune
New York Globe
New York Sun
New York Times
New York World
Omaha (Nebr.) *Enterprise*
Parsons (Kans.) *Weekly Blade*
Progres de l'Imerina (Paris)
Revue Bleu (Paris)
Richmond (Va.) *Planet*
St. Louis Advance
St. Louis American Eagle
St. Paul (Minn.) *Broad Ax*
Salina (Kans.) *Herald*

Selected Bibliography

Salt Lake City Broad Ax
Southern Argus (Baxter Springs, Kans.)
The Madagascar Mail
Topeka (Kans.) *Capital*
Topeka (Kans.) *Capital-Commonwealth*
Topeka (Kans.) *Colored Citizen*
Topeka (Kans.) *Colored Patriot*
Topeka (Kans.) *Commercial*
Topeka (Kans.) *Journal*
Topeka (Kans.) *Plaindealer*
Topeka (Kans.) *Tribune*
Topeka (Kans.) *Weekly Times*
Washington (D.C.) *Bee*
Washington Post
Western Recorder (Kans.)
Wichita (Kans.) *Eagle*
Wichita (Kans.) *National Reflector*

THESES AND DISSERTATIONS

Blake, Lee Ella. "The Great Exodus of 1879 and 1880 to Kansas." Master's thesis, Kansas State University, 1942.

Deacon, Marie. "Kansas as the Promised Land: The View of the Black Press, 1890–1900." Master's thesis, University of Arkansas, 1973.

Morton, Rashey B. "Negro Press of Kansas." Master's thesis, University of Kansas, 1938.

Smith, Leland. "Early Negroes in Kansas." Master's thesis, Wichita State University, 1932.

Waldron, Nell Blythe. "Colonization in Kansas from 1861–1890." Doctoral dissertation, Northwestern University, 1925.

ARTICLES

Abramowitz, Jack. "The Negro in the Populist Movement." In Sheldon Hackney, ed., *Populism: The Critical Issues.* Boston, 1971.

Argersinger, Peter H. "Road to a Republican Waterloo: The Farmers' Alliance and the Election of 1890 in Kansas." *Kansas Historical Quarterly* 33 (Winter, 1967).

Blyden, Edward W. "The African Problem and the Method of its Solution." In Howard Brotz, ed., *Negro Social and Political Thought, 1850–1920: Representative Texts.* New York, 1966.

Chaffe, William H. "The Negroes and Populism: A Kansas Case Study." *Journal of Southern History* 34 (August, 1968).

Cornish, Dudley T. "Kansas Negro Regiments in the Civil War." *History of Minority Groups in Kansas,* Commission on Civil Rights. Topeka, 1969.

Drake, Donald E. "Militancy in Fortunes *New York Age.*" *Journal of Negro History* 55 (October, 1970).

Eustis, James B. "Race Antagonism in the South." *The Forum* 6 (September, 1888–February, 1889).

"France and Madagascar." *The Literary Digest* 9 (May–November, 1894).

Garvin, Roy. "Benjamin or 'Pap' Singleton and His Followers." *Journal of Negro History* 33 (January, 1948):18–19.

Gatewood, Willard B., Jr. "Kansas Negroes and the Spanish-American War." *Kansas Historical Quarterly* 37 (Autumn, 1971).

Harlan, Louis R. "Booker T. Washington and the White Man's Burden." *American Historical Review* 71 (January, 1966).

Higgins, Billy D. "Negro Thought and the Exodus of 1879." *Phylon* 22 (Spring, 1971).

Meier, August. "The Negro and the Democratic Party, 1875–1915." *Phylon* 17 (Summer, 1956).

"Negro Immigration." *New West Monthly* 1 (April, 1879).

Roberson, Jere W. "Edward P. McCabe and the Langston Experiment." *Chronicles of Oklahoma* 51 (Fall, 1973).

Sanford, Henry A. "American Interests in Africa," *The Forum* 9 (March–August, 1890).

Sinkler, George. "Benjamin Harrison and the Matter of Race," *Indiana Magazine of History* 65 (September, 1969).

Taylor, Frederick. "Madagascar," *The North American Review* 158 (October, 1896).

"The French in Madagascar." *Harper's Weekly* 39 (July 6, 1895).

"The Release of Ex-Consul Waller." *Literary Guide* 12 (February 22, 1896).

Welch, Richard E., Jr. "The Federal Elections Bill of 1890: Postscript and

Prelude." *The Journal of American History* 52 (December, 1965).

Whiton, James M. "The Crime Against Madagascar." *Outlook* 57 (September 28, 1895).

Wickliffe, John C. "Negro Suffrage a Failure: Shall We Abolish It?" *The Forum* 14 (September, 1892–February, 1893).

Yost, Genevieve. "History of Lynchings in Kansas." *Kansas Historical Quarterly* 2 (May, 1933).

BOOKS

Andreas, A. T. *History of the State of Kansas*. Vols. 1 and 2. Chicago, 1883.

Athearn, Robert G. *In Search of Canaan: Black Migration to Kansas, 1879–1880*. Lawrence, 1978.

Bergman, Leola Nelson. *The Negro in Iowa*. Iowa City, 1969.

Blasingame, John. *The Slave Community: Plantation Life in the Antebellum South*. New York, 1972.

Brunschwig, Henri. *French Colonialism, 1871–1914*. London, 1966.

Cornish, Dudley T. *The Sable Arm: Negro Troops in the Union Army, 1861–1865*. New York, 1956.

Crain, Robert L., and Weisman, Carol Sachs. *Discrimination, Personality, and Achievement*. New York, 1972.

Dann, Martin E. *The Black Press, 1827–1890: The Quest for National Identity*. New York, 1971.

Du Bois, W. E. B. *The Souls of Black Folk*. New York, 1961.

Frazier, E. Franklin. *Black Bourgeoisie*. Glencoe, Ill., 1957.

Frederickson, George M. *The Black Image in the White Mind*. New York, 1971.

Garraty, John A. *The New Commonwealth*. New York, 1968.

Gatewood, Willard B., Jr. *Black Americans and the White Man's Burden*. Urbana, 1974.

Genovese, Eugene. *Roll, Jordan, Roll*. New York, 1971.

Gerber, David A. *Black Ohio and the Color Line, 1860–1915*. Urbana, 1976.

Grossman, Lawrence. *The Democratic Party and the Negro: Northern and National Politics, 1868–1892*. Urbana, 1976.

Hagan, Kenneth J. *American Gunboat Diplomacy in the Old Navy*. Westport, Conn., 1973.

Harlan, Louis R. *Booker T. Washington: The Making of a Black Leader, 1856–1895*. New York, 1972.

Healy, David. *U.S. Expansionism: The Imperialist Urge in the 1890s*. Madison, 1970.

Heggoy, Alf Andrew. *The African Politics of Gabriel Hanotaux, 1894–1898*. Athens, 1972.

Katzman, Donald M. *Before the Ghetto: Black Detroit in the Nineteenth Century*. Urbana, 1973.

La Feber, Walter. *The New Empire*. Ithaca, 1963.

Marks, George P. *The Black Press Views American Imperialism, 1898–1900*. New York, 1971.

McCormick, Thomas J. *China Market: America's Quest for Informal Empire, 1893–1901*. New York, 1967.

McGuinn, Nellie. *The Story of Kansas City, Kansas*. Kansas City, 1961.

Meier, August. *Negro Thought in America, 1880–1915*. Ann Arbor, 1963.

Painter, Nell Irvin. *Exodusters: Black Migration to Kansas after Reconstruction*. New York, 1977.

Penn, I. Garland. *The Afro-American Press and Its Editors*. New York, 1969.

Plesur, Milton. *America's Outward Thrust: Approaches to Foreign Affairs, 1865–1890*. De Kalb, Ill., 1971.

Porter, Kenneth Wiggins. *The Negro on the American Frontier*. New York, 1971.

Pratt, Julius. *The Expansionists of 1898*. Baltimore, 1936.

Priestly, Herbert I. *France Overseas: A Study of Modern Imperialism*. New York, 1938.

Quarles, Benjamin. *The Negro in the American Revolution*. Chapel Hill, 1961.

Redkey, Edwin S. *Black Exodus: Black Nationalist and Back to Africa Movements, 1890–1910*. New Haven, 1969.

Rice, Lawrence D. *The Negro in Texas, 1874–1900*. Baton Rouge, 1971.

Roberts, Stephen H. *History of French*

Colonial Policy, 1870–1925. Vol. 2. London, 1925.

Robinson, Ronald, and Gallagher, John. *Africa and the Victorians.* New York, 1968.

Simmons, William J. *Men of Mark.* Chicago, 1970.

Spear, Allan H. *Black Chicago: The Making of a Negro Ghetto, 1890–1920.* Chicago, 1967.

Thorpe, Earl E. *The Mind of the Negro: An Intellectual History of Afro-Americans.* Westport, Conn., 1961.

Weinberg, Albert. *Manifest Destiny.* Baltimore, 1935.

Weisbord, Robert G. *Ebony Kinship: Africa, Africans, and the Afro-American.* Westport, Conn., 1973.

West, Richard. *Back to Africa: A History of Sierra Leone and Liberia.* New York, 1971.

Weston, Rubin F. *Racism in United States Imperialism.* Columbia, S.C. 1972.

White, Brett. *American Opinion of France.* New York, 1927.

Williamson, Joel. *After Slavery: The Negro in South Carolina during Reconstruction, 1861–1877.* New York, 1975.

Wilson, Charles Morrow. *Liberia: Black Africa in Microcosm.* New York, 1971.

Woodward, C. Vann. *The Strange Career of Jim Crow.* New York, 1966.

Zornow, William Frank. *Kansas: A History of the Jayhawk State.* Norman, 1957.

Index